AF378228

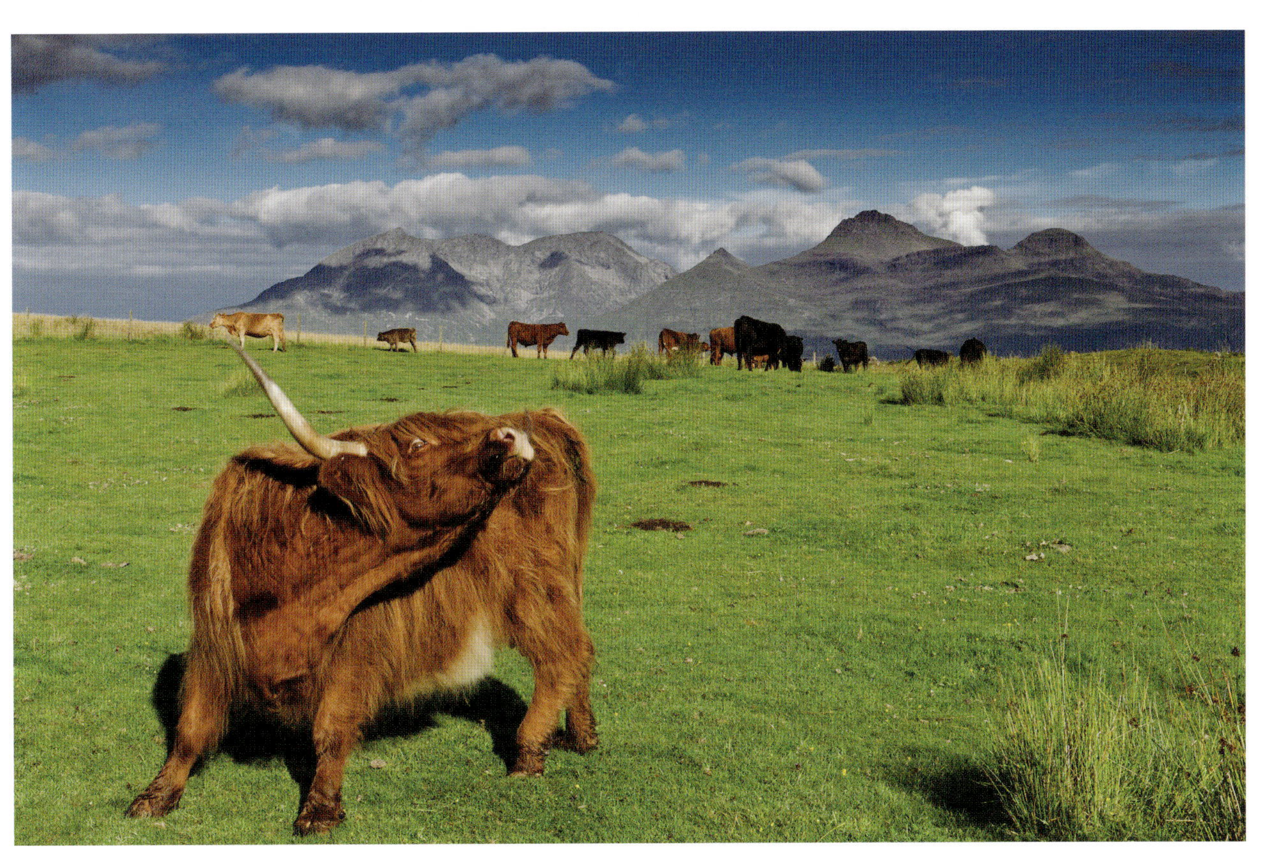

First Published April 2019

by

Allan Wright Photographic

www.allanwrightphoto.com

Scotland

ISBN: 978-1-905683-95-6

Printed by Skleniarz, Poland

ACKNOWLEDGEMENTS

Design: Michael Melvin, Melvin Creative Ltd

Editing associate: Carol Carr PR

SCOTLAND'S ISLANDS

ALLAN WRIGHT | MARIANNE TAYLOR

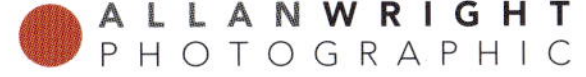

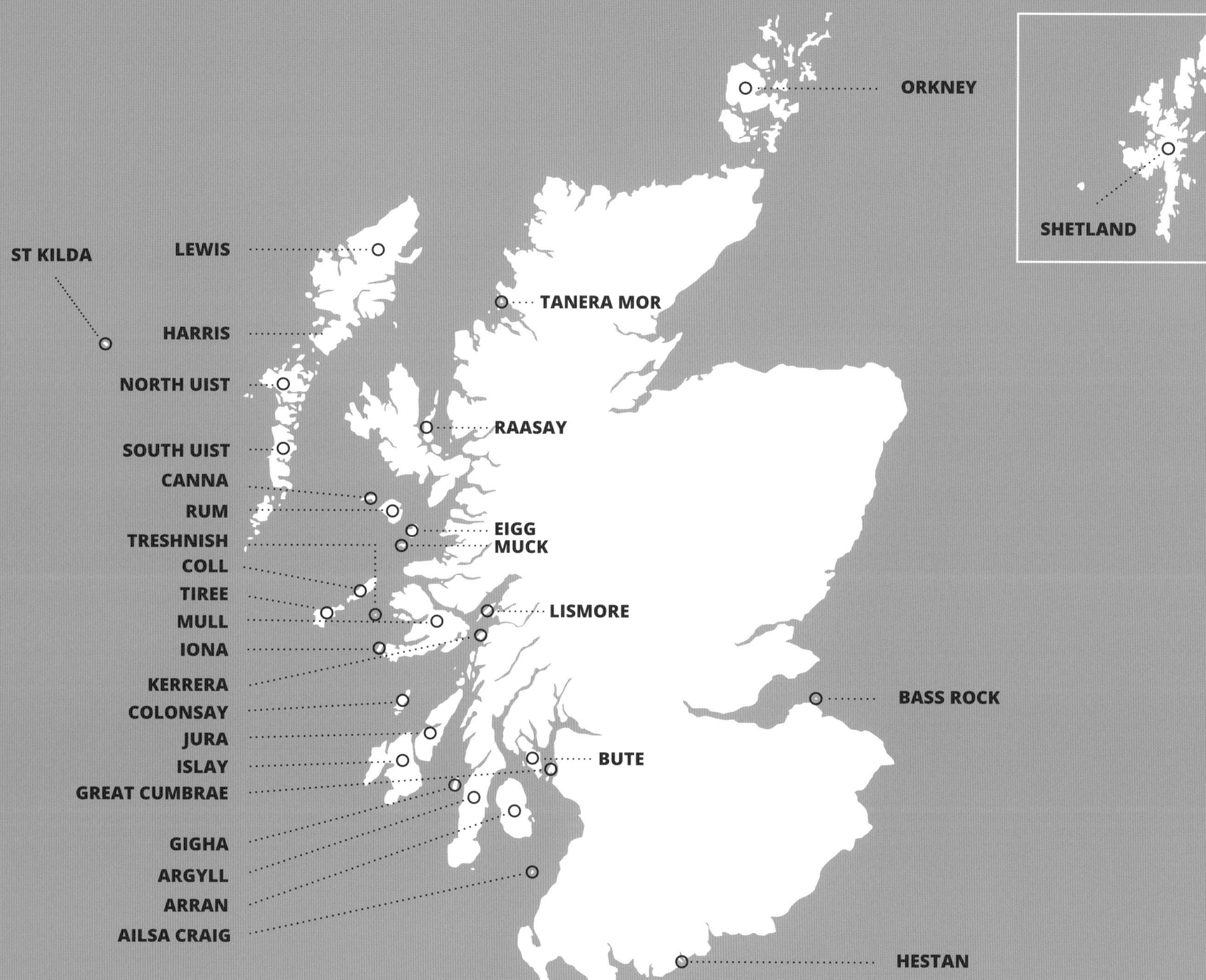
ORKNEY
SHETLAND
ST KILDA
LEWIS
HARRIS
NORTH UIST
SOUTH UIST
CANNA
RUM
TRESHNISH
COLL
TIREE
MULL
IONA
KERRERA
COLONSAY
JURA
ISLAY
GREAT CUMBRAE
GIGHA
ARGYLL
ARRAN
AILSA CRAIG
TANERA MOR
RAASAY
EIGG
MUCK
LISMORE
BUTE
BASS ROCK
HESTAN

PREFACE

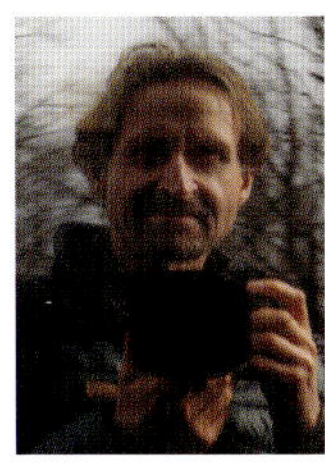

My earliest and most unforgettable exposure to the magic of Scotland's islands occurred in the late sixties at Machrie on the Isle of Islay. I have vivid memories of the longest beach you could imagine, a golf course fully inhabited by sheep, and a wonderfully idiosyncratic hotel whose kilted laird Bert Marshall would be found sat on a bench, gnarly crook in hand, surveying his minor Gaelic empire. Thus began a relationship with the "Queen of the Hebrides" which at my last count has extended to sixteen visits. As a Glasgow teenager, I fell victim to the tradition of taking boozy, bank holiday weekends on the Isle of Arran. Aside from all the bar banter and madness, these sorties further connected me to that special "island time" feeling one reliably experiences as soon as the ferry sets sail.

It's perhaps fitting that since those days I have been in no great hurry to complete my personal island odyssey. Some of my favourite images in this portfolio date back to the mid 80s, the majority were obtained in the past twenty years. Even as a Scottish landscape photographer, I've never really followed a particularly structured approach to my island bagging. Each visit came in its own time according to business opportunities and ad hoc inclination. Awareness over the last two years of a wish to achieve completion of some kind however, caused me to sharpen up my shooting schedule.

This portfolio exists by virtue of being held captive by the beauty and atmosphere of these islands and whereas I enjoy my job immensely, it is still work. In general and in practice I will claim that it is the land that seems to speak to me, although I do also shorten the odds by making precise logistical calculations for some shots. It is humbling and gratifying to be able to capture a glimpse of the fleeting beauty and the inherent lyricism of a particular subject. The famously changeable nature of Scottish light, especially on the West Coast, means that an alertness, and readiness to move when opportunity strikes, is very much part of the game. I see my role in this process as a receiver transmitter, summed up well by Yen Arthurs-Bertrand whose statement: "The Earth is Art, The Photographer is only a Witness," speaks volumes about the role we photographers play in creating landscape consciousness. People have often asked me: "Do you have a favourite Island?" I confess I enjoy trying to answer this question but concede that I generally fail to offer any such clarity. Maybe my three day visit to the St Kilda archipelago was the most intense and other worldly experience that deeply touched me but then, my time on the Isle of Coll was so delightful, I could easily rate that among the top few. On the other hand Mull quite simply has it all. Islay for sure is in my blood and Jura remains for me an intriguing and vast unconquered wilderness. Gigha is rich and colourful in many ways and my time on Eigg was so fascinating that days spent there simply flew past like a dream. Rum was powerful and anachronistic, symbolic of both human folly and nature's dominion. Golden hours on Tiree with its vernacular cottages,

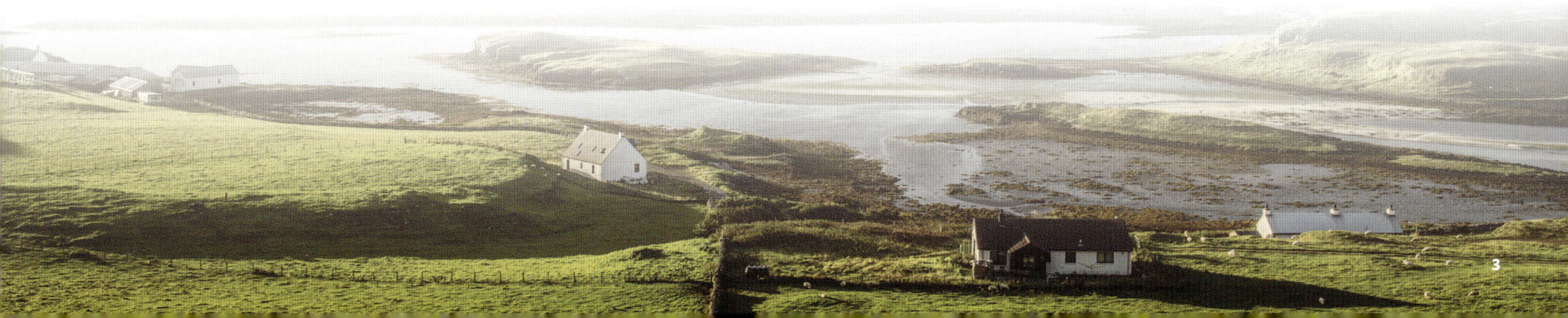

crofting traditions and exquisite beaches are also etched in my memory. Lewis's mist, moorland and raw coastlines set in the deepest historical context had a profound effect. The Uists were quite simply enchanting with their remote beaches, achingly beautiful sunsets, and aquamarine supremacy, all under vast, heavenly skies. The open-ended sortie south via Barra to Vastersay has no equal, although I would single out Berneray off North Uist for delivering the most intensely visual Hebridean ramble you could ever wish for. I will return.

Raasay offers a superb little adventure edified by the amazing real-life tale of the famous crofter Calm McLeod's road-building feat. Its giant of a neighbour, the customarily named Isle of Skye, is deliberately not included in this book. Partly because there is debate about its legitimacy as an island given its more recent acquisition of a road bridge, but also because I have in print a book of my photographs devoted to the same, published in 2017. It is entitled: Skye - A Photographic Communion.

It was only in 2018 that I finally took the time to let the northern isles of Orkney and Shetland get under my skin. It was early summer, with the characteristic generous light afforded by that time of year in the far North. Orkney left me hungry for more; such fertility from farming, archaeology,

and wartime history and bird life on the endless stunning cliff walks. Time constraints prevented me from visiting some of the many smaller islands that constitute Orkney - for another time maybe. Shetland is a long way north from here. It's impossible to escape its Nordic connections. And no more so than when one steps back and takes stock of the particularly confident, practical style of architecture much in evidence there. The scale of Shetland's rugged coastline and moorland wilderness with associated wildlife is impressive. I took in all the main islands but it would take many weeks to achieve any sense of completion there.

I also include the tiny but locally iconic islands of Heston in my home region of Galloway, the ever visible Ailsa Craig, Tanera Mor one of the Summer Isles and of course last but not least East Lothian's Bass Rock. Such is their lure, I now realise that I will probably never genuinely feel that I have 'done all the islands,' regardless of my initial urge. I will return. And I wish for myself and all others who love Scotland's islands, many happy returns indeed.

Allan Wright
April 2019

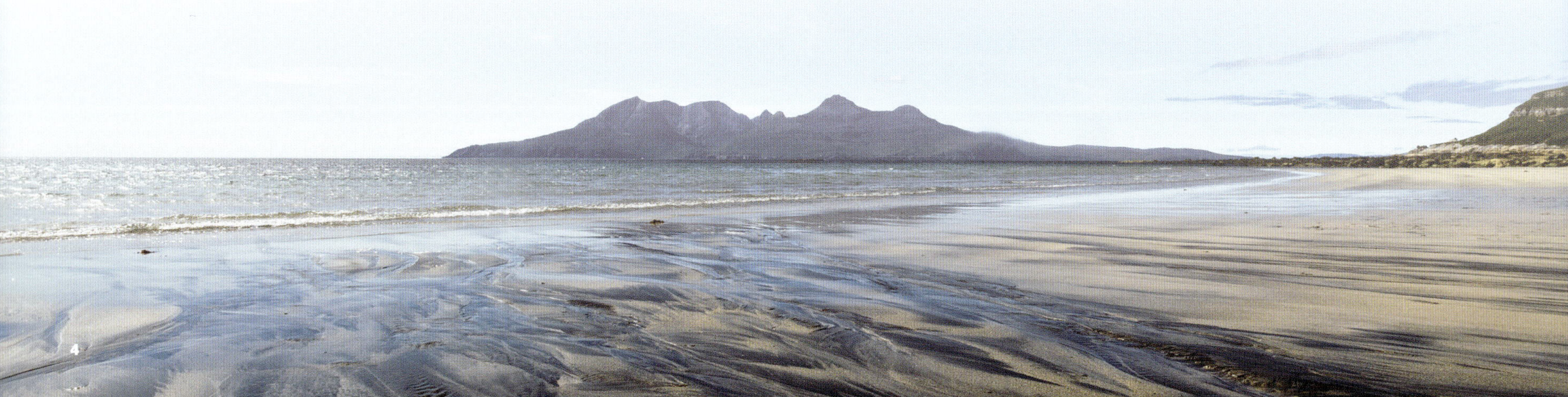

INTRODUCTION

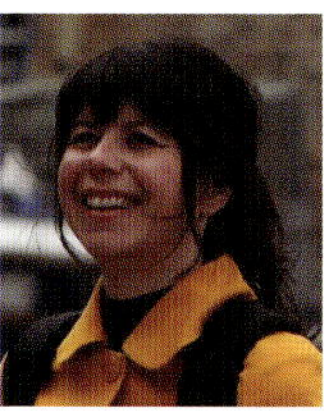

THE aquamarine waves swell in and out, crashing crystal clear on sand that stretches as far as the eye can see, white and powdery as any Caribbean dream. It's 3pm in December and the sun is already setting behind the hills, turning the sky to a cobalt blue straight from the brush of Matisse.

The handful of souls dotted on the beach today, human and canine, know what to expect from this extraordinary place. Luskentyre in winter is bracing, to be sure; the wind can get up at any time here on the Isle of Harris, the sky can switch from blue to slate without warning, snuffing out the light and unleashing the sort of hoolie that keeps you inside for days. In summer, though the sunsets seem to go on forever it never really gets dark.

That's what draws folk here in all weathers in every season, the drama of the natural light show, the drama of the sea, the steadfastness of the mountains beyond. Perhaps above all, the comfort of your own smallness. When I think of Scotland's islands what always comes to mind first is that rarely achieved feeling of living in the moment, of weather and landscape encompassing and overpowering everything in its wake, including the people. Especially the people. It is striking that almost everyone you talk to about the islands, be they inhabitant or visitor, young or old, male or female, will invariably bring the conversation round to these three themes: landscape, weather and community, and all are highlighted in this book.

You won't see people in the pages of this visual odyssey, yet their presence is indelible in the boats, tractors and fences, the white-washed cottages, churches and distilleries. The standing stones and ancient remains remind us that island communities have been surviving, sometimes thriving, for many thousands of years, bringing up families, working the land and the sea, worshipping, celebrating, mourning and fighting. The abandoned settlements, meanwhile, highlight a past in which communities ultimately did not thrive, and it's both interesting and sad to note that many of Scotland's islands were more populated in the past than they are now.

The changes in fortunes and demographics over the centuries are many and complicated, as complex and diverse as the 790-plus islands themselves. They vary in size, geography, population, language, history, tradition, economy and prosperity, situated in different groupings and bodies of water, some closer to the mainland than others. The climate and seasons affect them in very different ways, as do their geographical and political influences; Islay off the south west of Scotland, just 24 miles from the Irish coastline, is clearly very different from Shetland, in the far north east, halfway to Norway and not part of Scotland till the 15th century.

Some islands move your soul more than others; a certain walk taken at a certain time of year with a loved one lingers long in the imagination, a special sunset over a favourite bay cries out to be relished over and over again. How wonderful that the exploring, appreciating and comparing of the islands takes a lifetime. My own introduction to them came, like that of so many other Glaswegians, in early childhood during cheerful Fair Fortnight holidays in the Firth of Clyde – Millport on Great Cumbrae and Rothesay on Bute - where bike rides, ice cream floats and sails on the Waverley made memories. The bond was strengthened in my early-20s when, seeking respite from difficult times, I packed a rucksack in the summer of 1996 and took off in a Fiat Panda. I hoped a weekend away on Arran would sort my head out. It did. But I just kept going and six weeks and a maxed-out credit card later, I'd also fallen in love with Islay and Jura, Eigg and Rum, Mull, Iona, Skye and Raasay.

Over the next few summers I explored Tiree and Coll, Lewis and Harris, Barra and the Uists for the first time, and more recently I've had the pleasure of exploring Orkney and Shetland. Like many city dwellers who love the islands I also managed to engineer close friends who live on one, and I am fortunate enough to spend time on Harris every year, usually in winter.

What draws this townie back again and again? The same thing that probably attracts most dreamers, an addiction to that feeling of being in the moment I referred to earlier, the comforting recognition of one's own tiny place in things. I also can't live for long without with the flora and fauna, the majestic eagles flying across the mountains, the wild flowers growing in the machair, the shimmer of the dolphins swimming alongside your boat, the seals sunbathing on the rocks. Animals, wild, domestic and everything in between, somehow seem all the more remarkable on the islands, whether it's the deer swimming from islet to islet off Islay or the hardy wee Hebridean sheep stoically munching in 70 mph winds on Lewis.

The history of the people draws me in, too. Speak to islanders and the stories you'll hear passed down the generations will inevitably feature hard lives lived on the edge of the world. But what's even more striking is how folk have always adapted. And in doing so they've found innovative ways to live and work. Never more so than now. Think of the contemporary Harris Tweed designs that sit alongside the traditional patterns and adorn catwalks in Paris, Milan and Tokyo. Think of the island whisky distilleries using social media to market the uniqueness of their product, enticing visitors and income from around the world. Consider the way our digital world has created opportunities for people to thrive in island communities, from web designers to renewable energy providers to crofters, and the arts festivals and stunning restaurants that add to the vibrant culture for locals and visitors alike.

Scotland's changing political landscape, the journey towards self-determination that started with the vote for devolution and the establishment of a Scottish Parliament in the late 1990s, also continues to have a profound effect on the life of the islands. In 2018 Ulva, off the coast of Mull, became the latest island to successfully complete the community buy-out process that has already put Eigg, Rum, Gigha, Great Bernera, as well as parts of Lewis and Harris, into the hands of the people that live there. No doubt the success of the scheme so far will inspire others to press for change. Eigg, which in 2017 celebrated 20 years of community ownership, has seen its population rise by more than 55 per cent in that time, while retaining and attracting more young people with better job opportunities and more affordable housing. The island is also leading the way environmentally by producing much of its own energy, this tiny island of 87 people has much to teach the mainland, not least that people power really does work.

Positive moves have also been afoot to save the Gaelic language – historically spoken in the Hebrides - from extinction, with many schools on the islands embracing the language once again, and community centres offering evening classes to all. The long waiting lists for the expanding number of Gaelic schools in Glasgow shows that many Scots, not to mention people of international heritage living in Scotland, want the language to be part of their lives.

The world has certainly woken up to the beauty of Scotland's islands, and tourism is booming across the Hebrides, the Northern Isles and on Arran. In years gone by a trip to the islands would likely be a rather primitive affair in terms of accommodation and food. How things change. Our islands are home to some of the best restaurants, hotels and Airbnbs in the country, showcasing wonderful local produce and world-class hospitality. Eating scallops and langoustines straight out of the loch on Skye, or enjoying a dram by the fireside on Islay, are two of life's great pleasures. Such experiences used to be well-kept secrets, too, but are now as likely to top global food and travel lists as Scotland's reputation – and visitor numbers – continue to soar. Packed Cal Mac ferries are good news for island economies, of course, though questions remain about whether the infrastructure can cope. Whether fragile eco-systems will be adversely affected by tourism also causes concern.

Not for the first time, Orkney was recently voted the best place in Britain to live, commended for its affordable property, excellent education, high employment, vibrant cultural scene and community cohesion. I can think of other Scottish islands that offer a similarly high quality of life. It's telling that in this era of mega-cities and unlimited digital networking, urban isolation is also on the rise and it is our most remote places that are often seen to provide the things so many of us crave: community and authenticity. They are precious things indeed and we must preserve and invest in them so that Scotland's islands can continue to thrive in the years to come.

Marianne Taylor

Marianne Taylor is a Glasgow-based journalist and broadcaster. She writes mainly for The Herald but has also worked for the Guardian, the Times and Die Welt, covering politics, culture, society and travel. She is a regular contributor on Radio Scotland and has been an enthusiastic explorer of Scotland's islands for most of her life.

Marianne Taylor photo courtesy of Gordon Terris, Herald and Times Group.

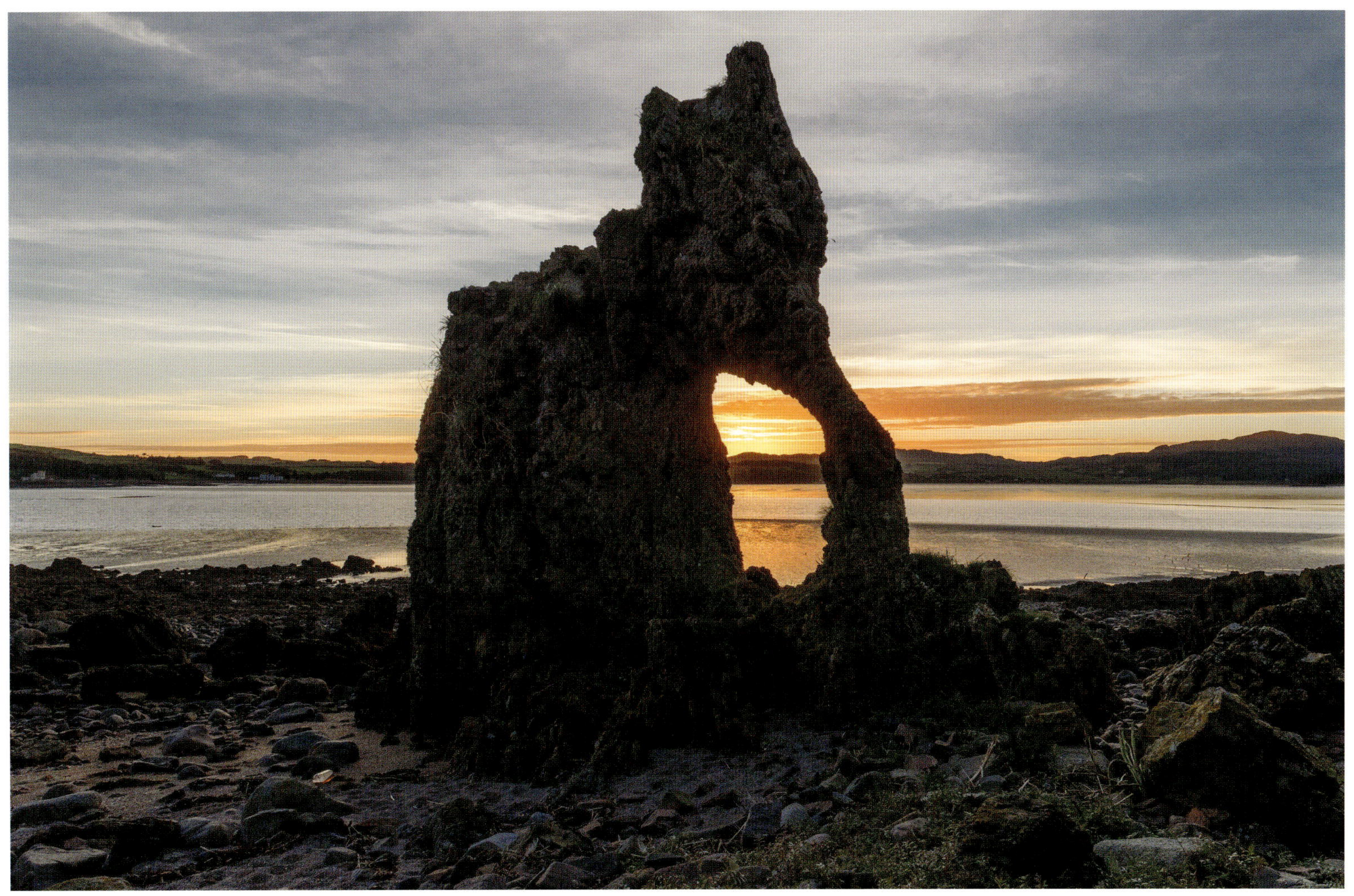

A natural archway on the north shore of Hestan Island, which lies at the southern tip of the River Urr estuary in the Solway Firth. The island was an inspiration for Victorian adventure novelist S R Crockett.

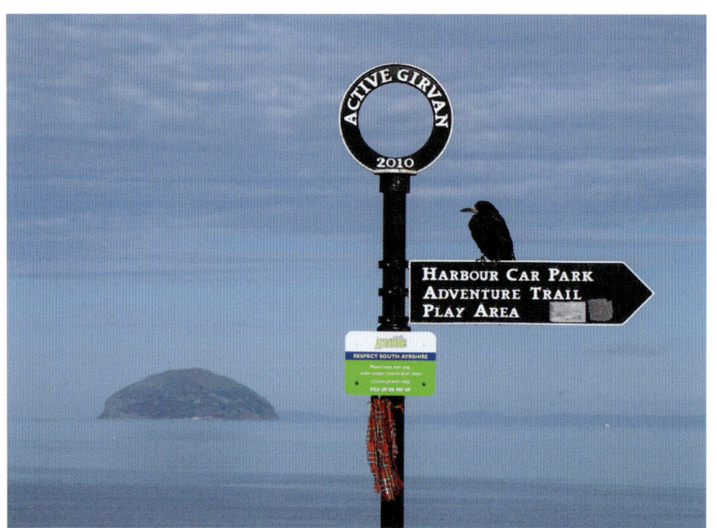

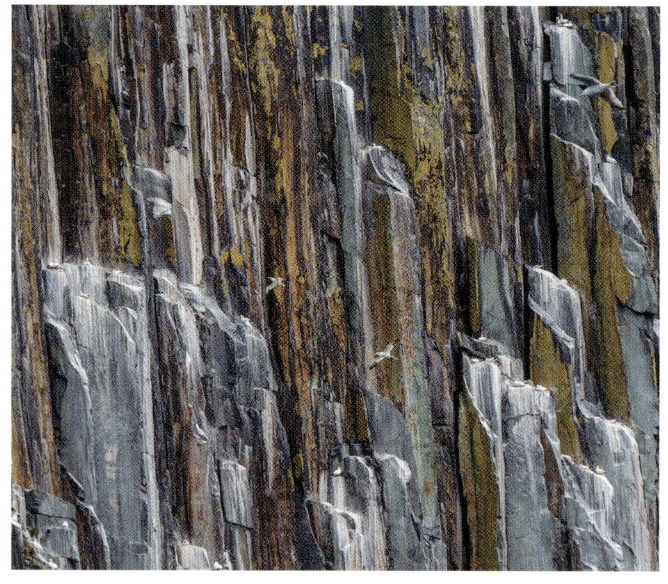

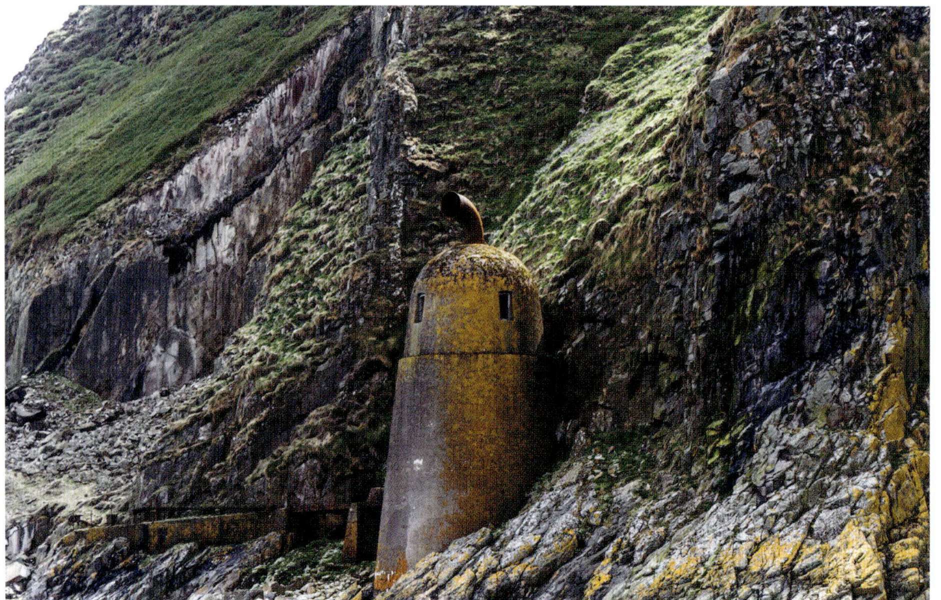

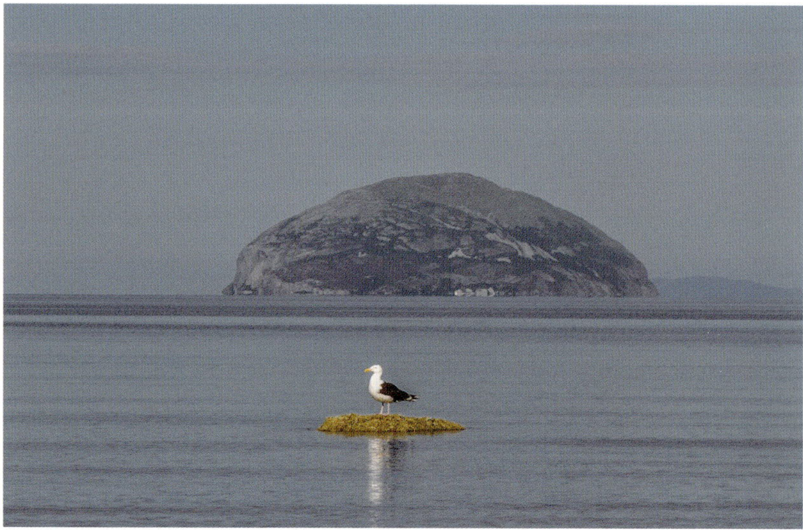

Ailsa Craig owns the horizon for much of South Ayrshire. Famed for its Blue Hone granite, used to make curling stones, it elicits both curiosity and familiarity.

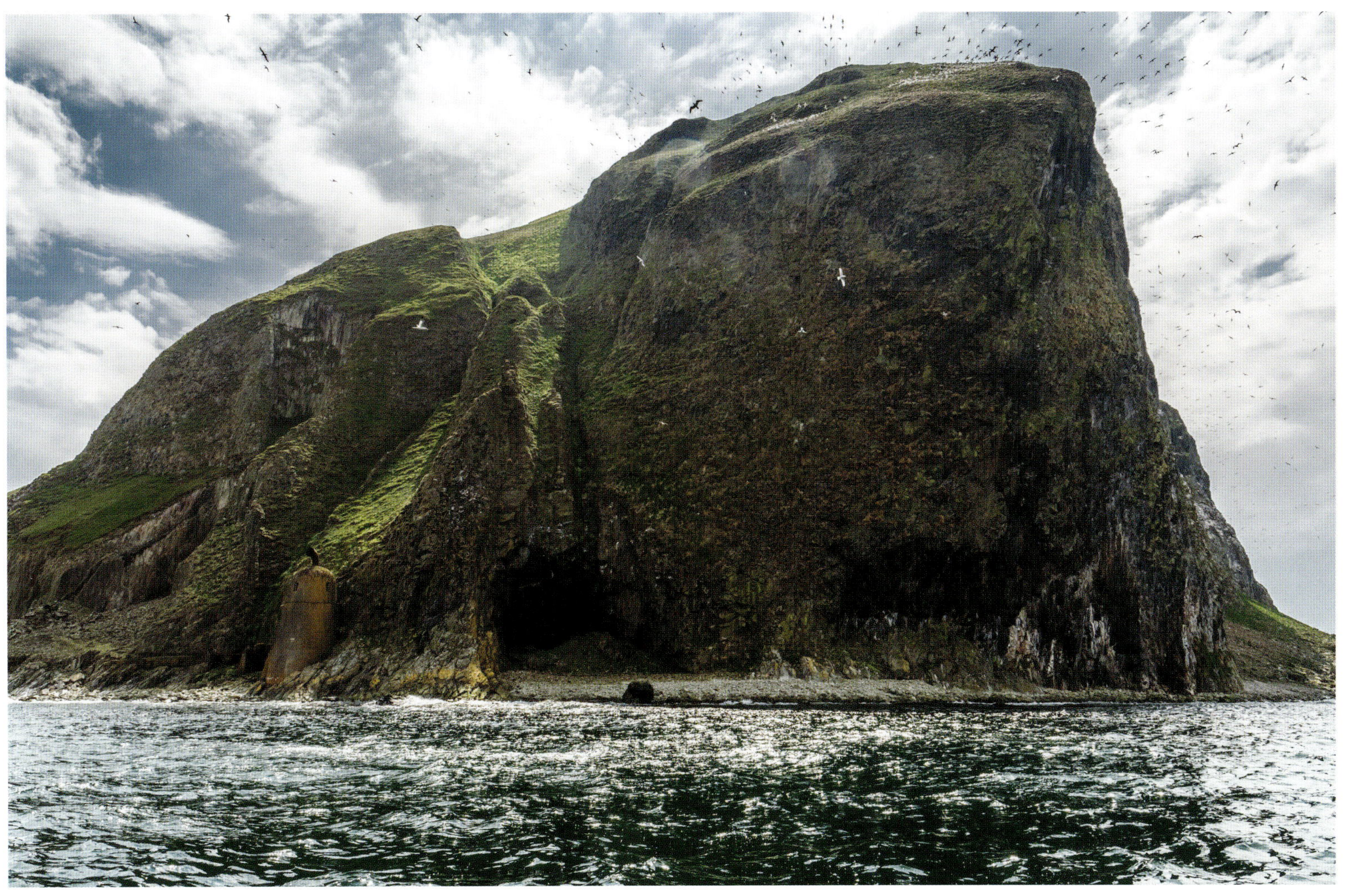

Day trippers from Girvan are often surprised to find that the rock offers a more dramatic structure than the benign dome it appears to represent from the mainland.

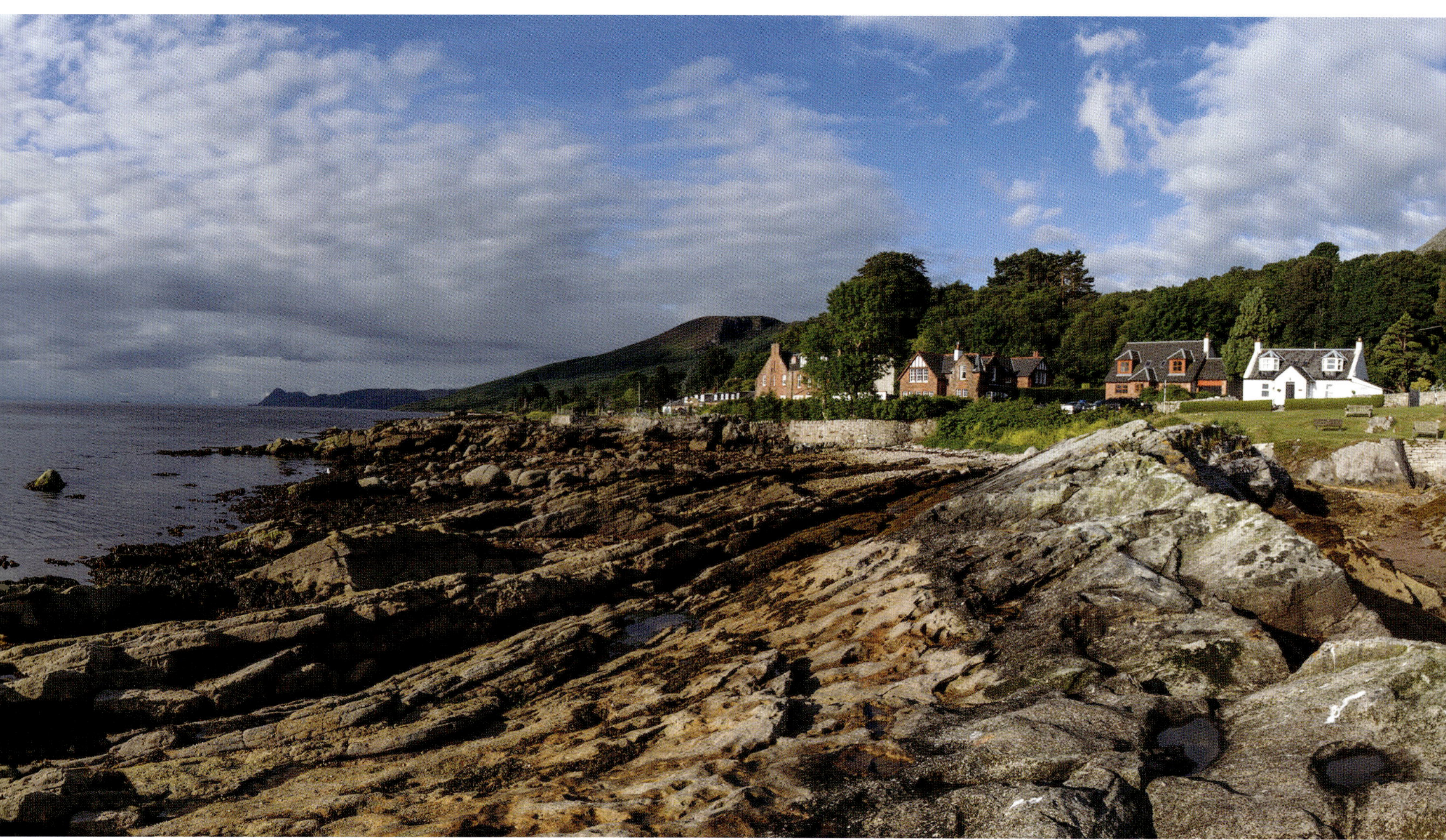

The harbour at the village of Corrie is about as cute as Scottish harbours get.

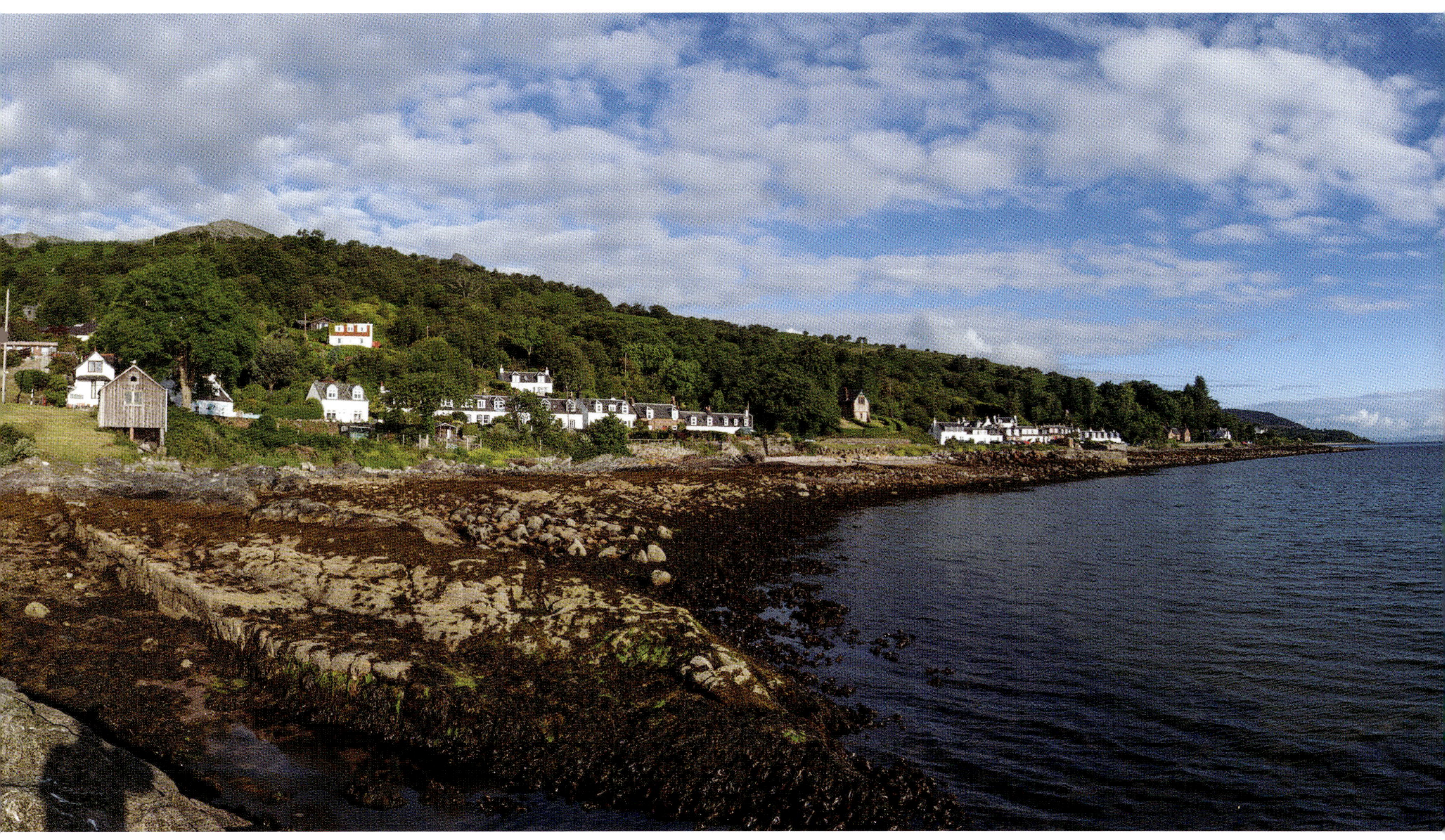

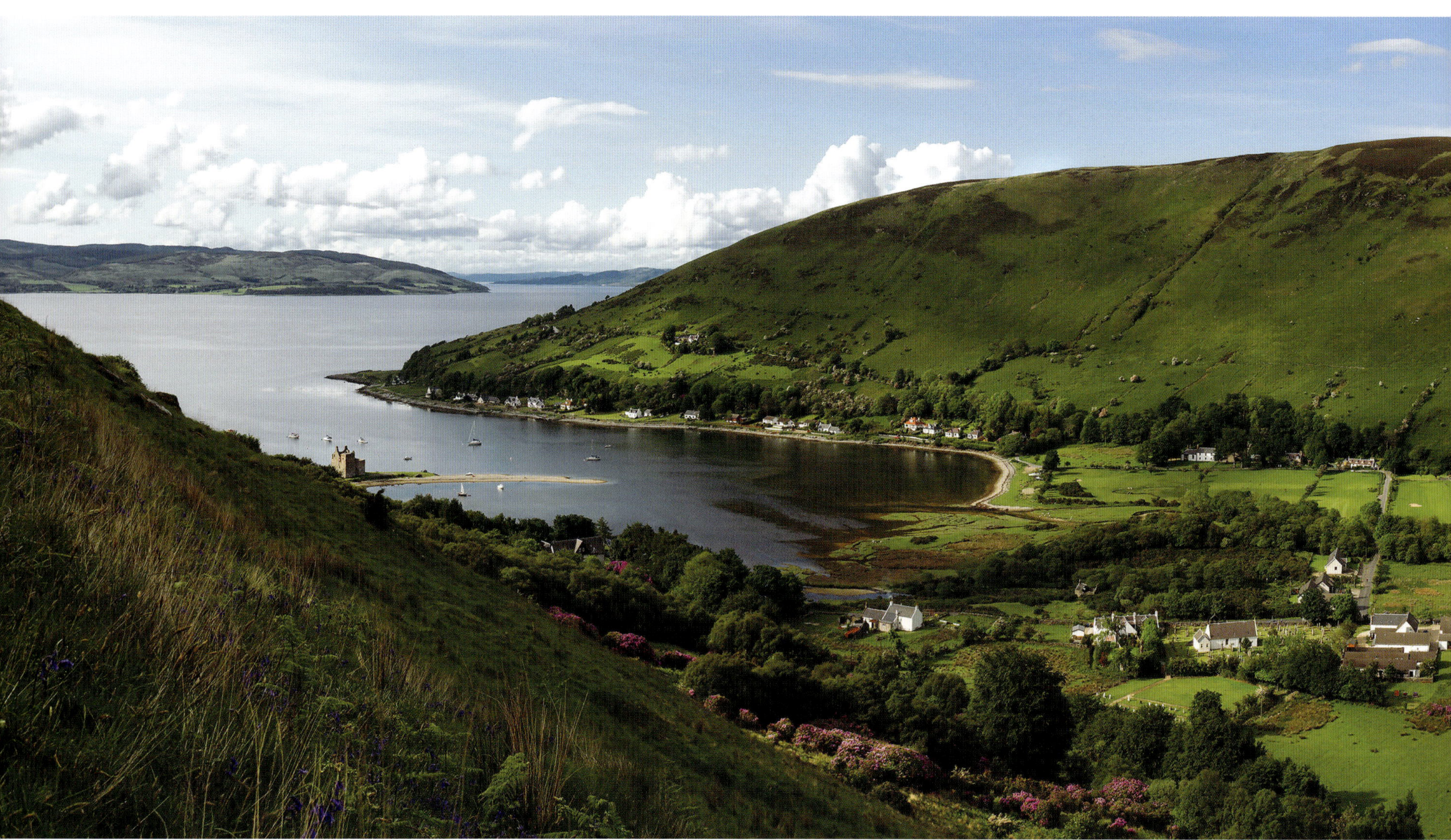

Beautiful Lochranza, on the north coast of Arran, boasts a castle and a world-renowned distillery.

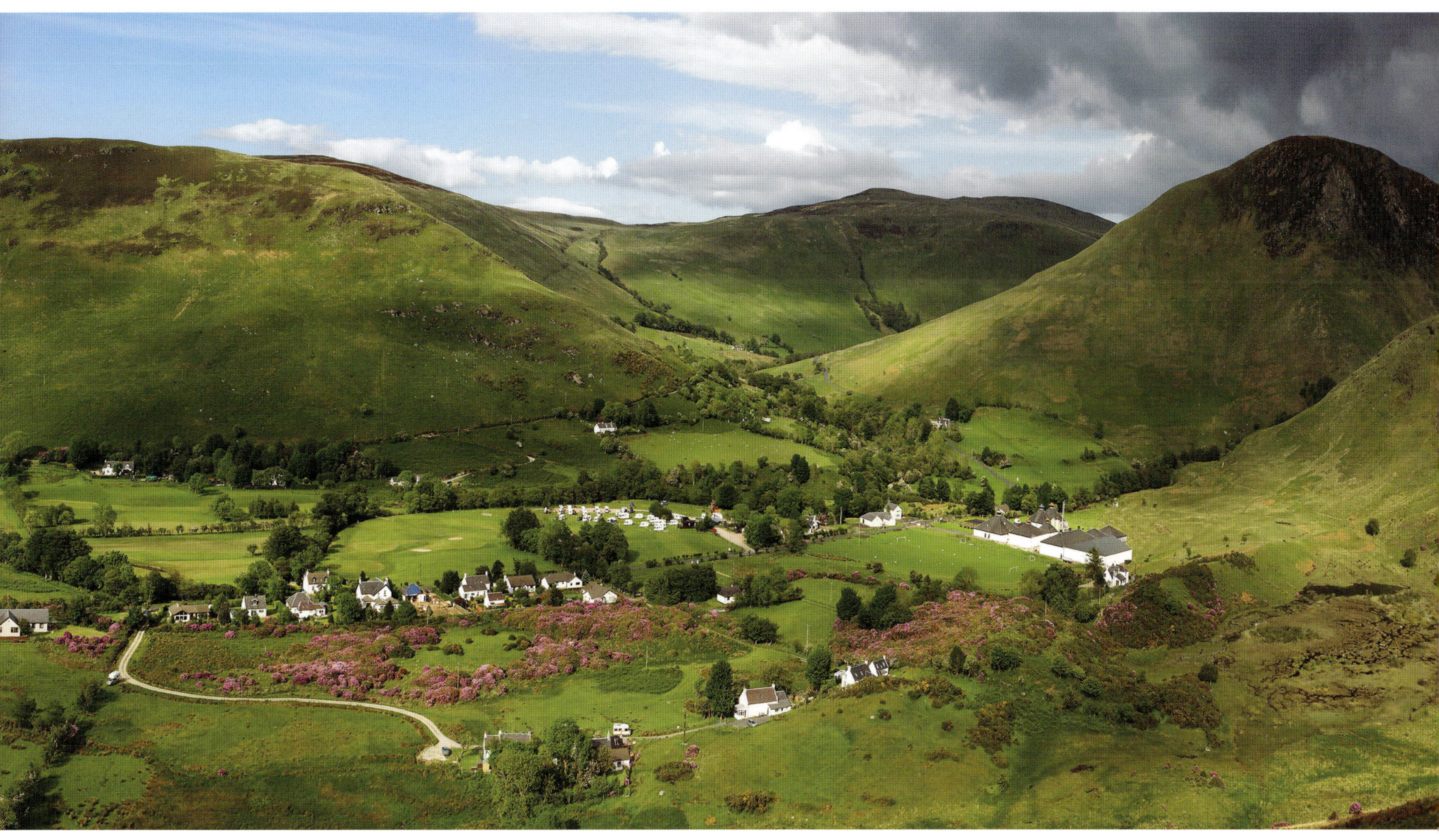

Lochranza Castle and a fresh bloom of thrift

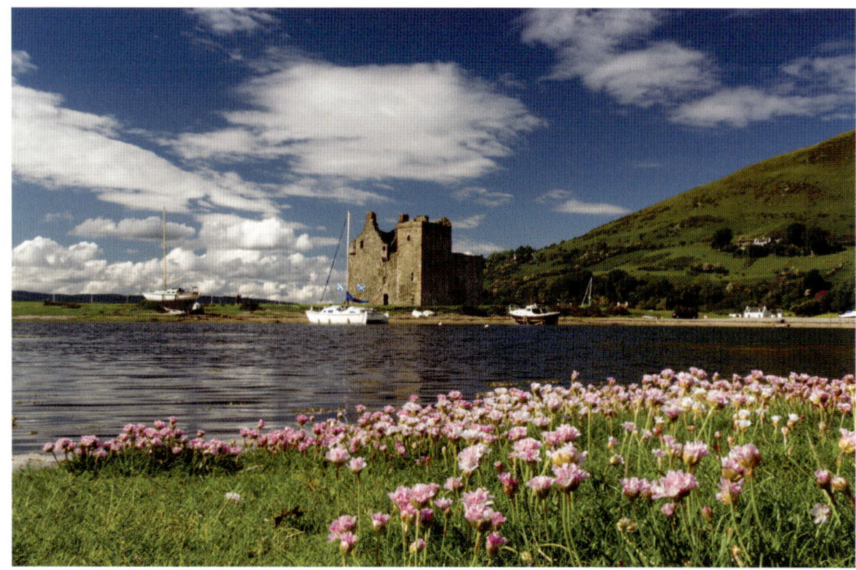

The atmospheric Machrie Moor Standing Stones give an insight into Arran's Neolithic past.

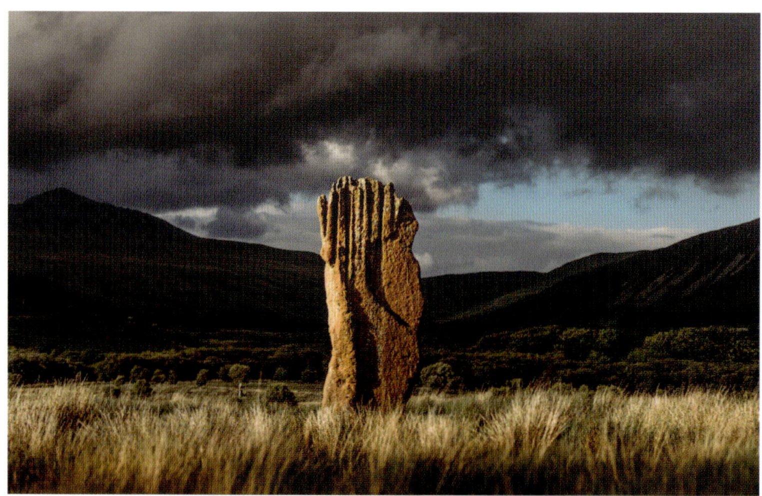

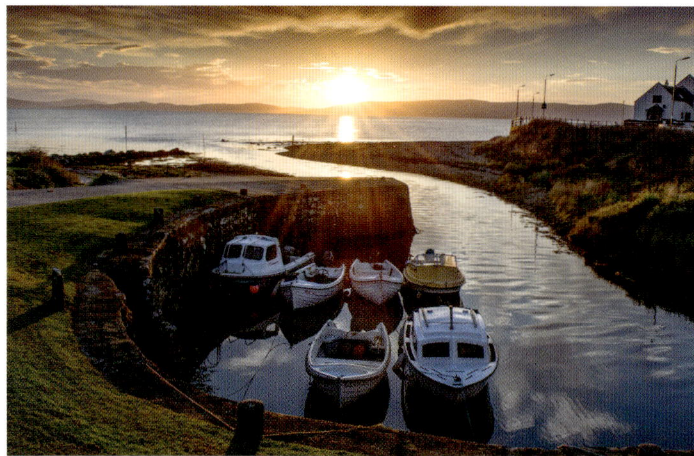

Captivating Blackwaterfoot harbour

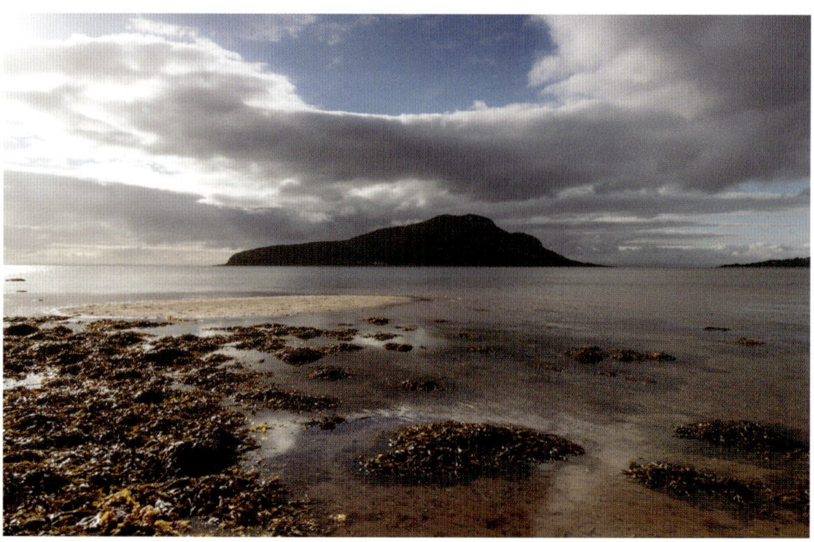

Holy Isle, now a Buddhist Community, presides over the horizon on the island's eastern coast. It is seen here from the Lamlash shore.

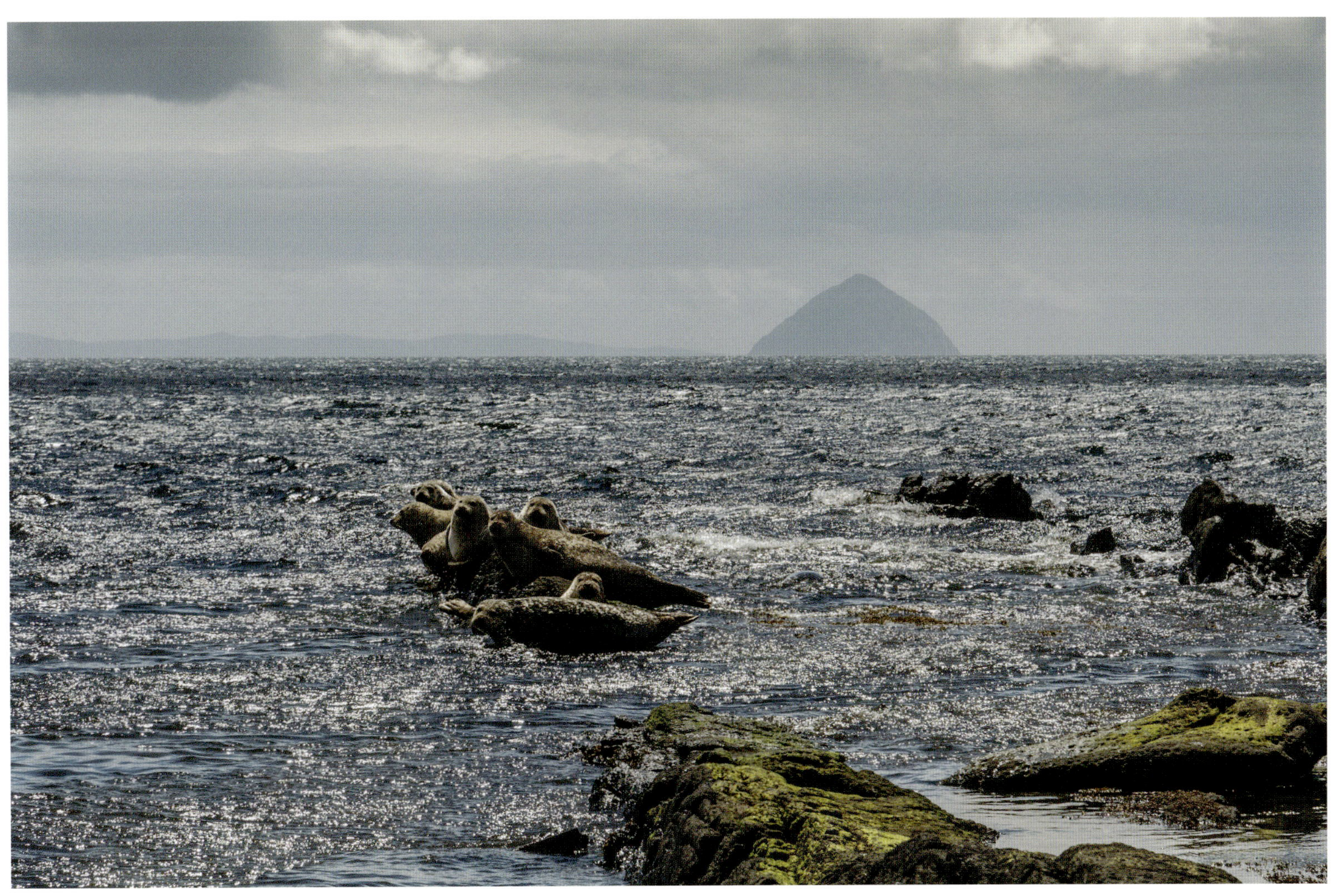

Seals often feature in the magical ramble from Kildonan to Bennan Head.

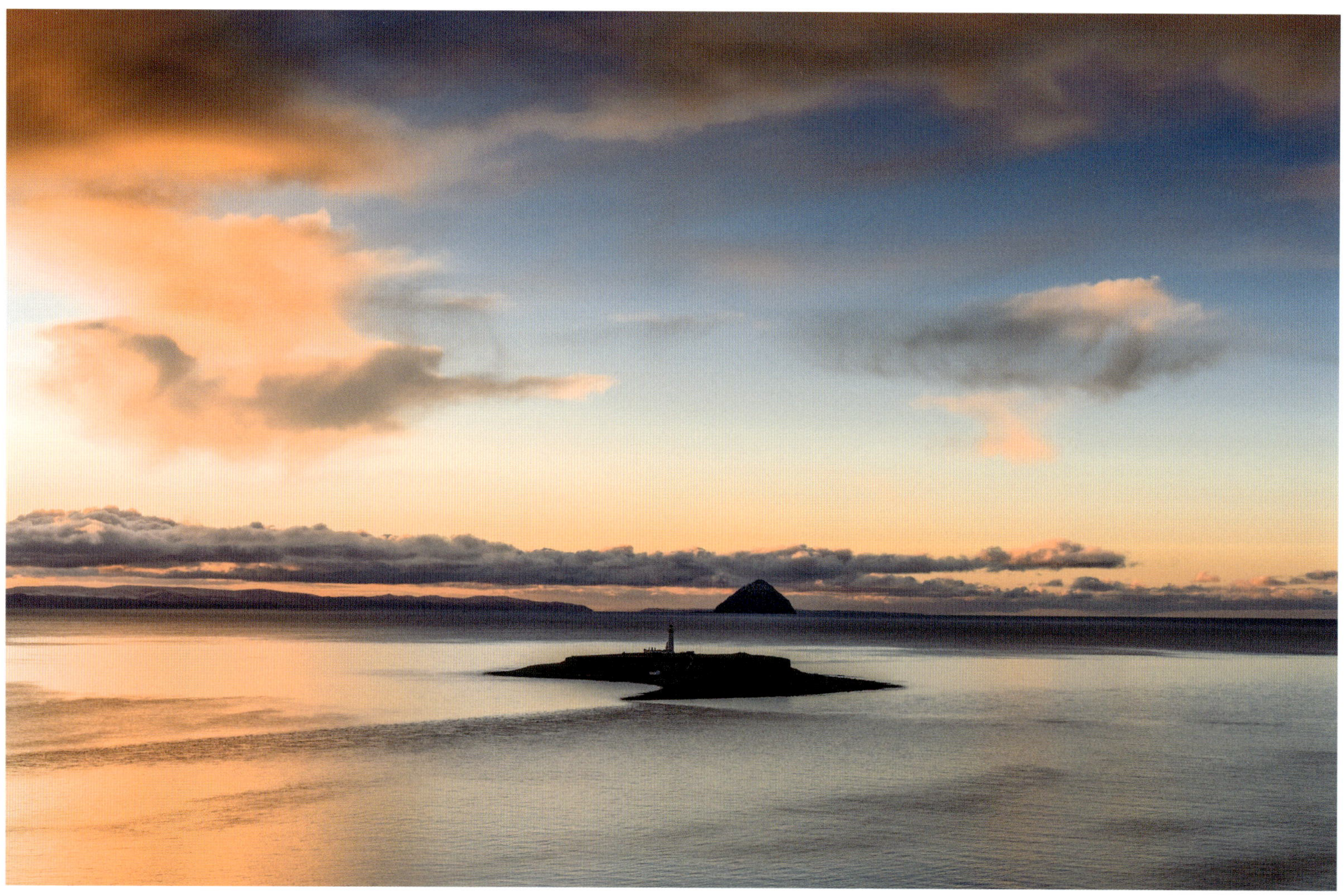

Pladda Lighthouse and Ailsa Craig make for an elegant partnership.

Diagonal flanks cross Ben Nuis, with views to Holy Isle.

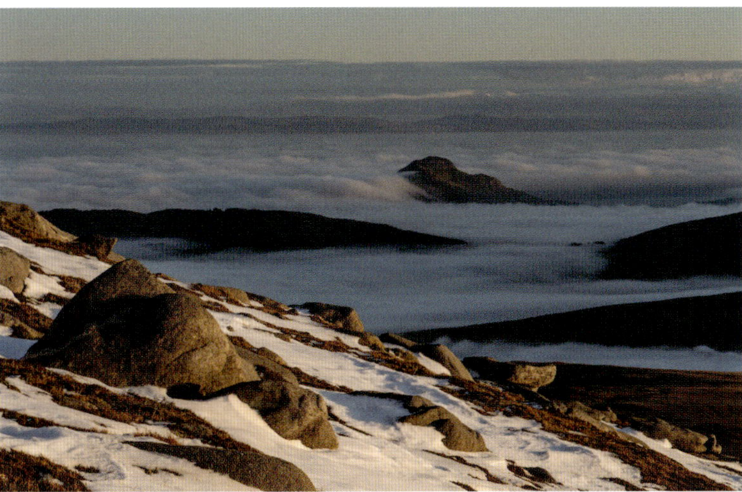

Cormorants on Cleats Shore gaze across to Ailsa Craig.

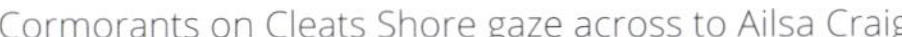
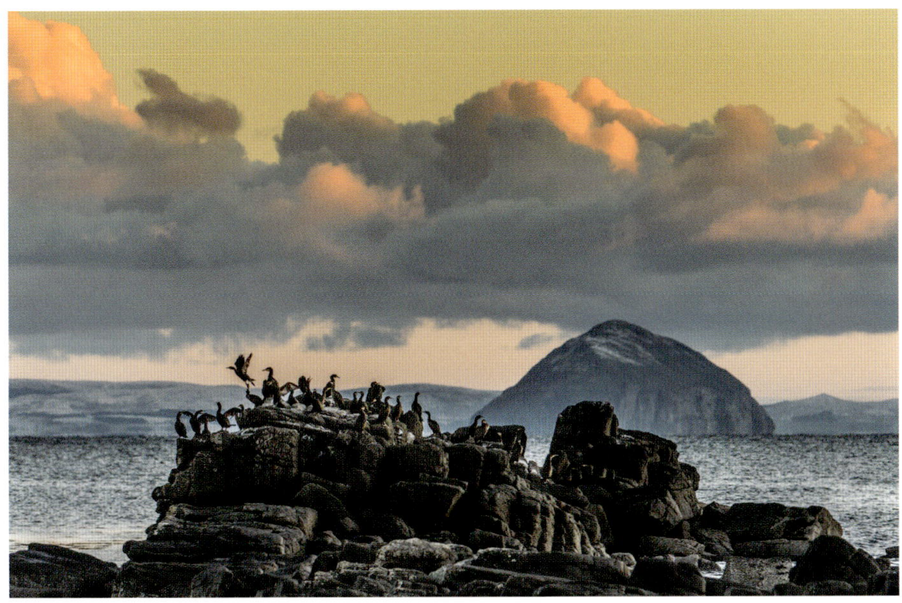

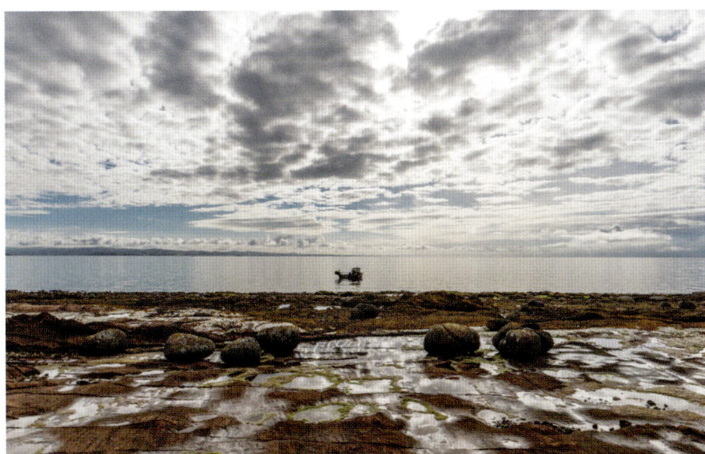

Daybreak with an inshore creeler poised on the Corrie shoreline.

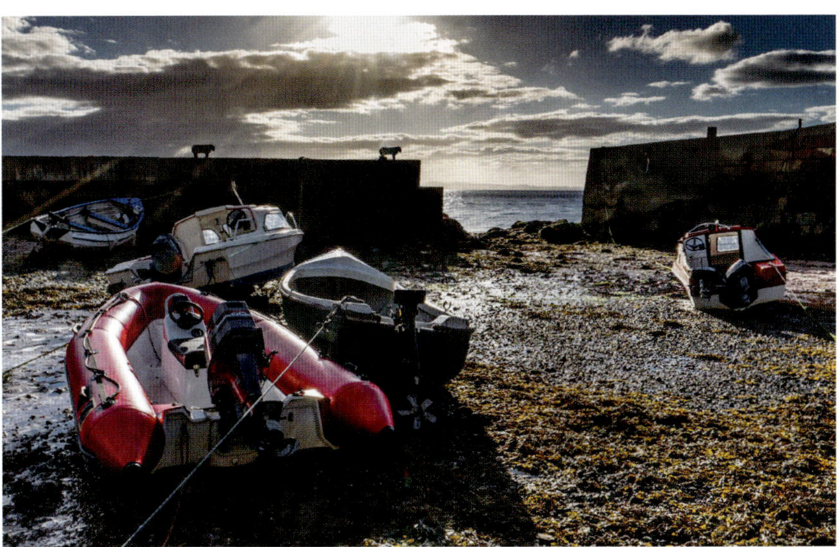

Small boats and cast-iron ewes define Corrie's northern harbour.

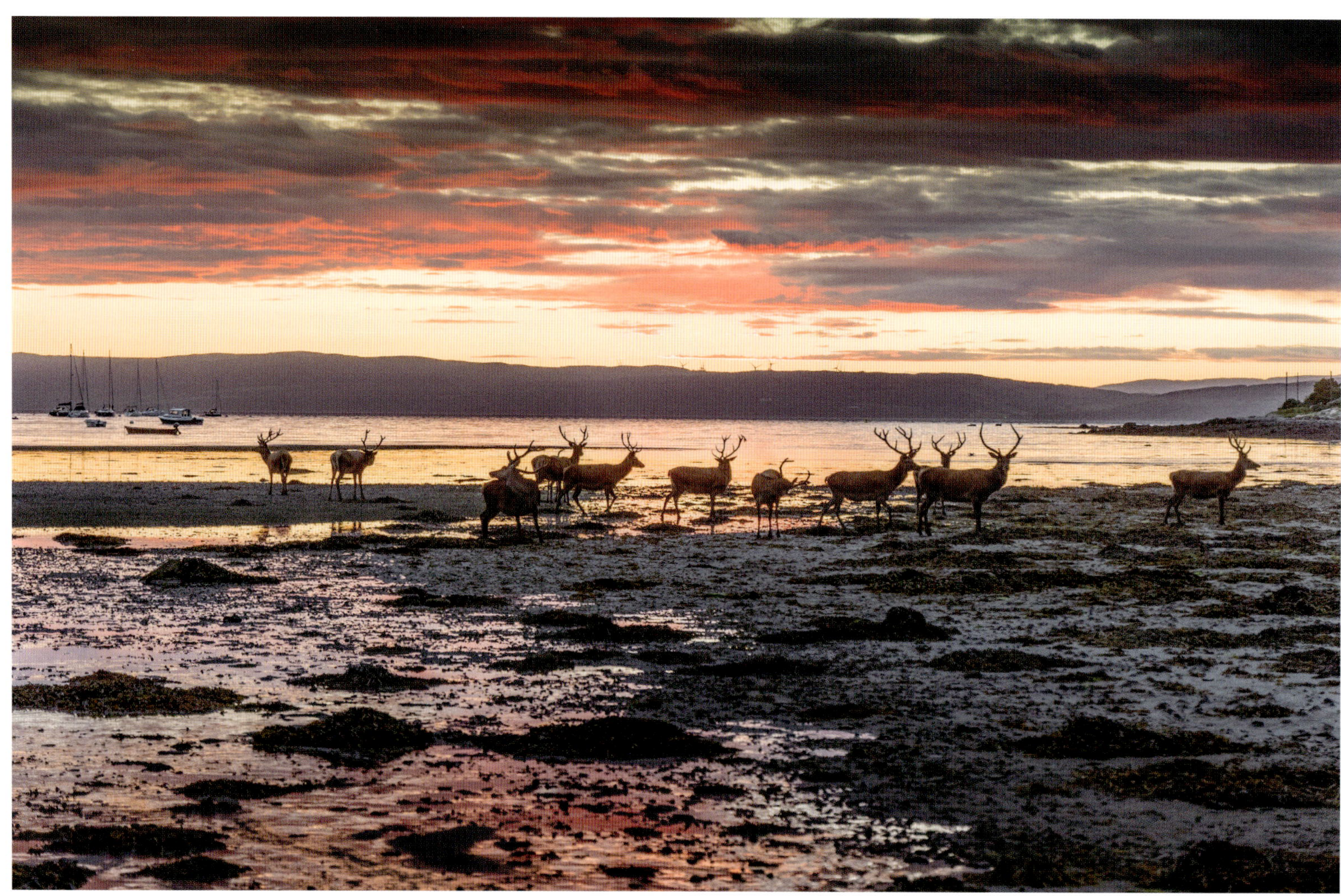

A Lochranza stag party makes its way back to dry shore.

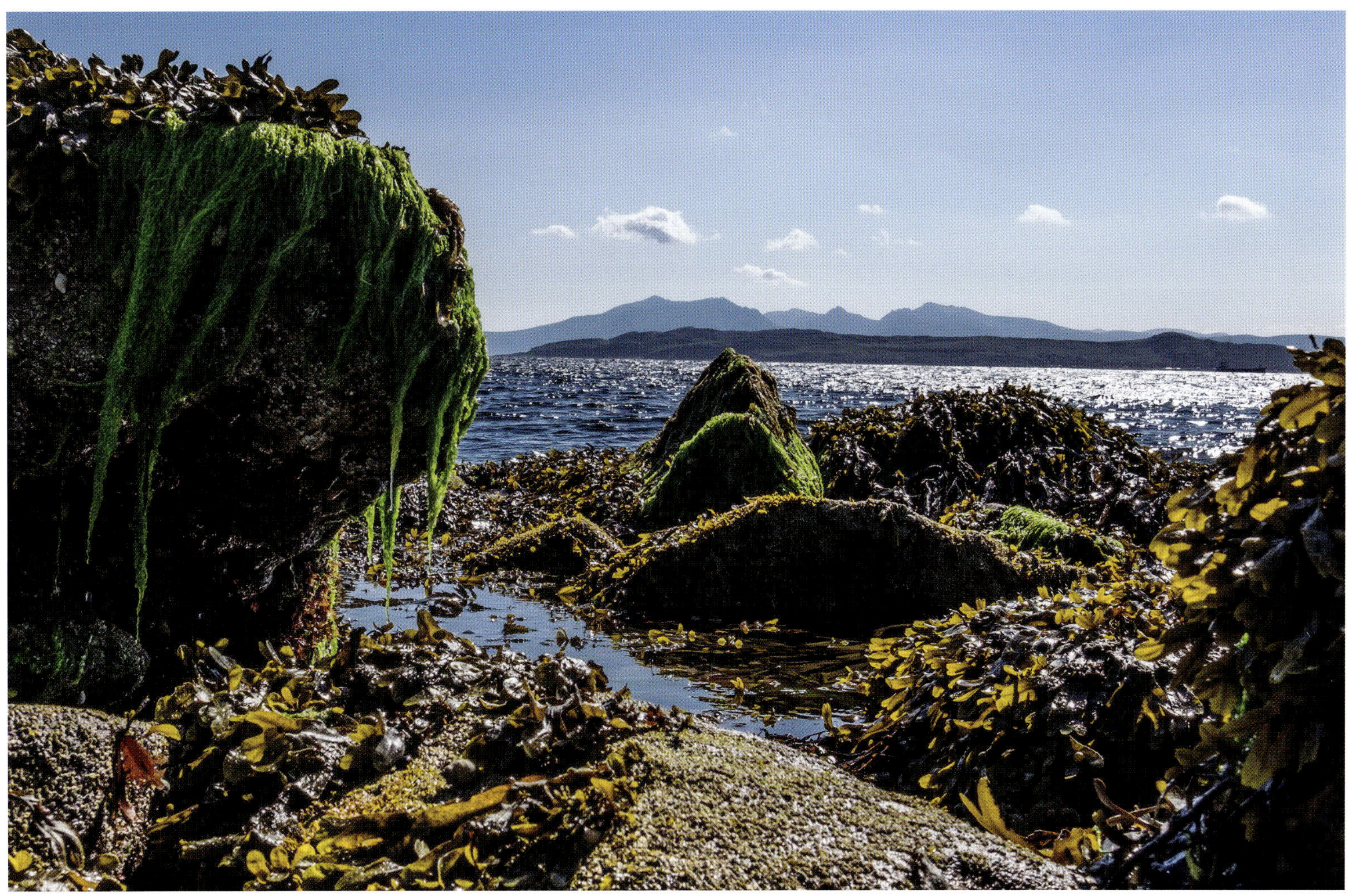

The lush shoreline at Bell Bay with glimpses of Bute and the Arran mountains

The ubiquitous oyster catchers at Fintry Bay

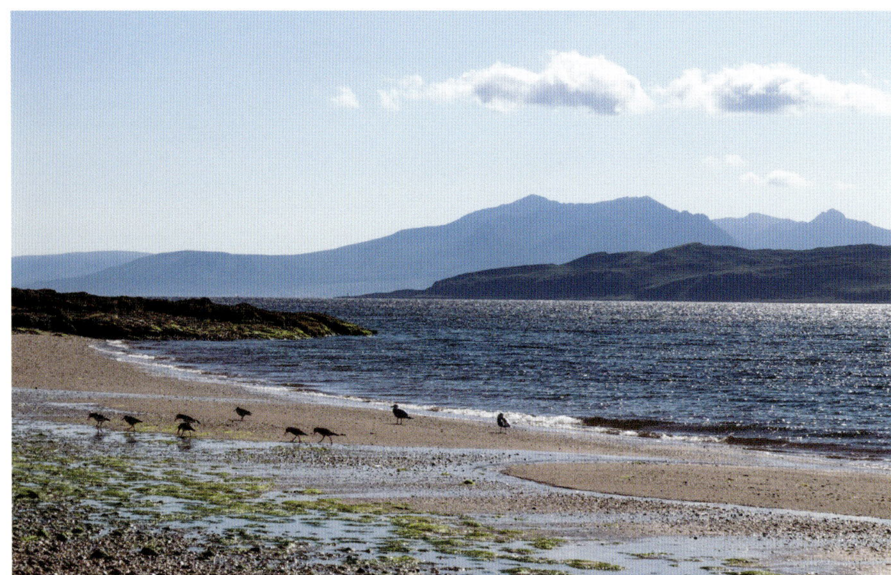

Victorian Villas line the shore around Kames Bay in Millport

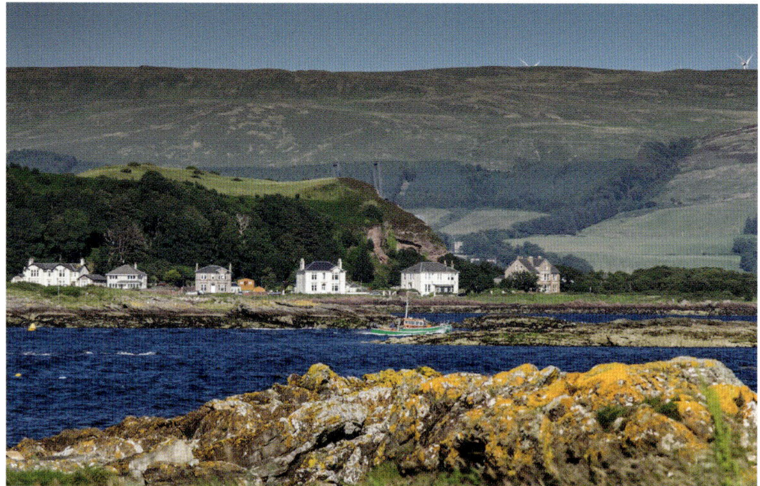

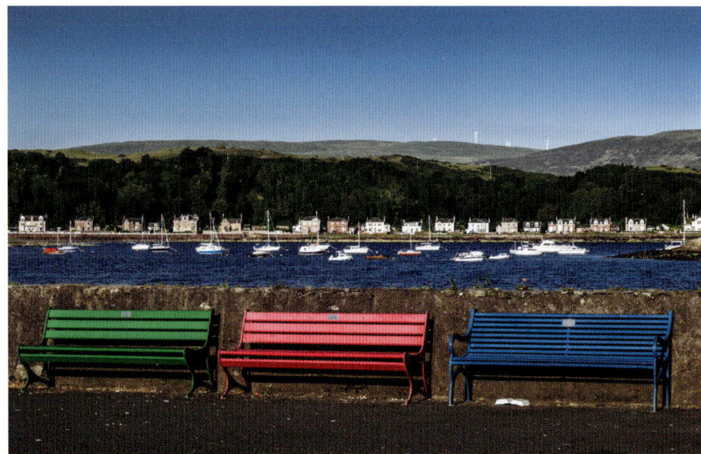

Colourful benches, moorings and the marine parade at Millport

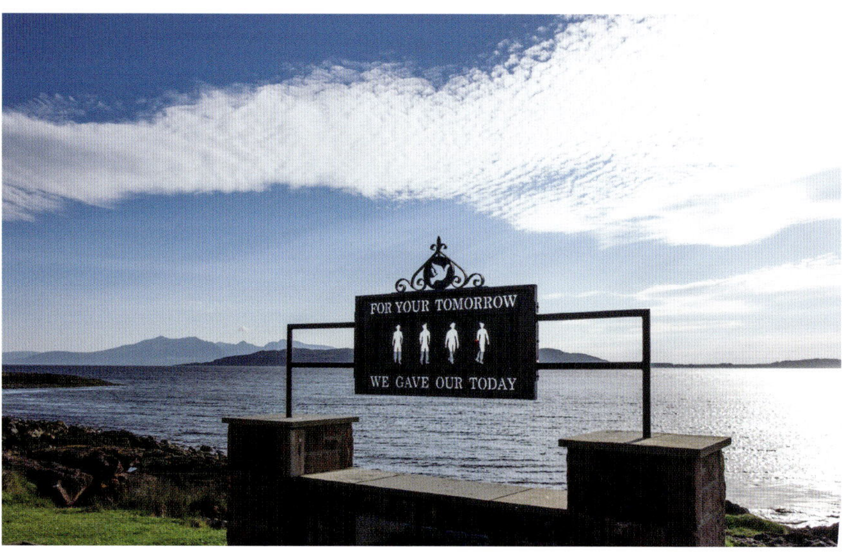

One of two war memorials at Millport

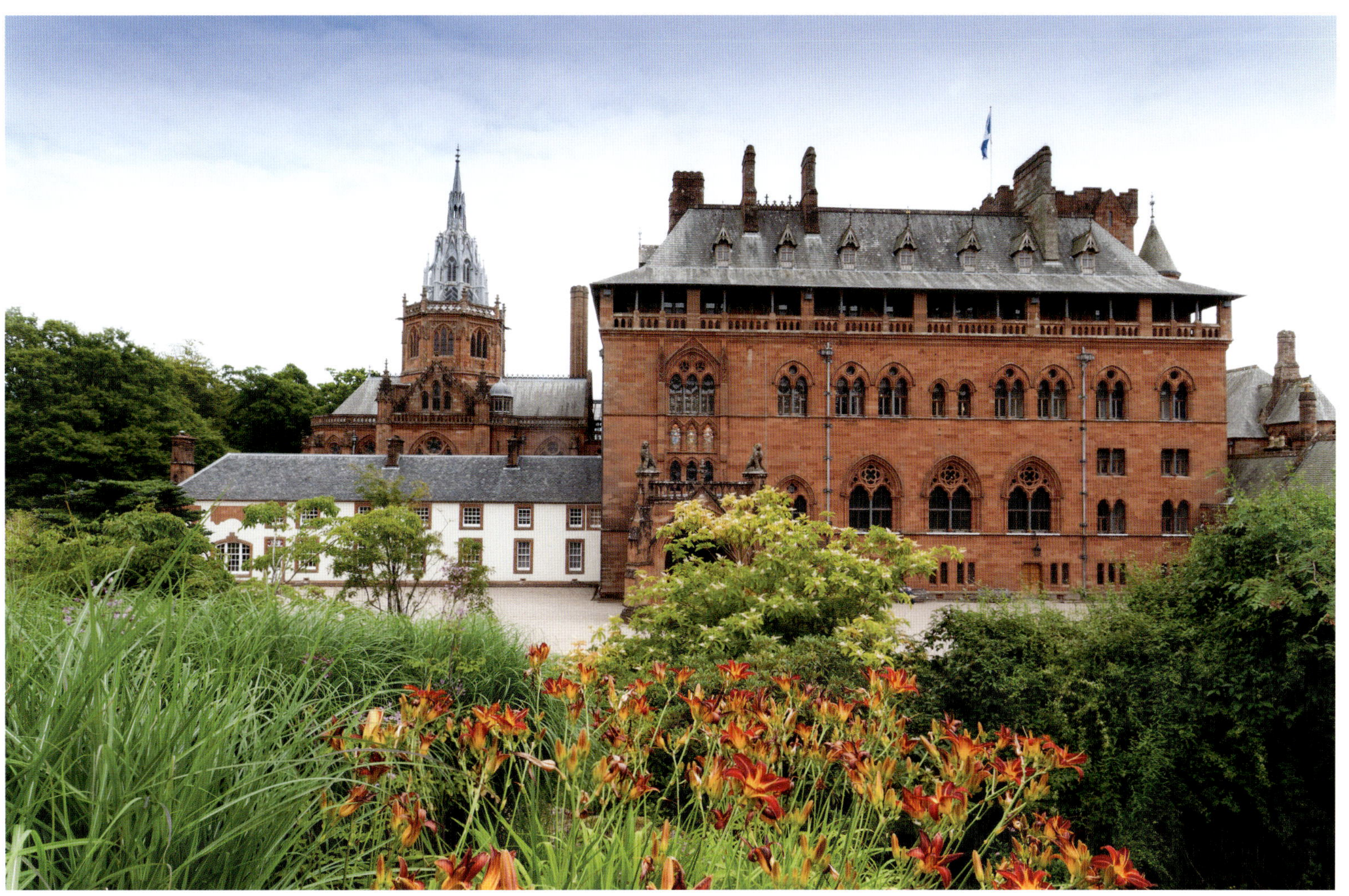

Palatial Mount Stuart, seat of the Stuart family of Bute

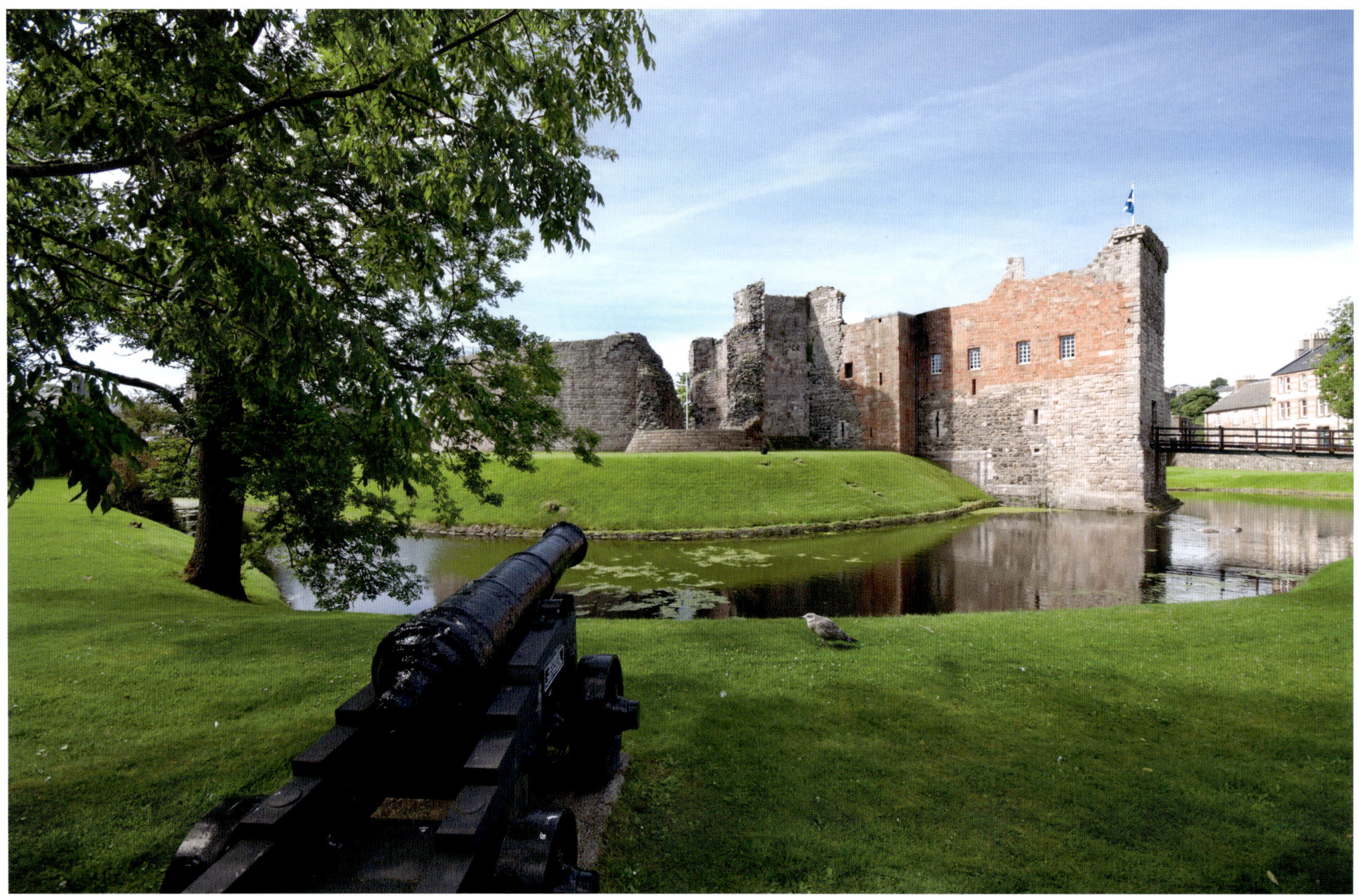

Rothesay Castle and moat

Ettrick Bay, Midpark Island & Arran Mountain profile

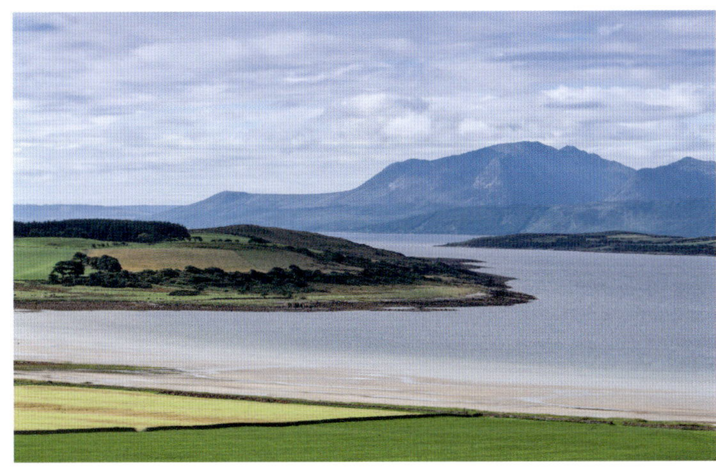

Victorian grandeur along the Rothesay seafront

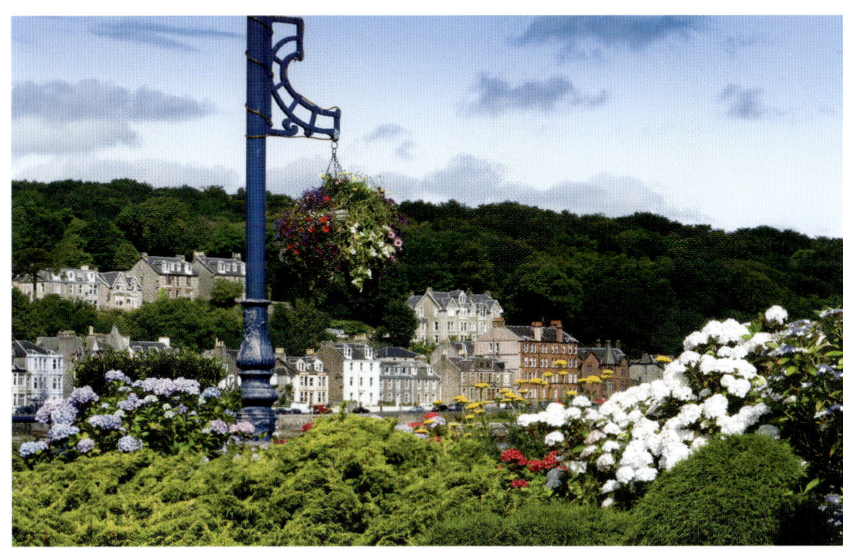

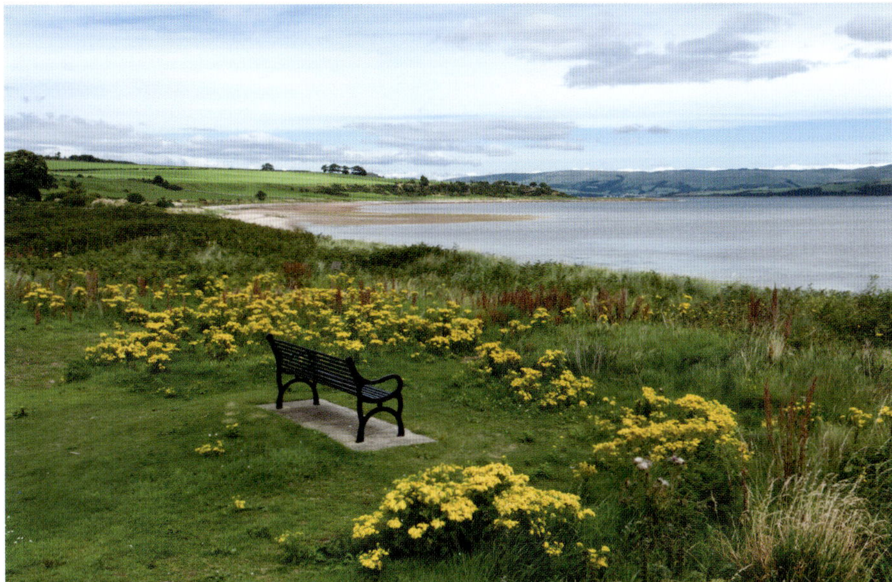

Stop a while at Kilchattan Bay

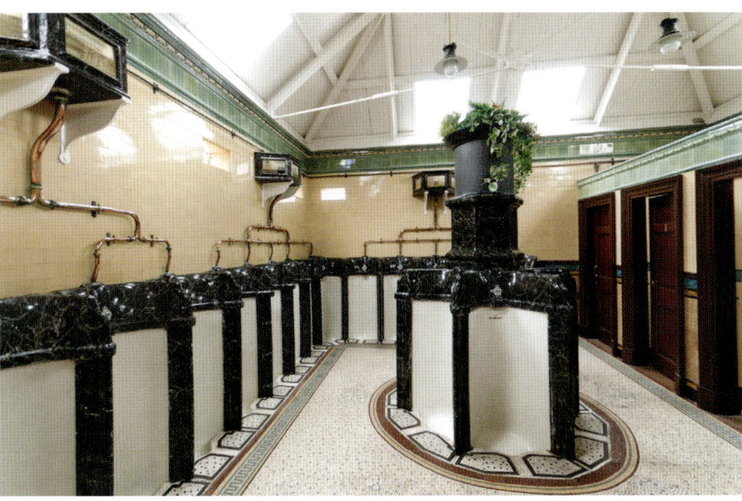

Rothesay's lavish Victorian public toilets are a work of art

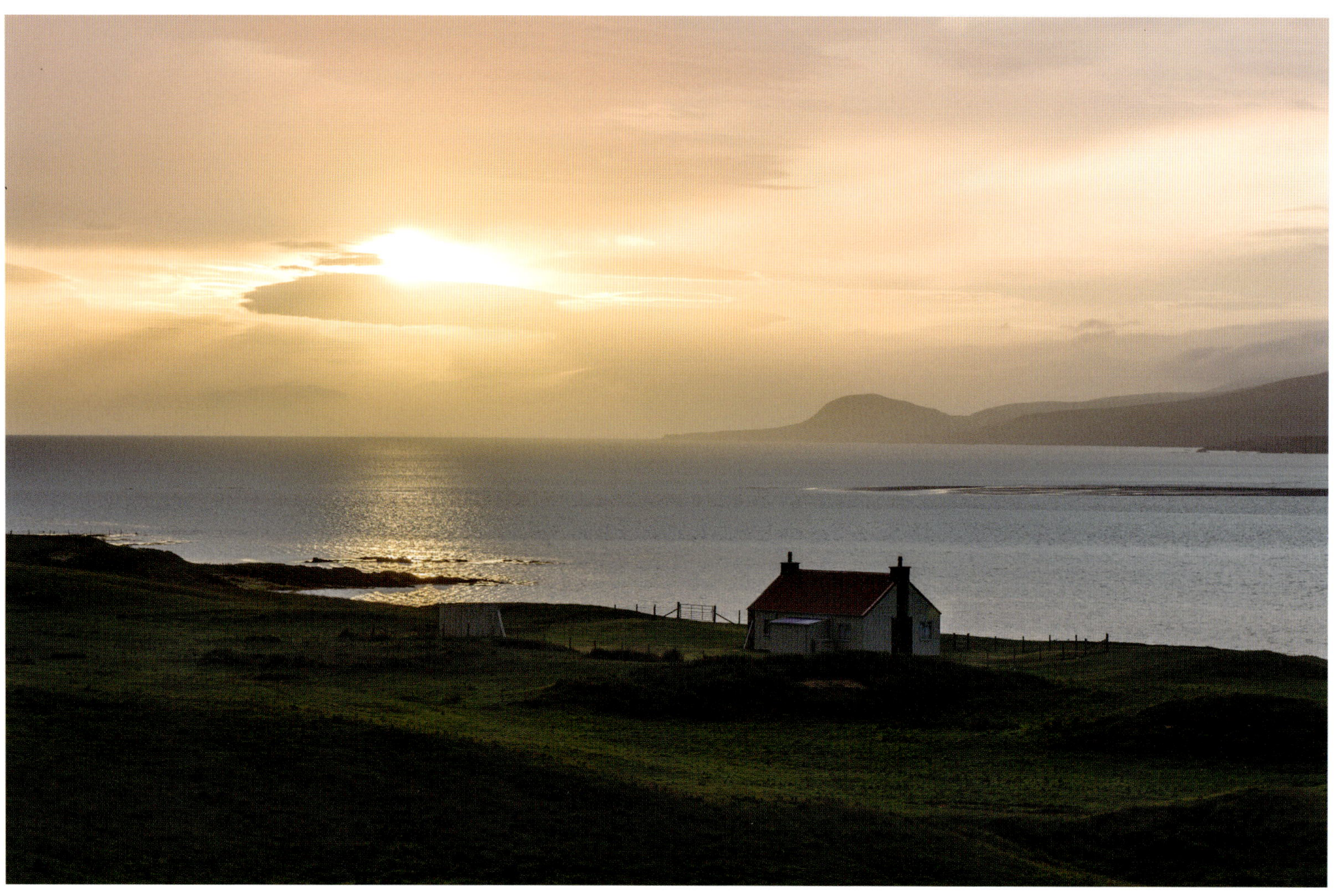

A holiday cottage on the shores of Loch Gruinart

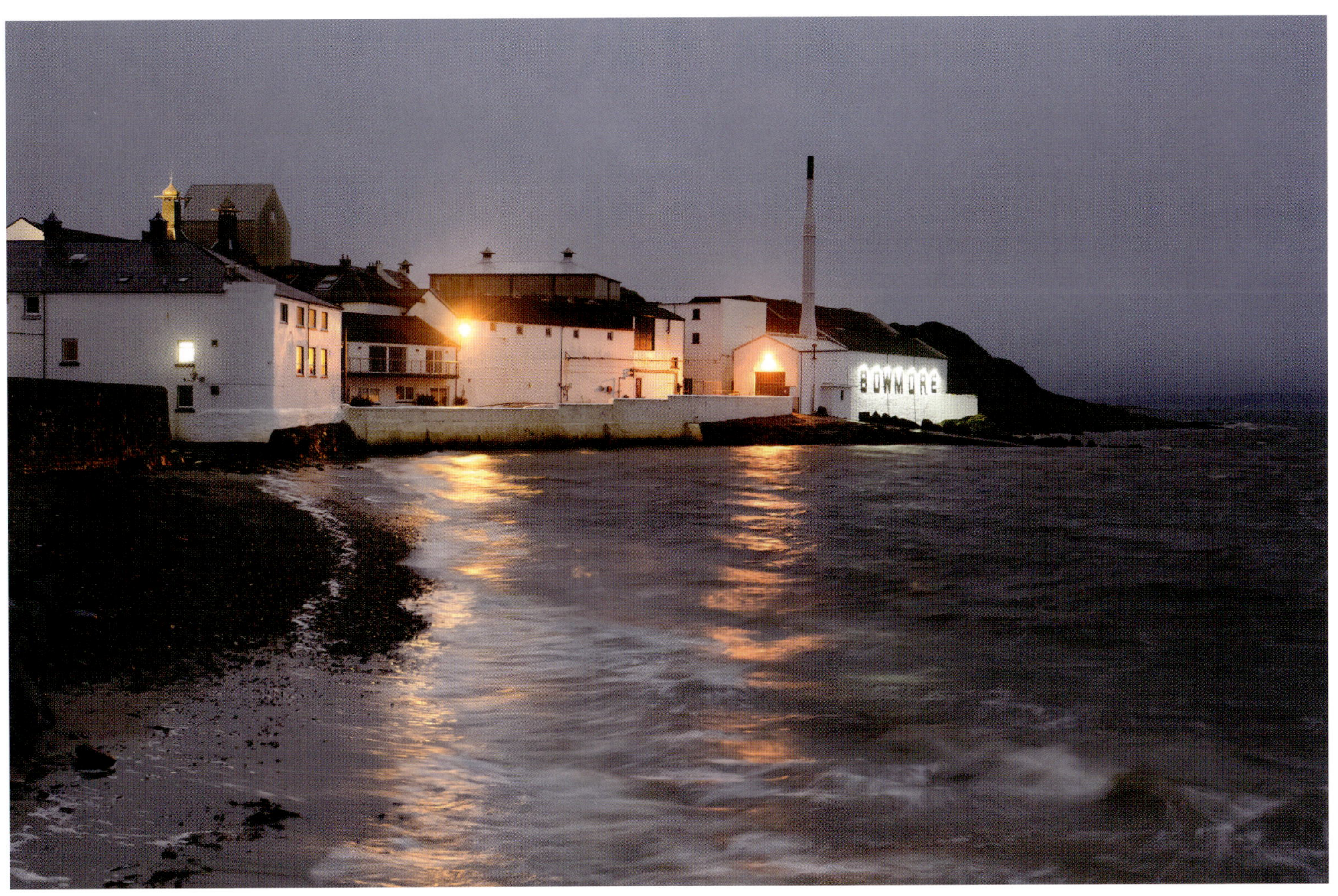

The Bowmore distillery was founded in 1779.

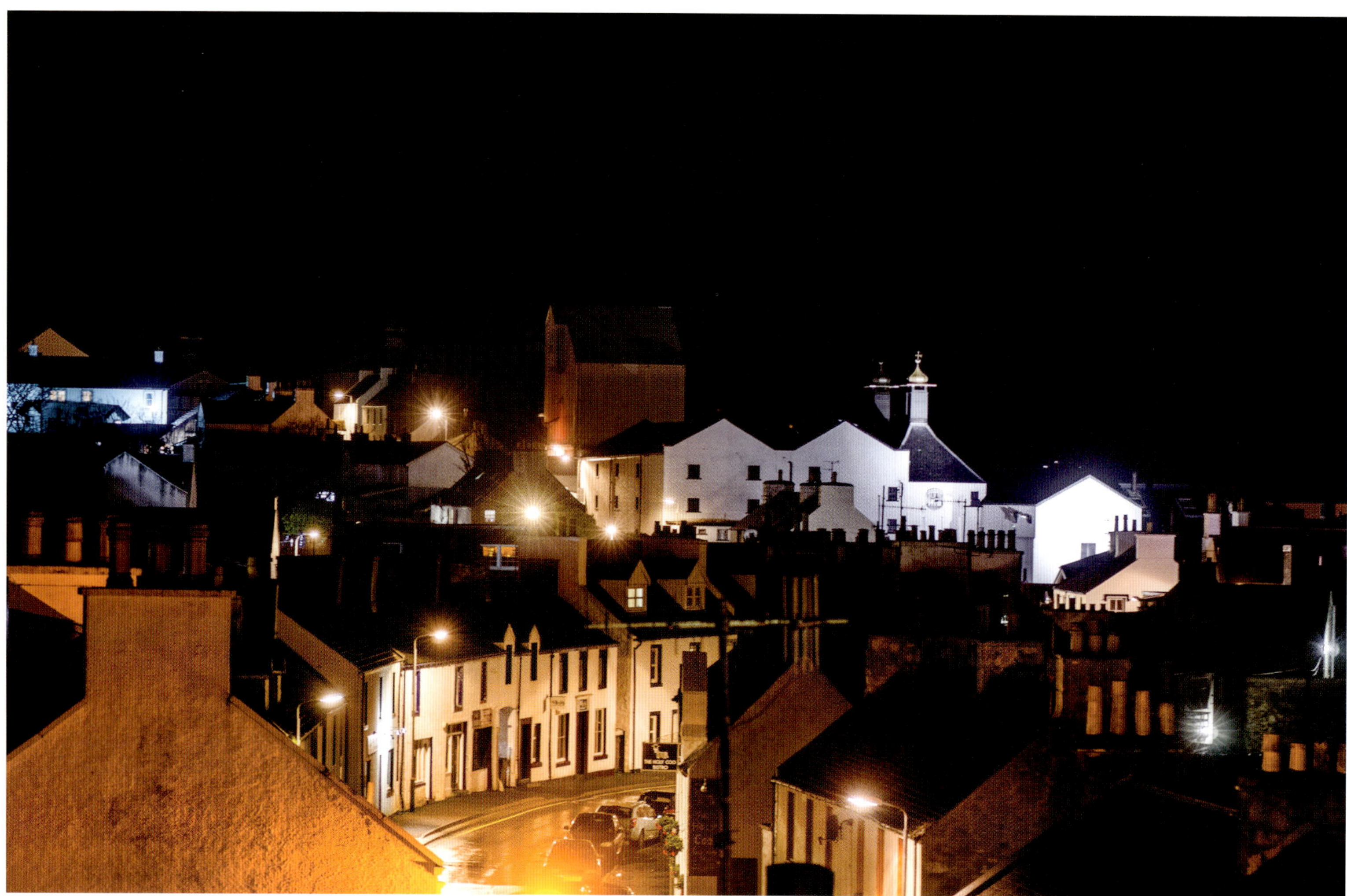

Bowmore by night

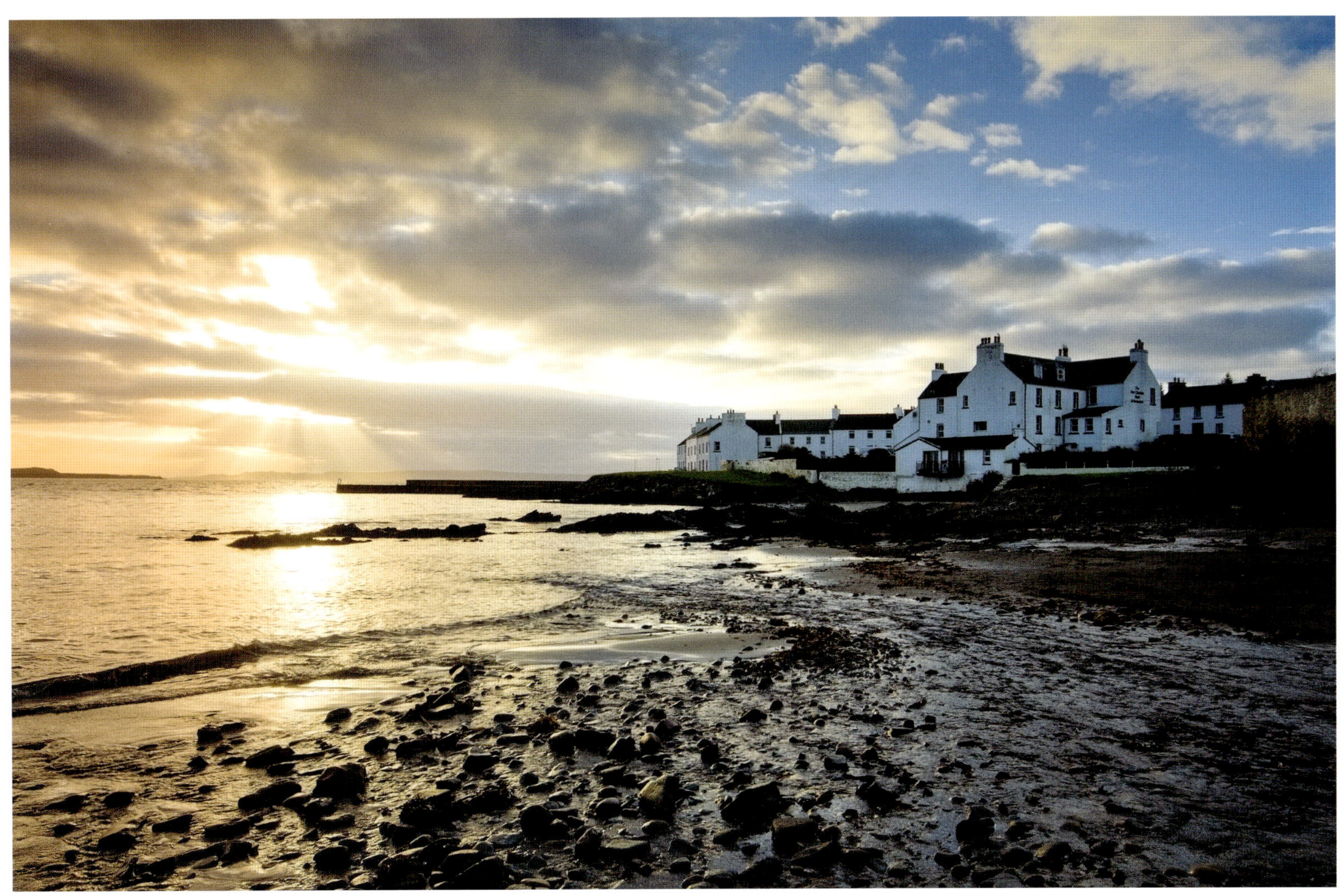

Port Charlotte

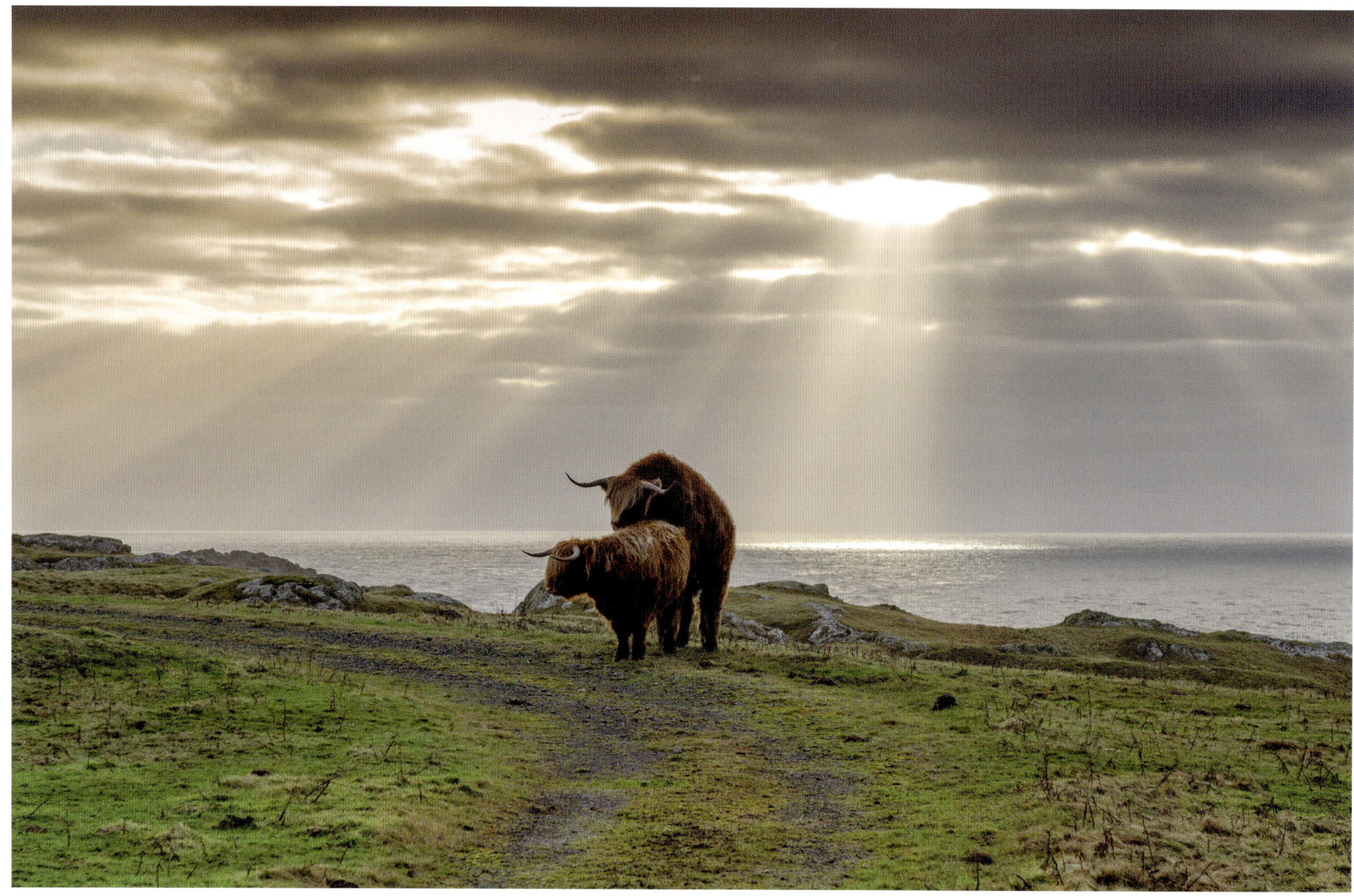

Island romance, Port Wemyss

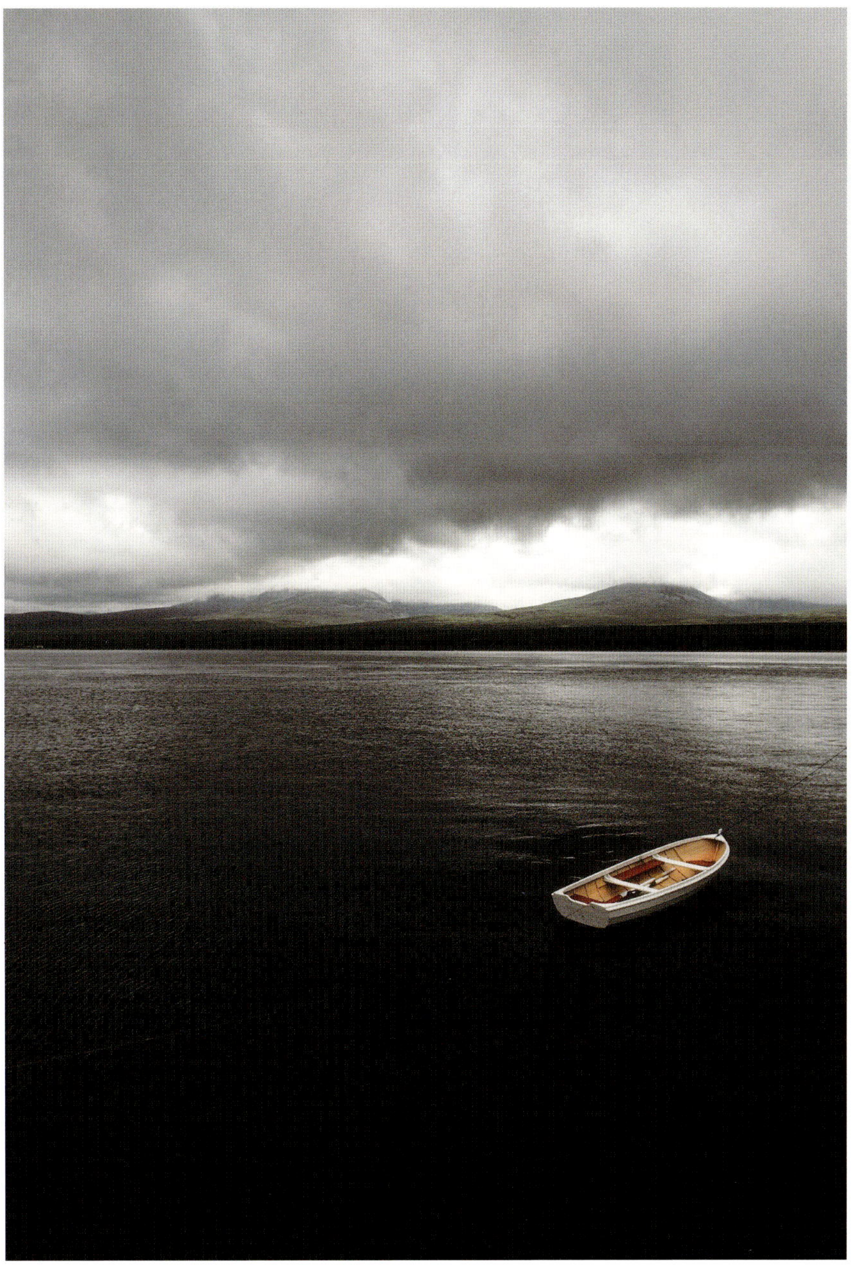

A dinghy on the grey sea at Caol Ila

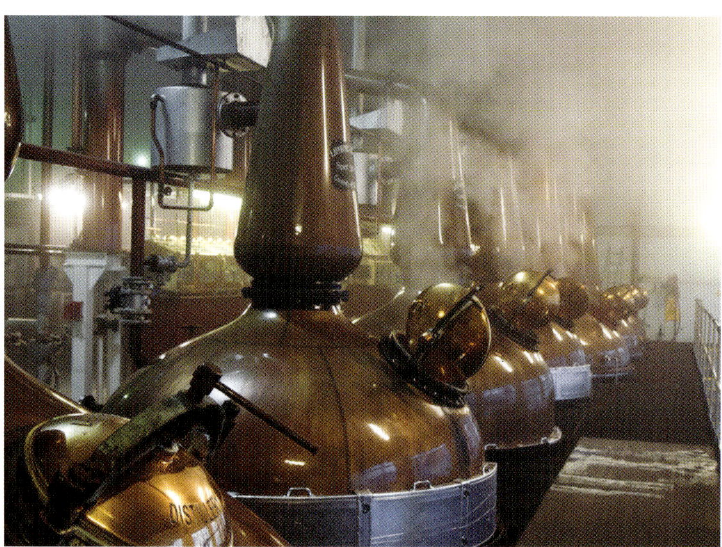
The working stills at Laphroaig distillery

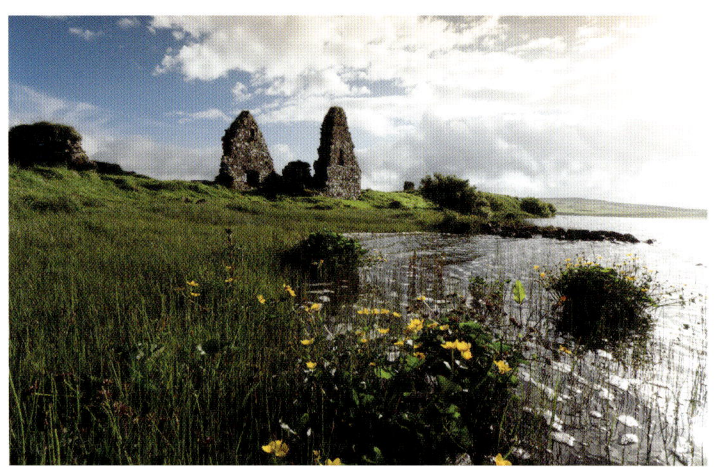
Finlaggan, the original seat of the Lords of the Isles

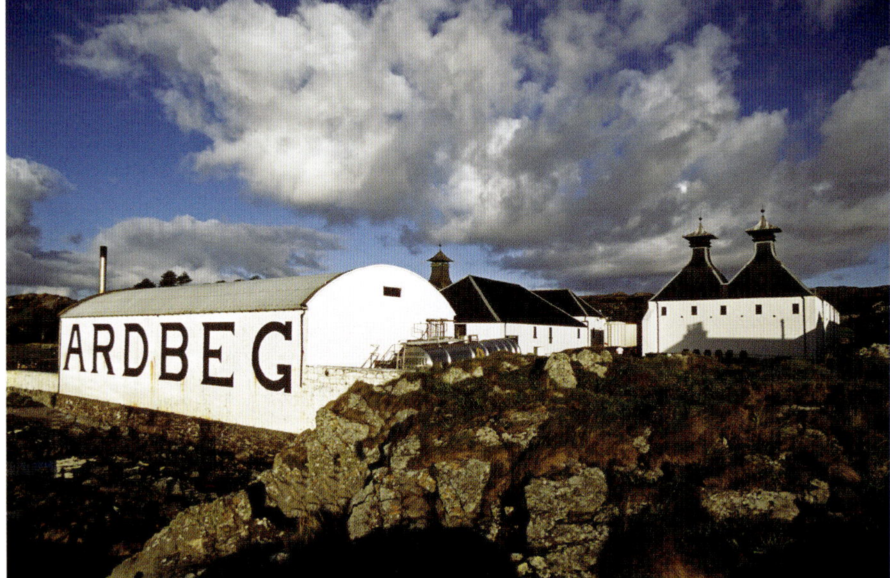
Ardbeg distillery has been producing whisky since 1798.

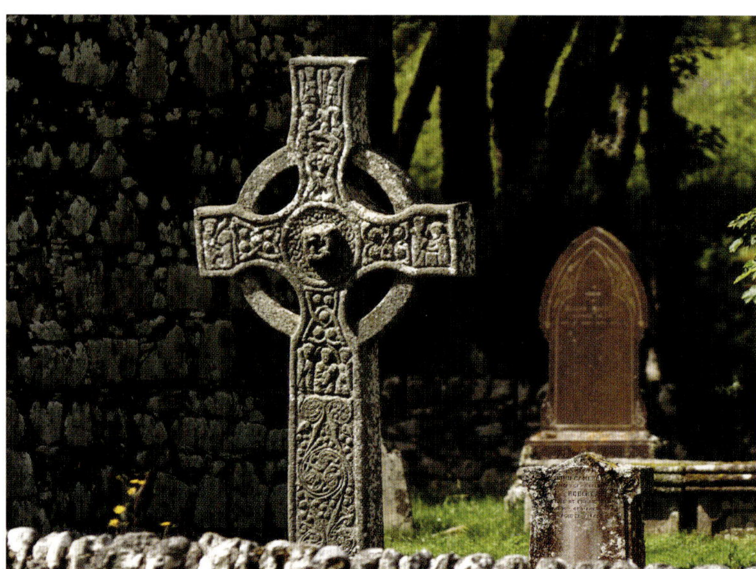
The Celtic cross at Kildalton

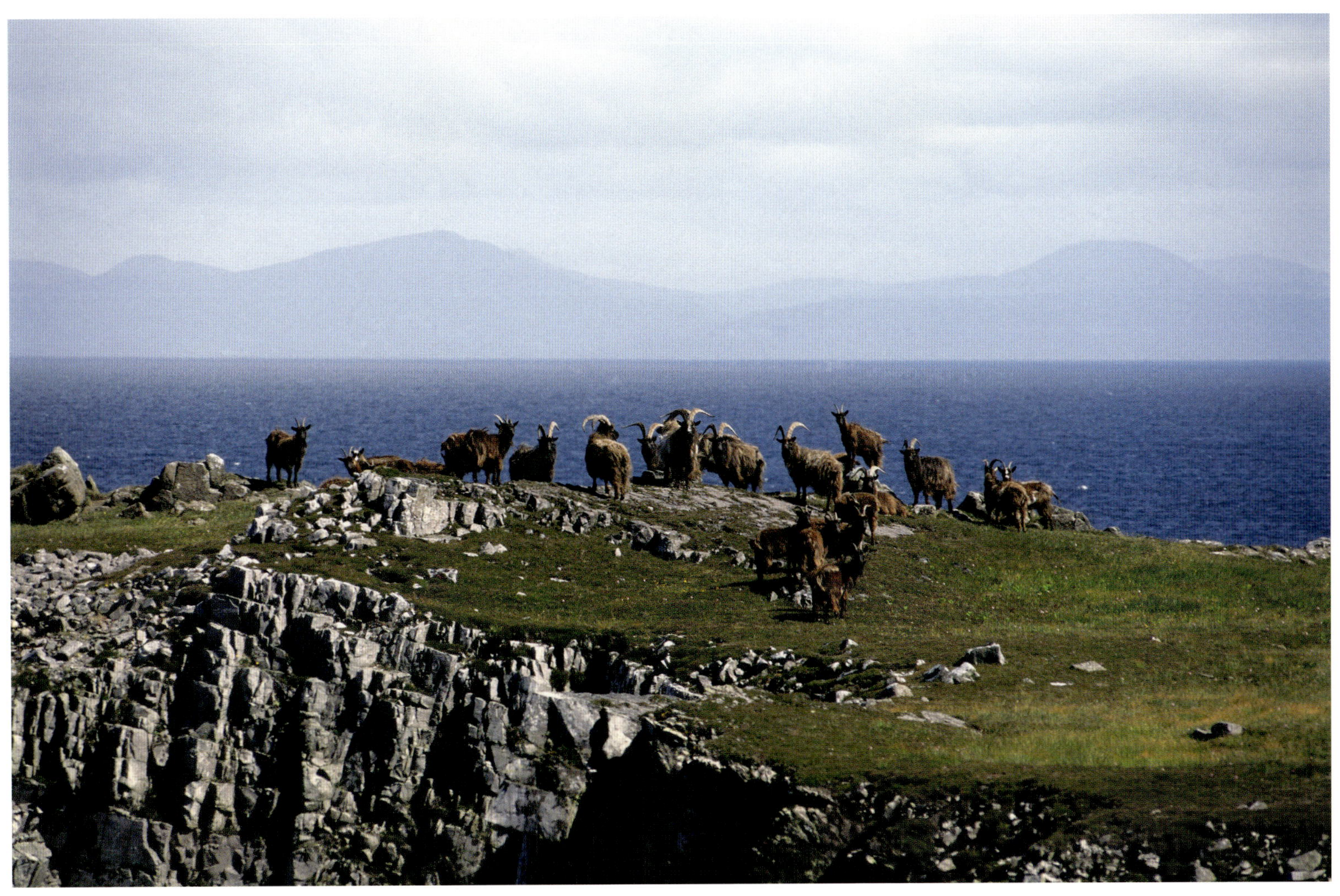

A shaggy and pungent feral goat herd highlight the genuine wildness
of Jura's vast western shore, with Mull on the horizon.

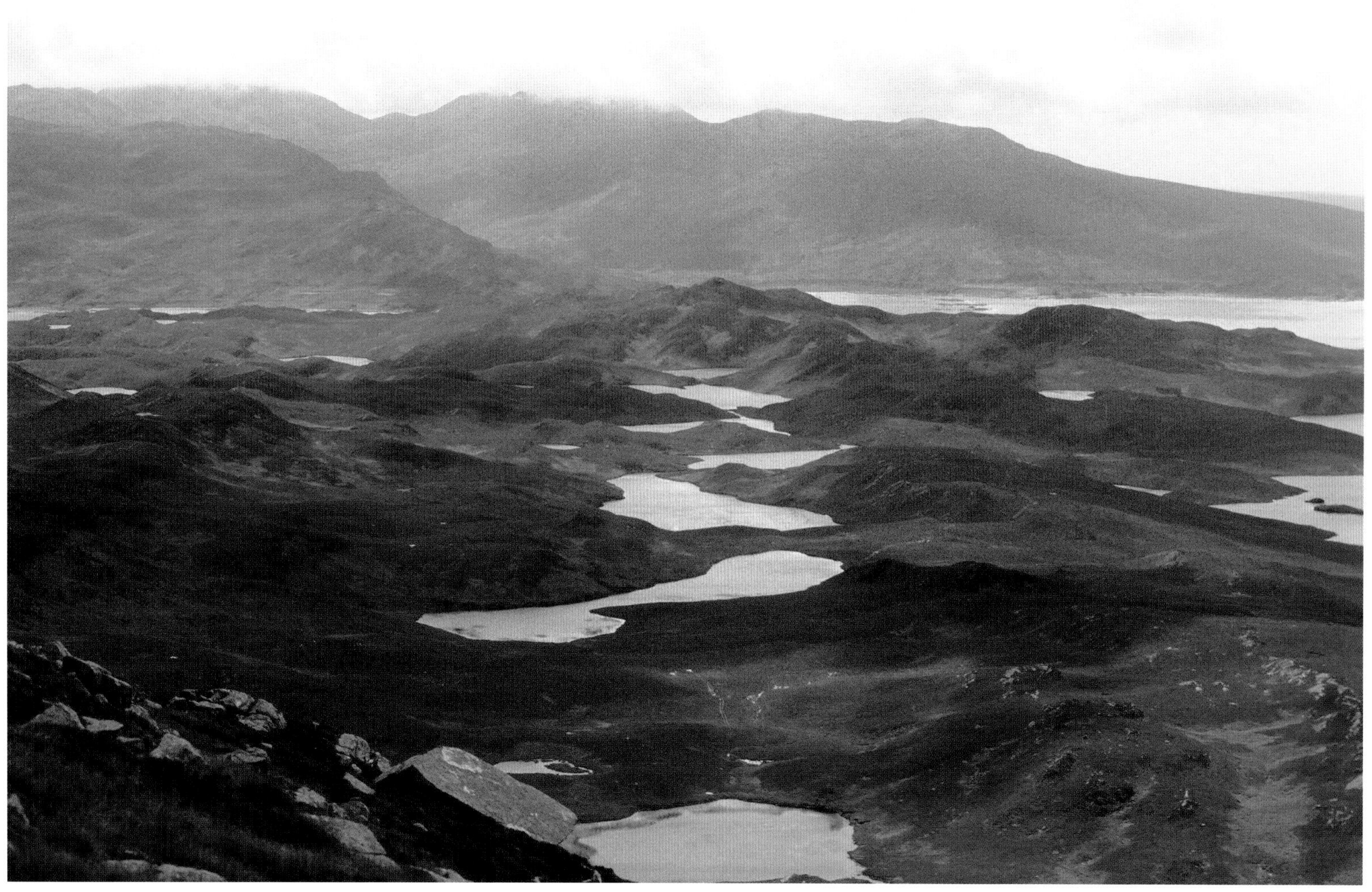

A cluster of remote lochans, some named, some not, looking
south across Loch Tarbert to the misty Paps of Jura.

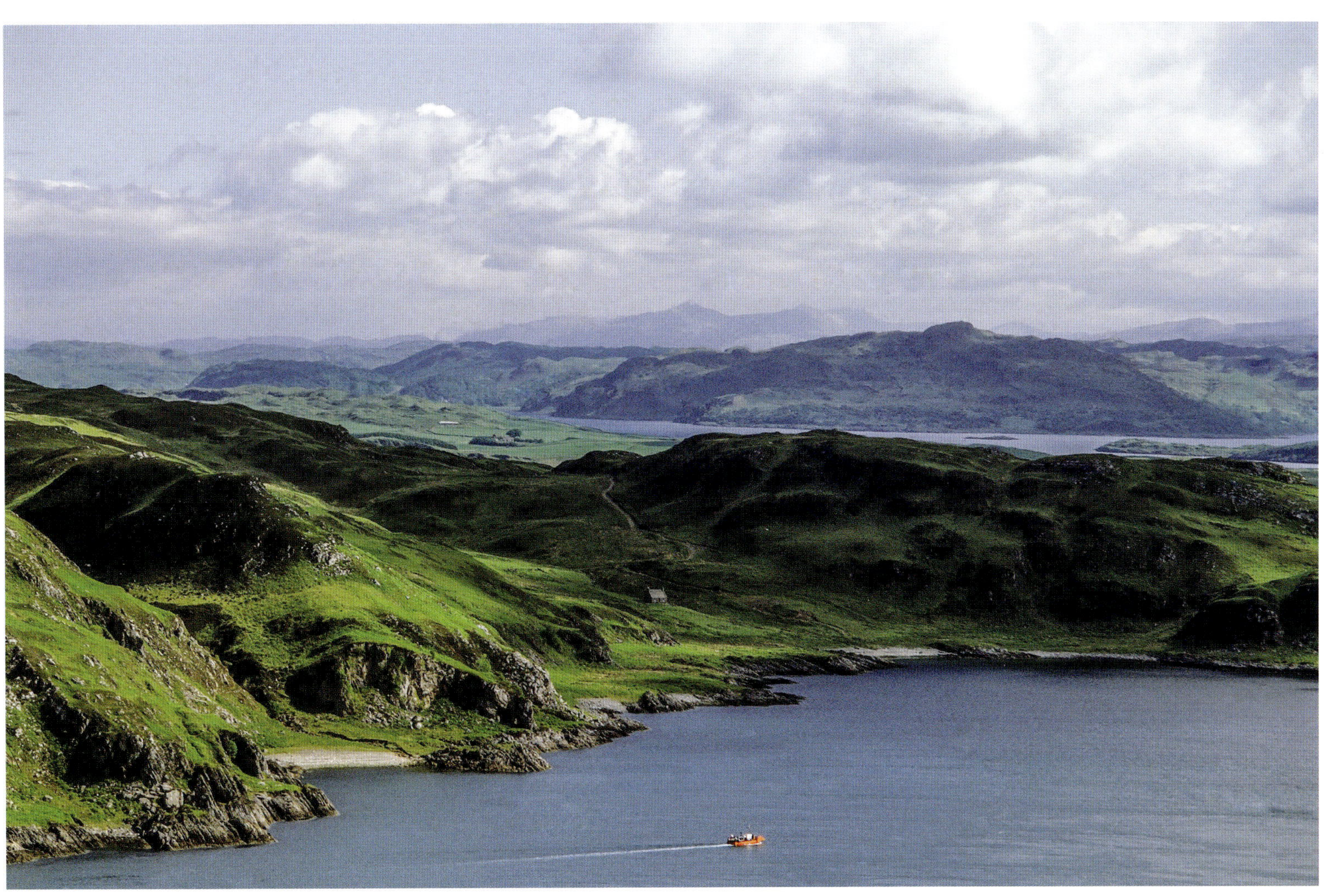

A lonely bothy on uninhabited Scarba from the most Northerly point
of Jura, with the deceptively calm Corryvreckan below

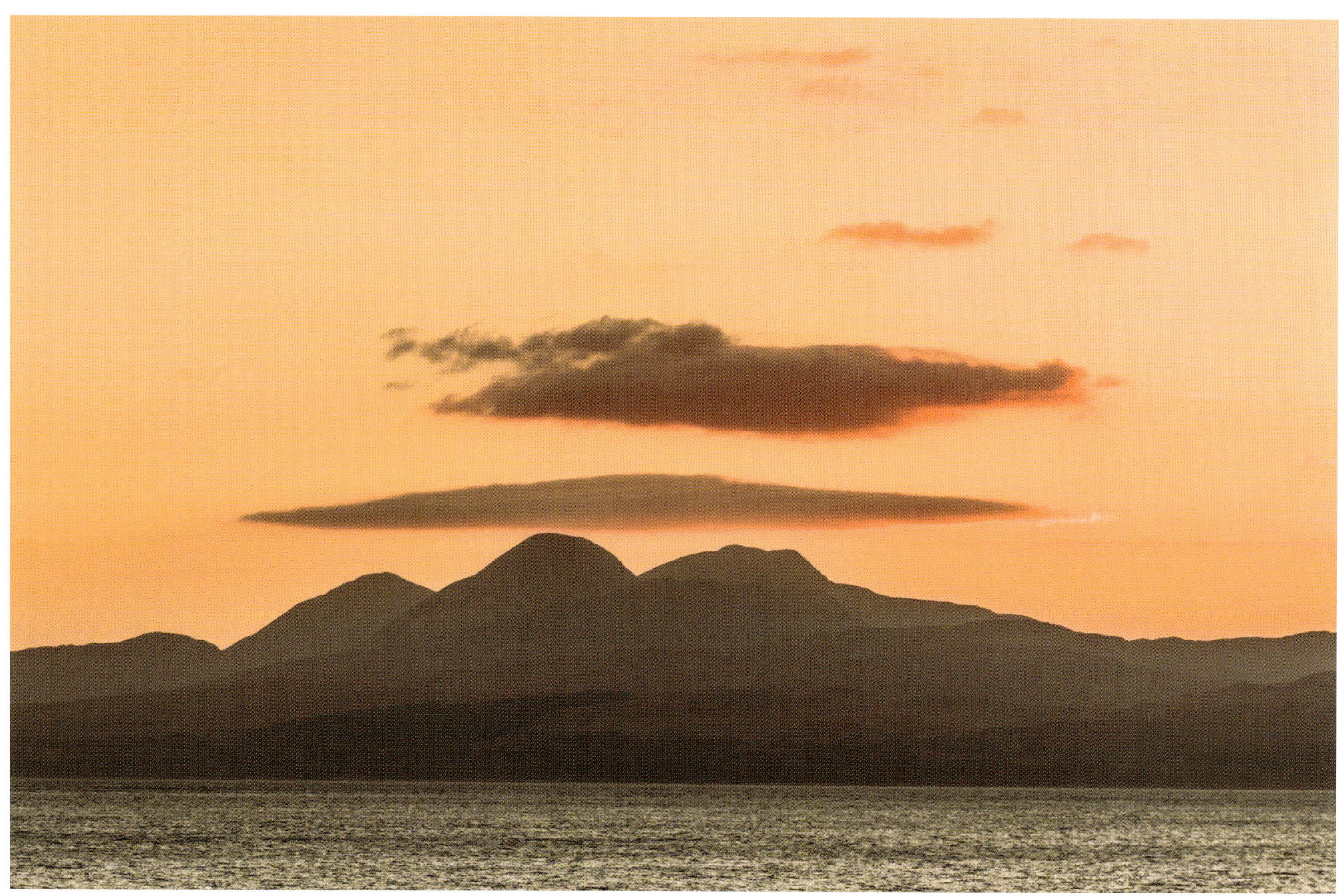

The harmony of the Paps, caught here from Keilmore on the Knapdale peninsula.

The long and winding road on Jura

Barnhill farm cottage, where George Orwell wrote 1984.

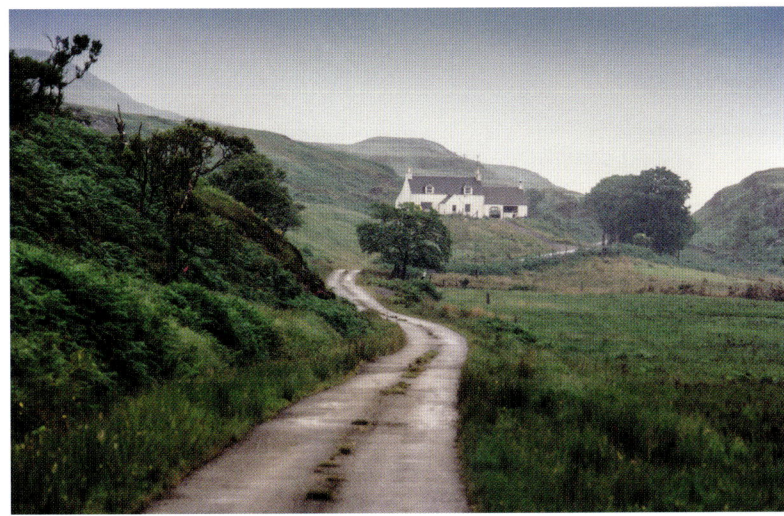

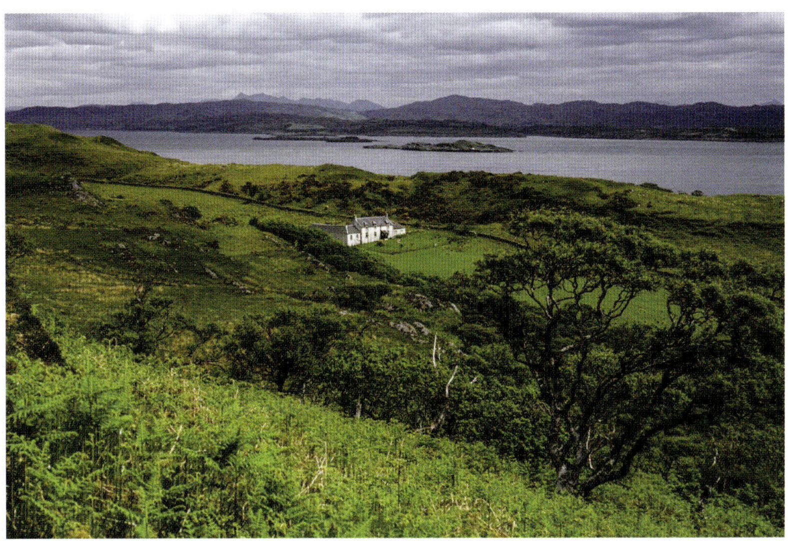

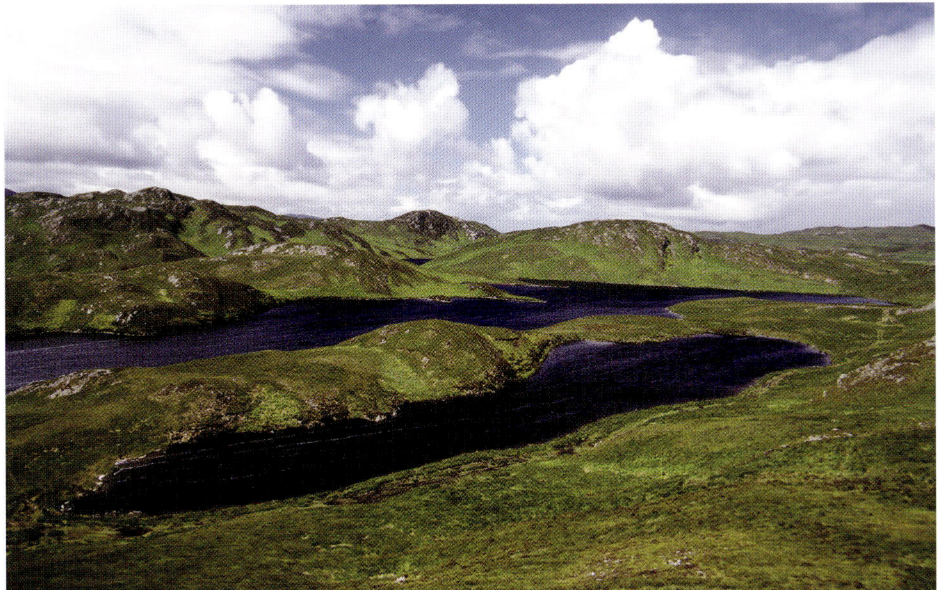

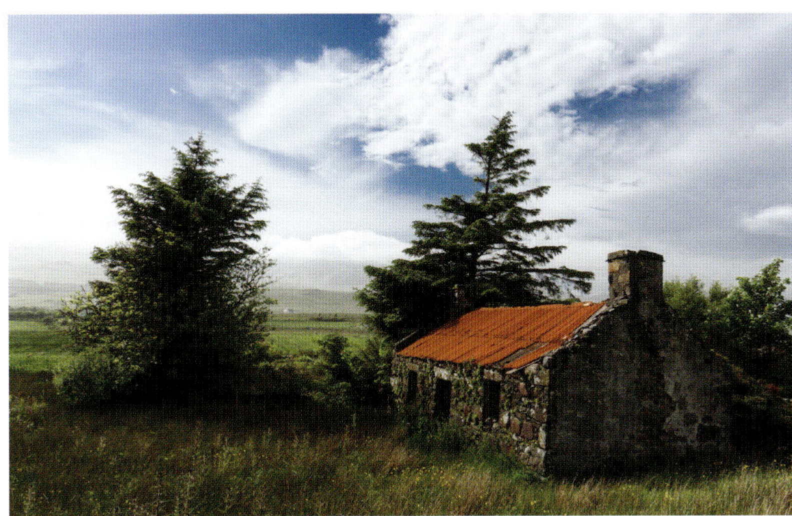

Abandoned Hebridean steadings, akin to earlier blackhouses, in south eastern Jura

Loch Righ Meadhonach and Loch Righ Mor in the heart of Jura

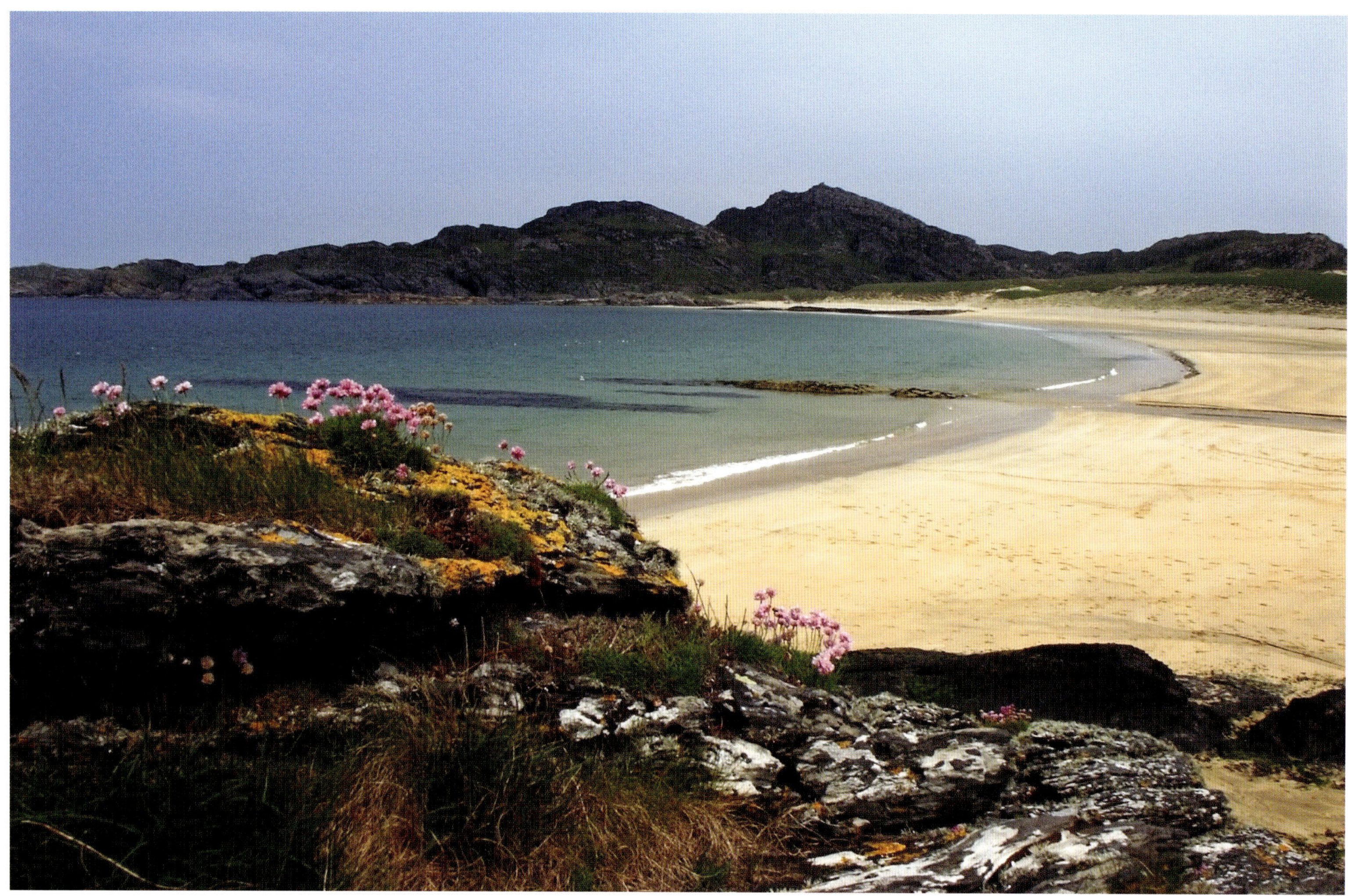

The quintessentially Hebridean Kiloran Bay is a sweet spot for most.

The pristine shoreline at Garvard

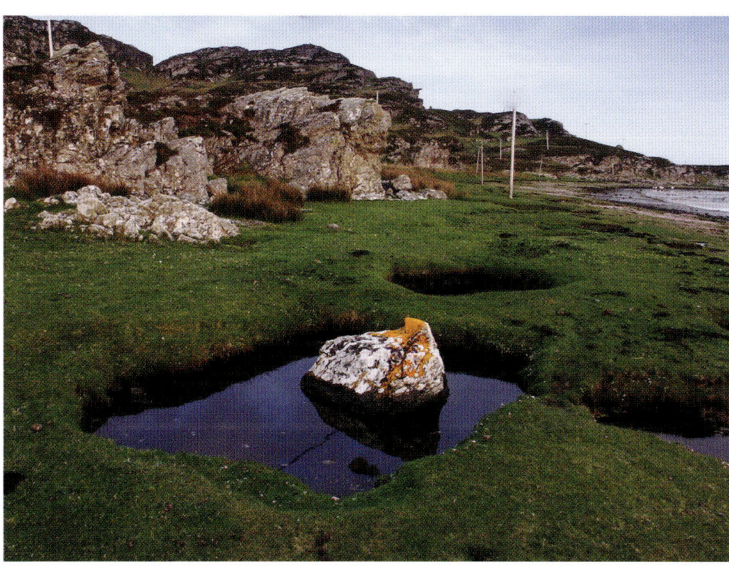

A standing Stone at Garvard, overlooking Oronsay, with the Paps of Jura in the background.

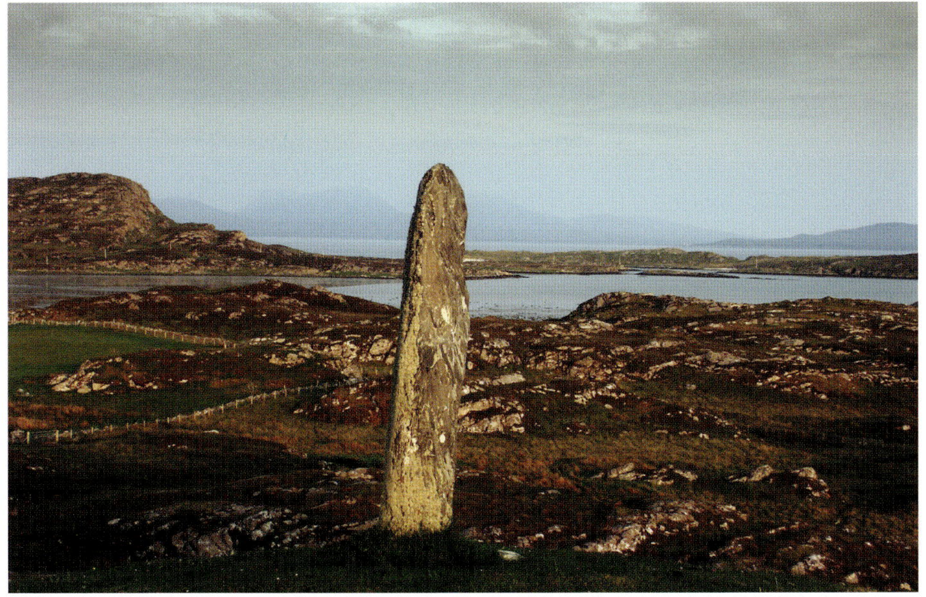

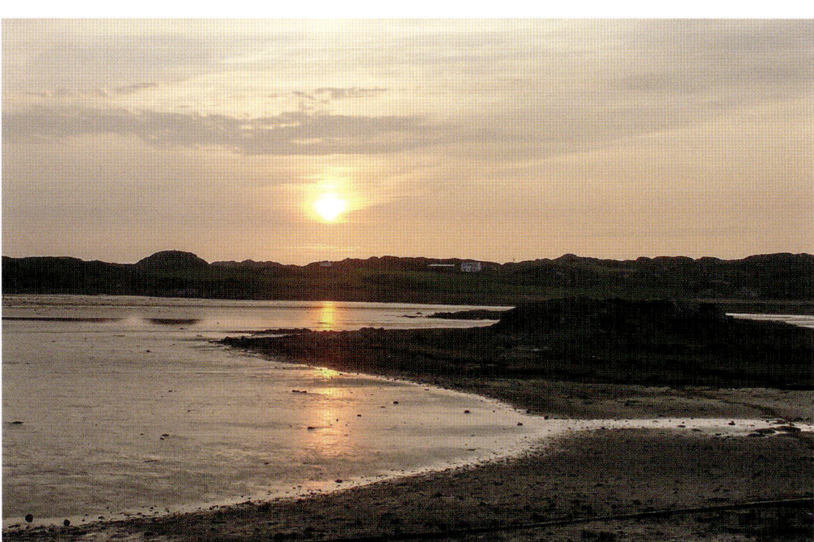

Oronsay is accessible with the tides

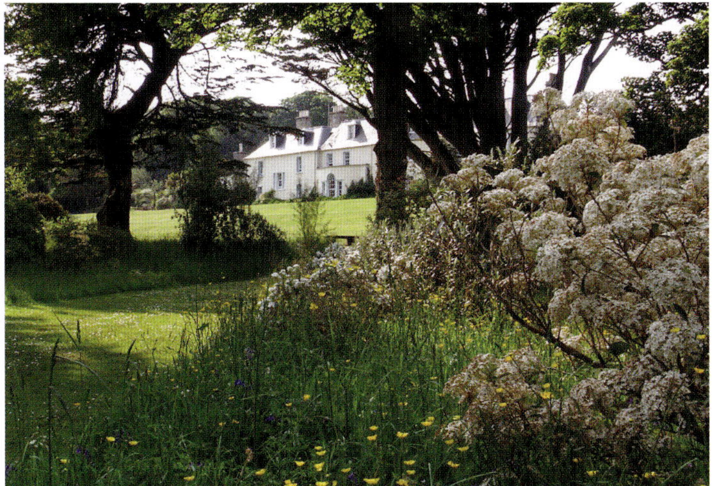

The tranquillity of Jura House with its sumptuous garden.

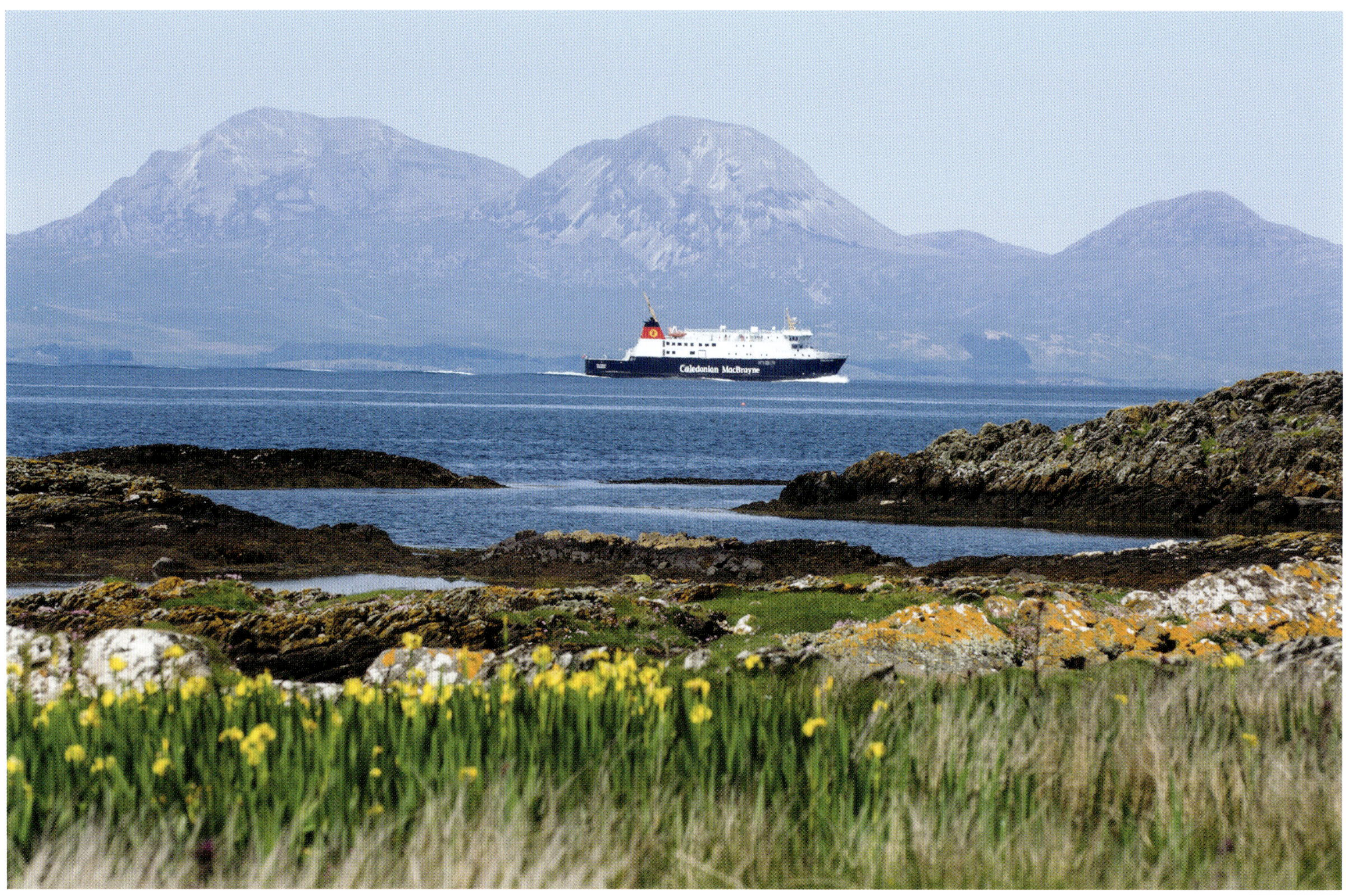

CalMac's MV Finlaggan sails between southern Jura and the northernmost tip of Gigha.

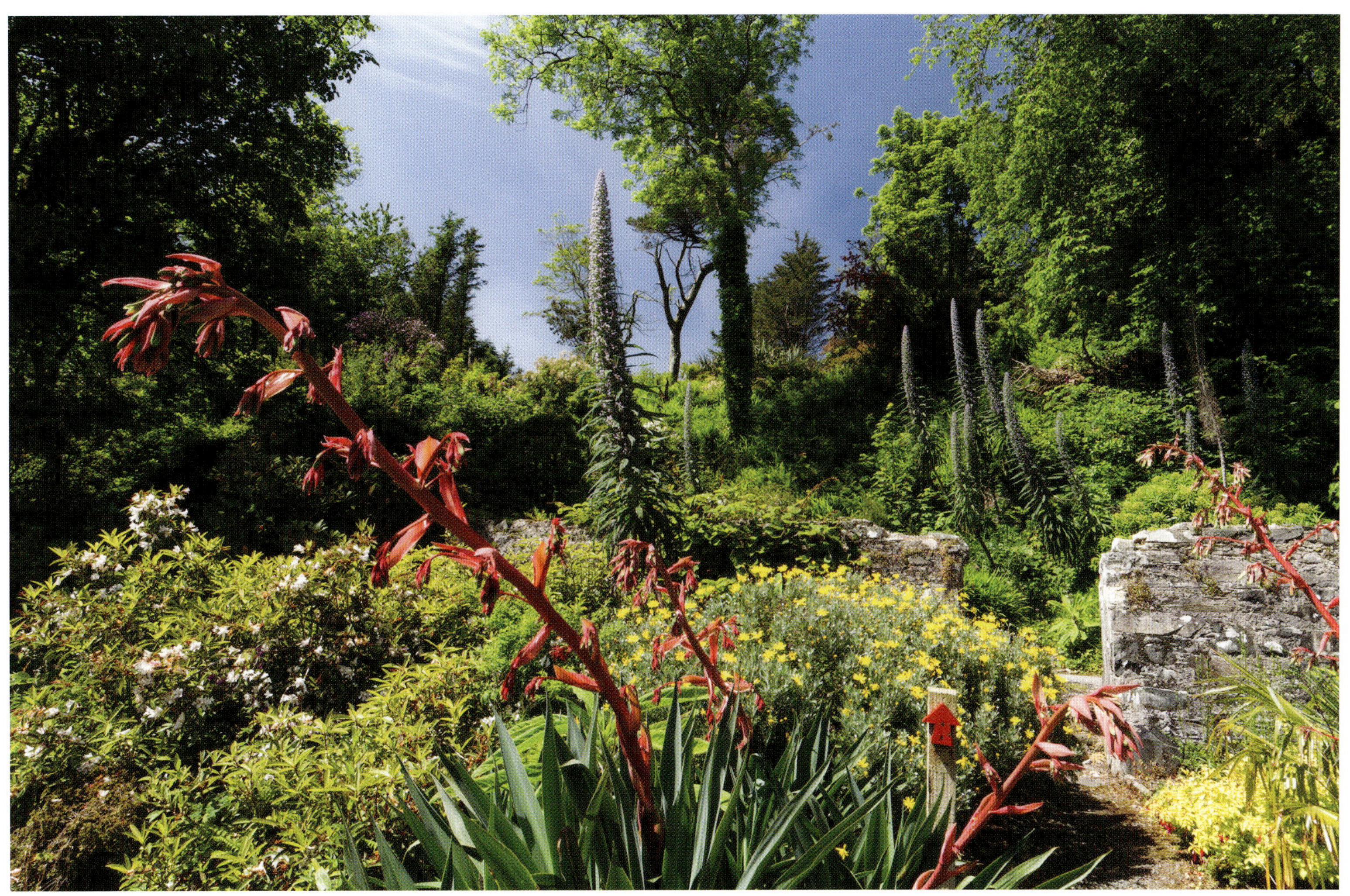

Exotic Achamore Gardens, created by Colonel Sir James Horlick and Kitty Lloyd Jones in 1944

Lush greens and aquamarines adorn the fertile shores of Gigha.

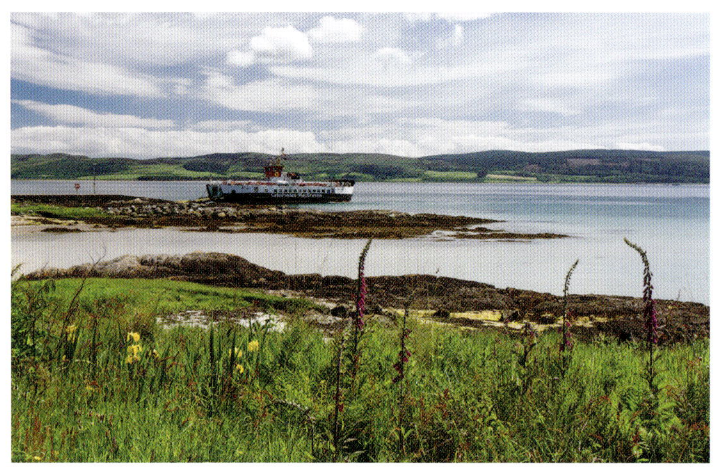

Achamore House

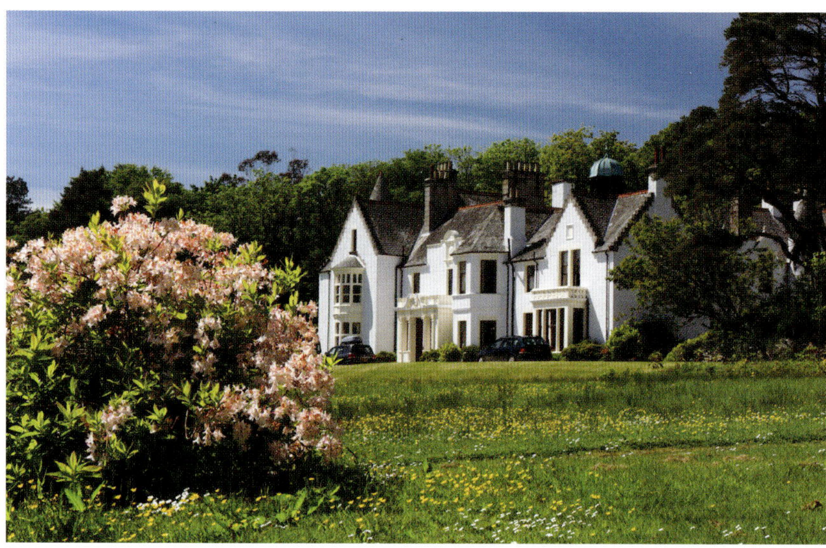

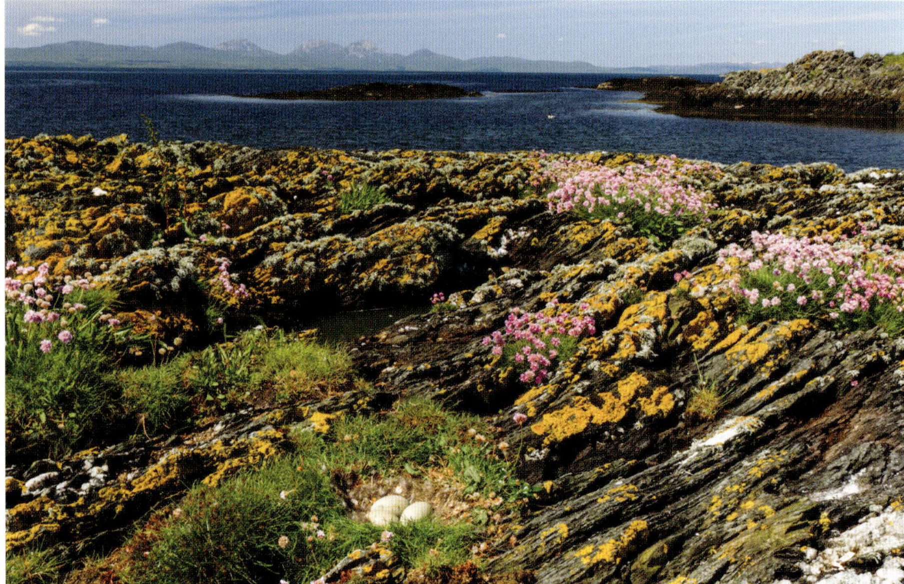

Goose nest among the thrift, West Tarbert Bay.

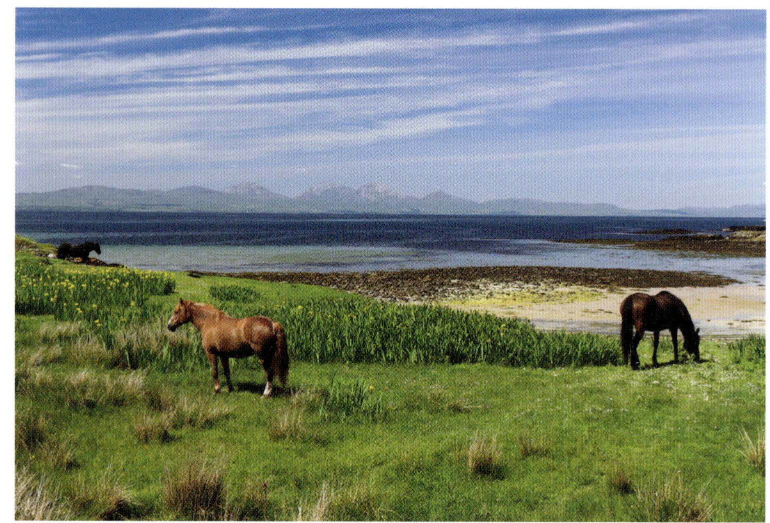

Abundant pasture by the shore

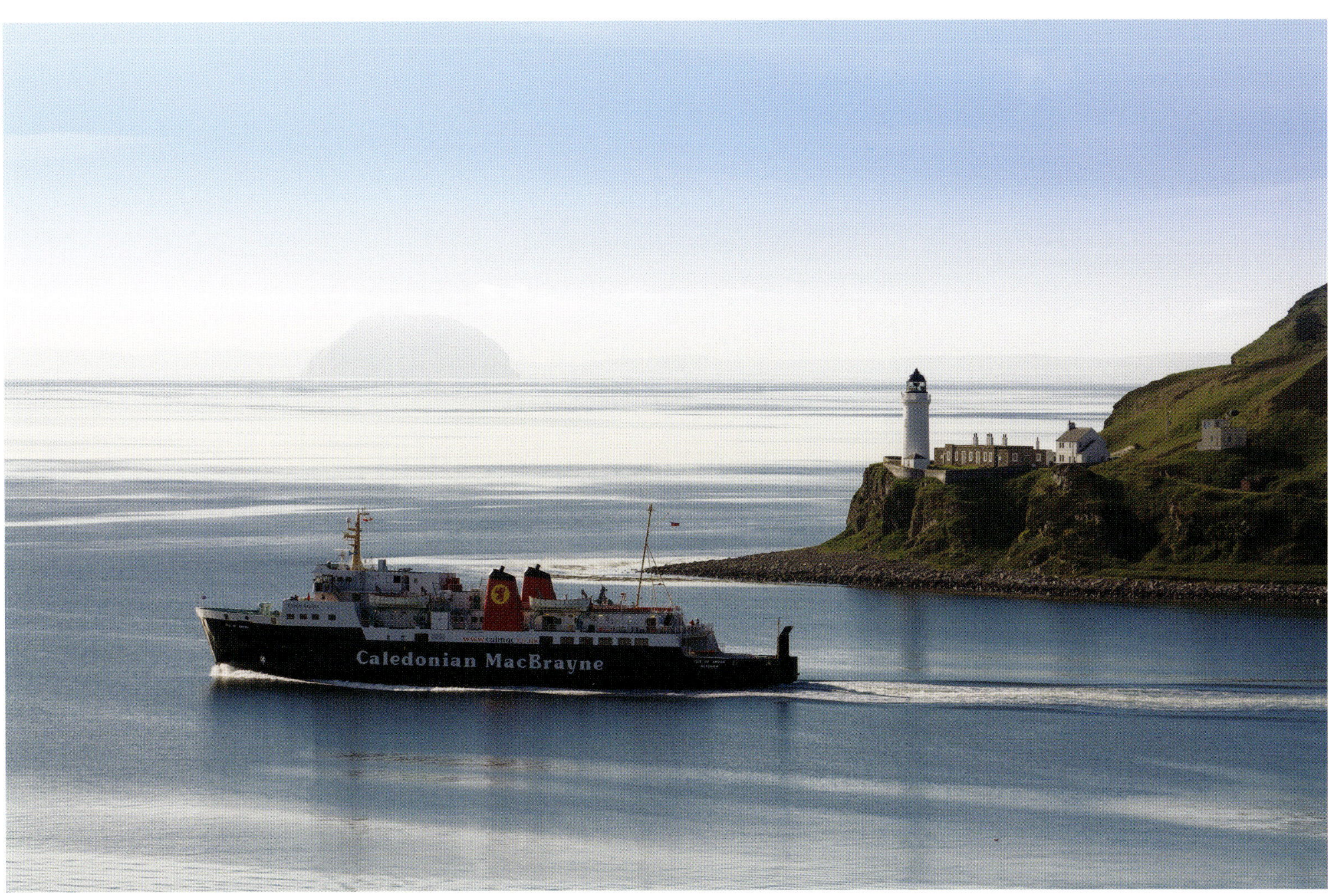

MV *Isle of Arran* slips gracefully past Davaar Island lighthouse. An almost
ethereal Ailsa Craig on the horizon defines its trajectory.

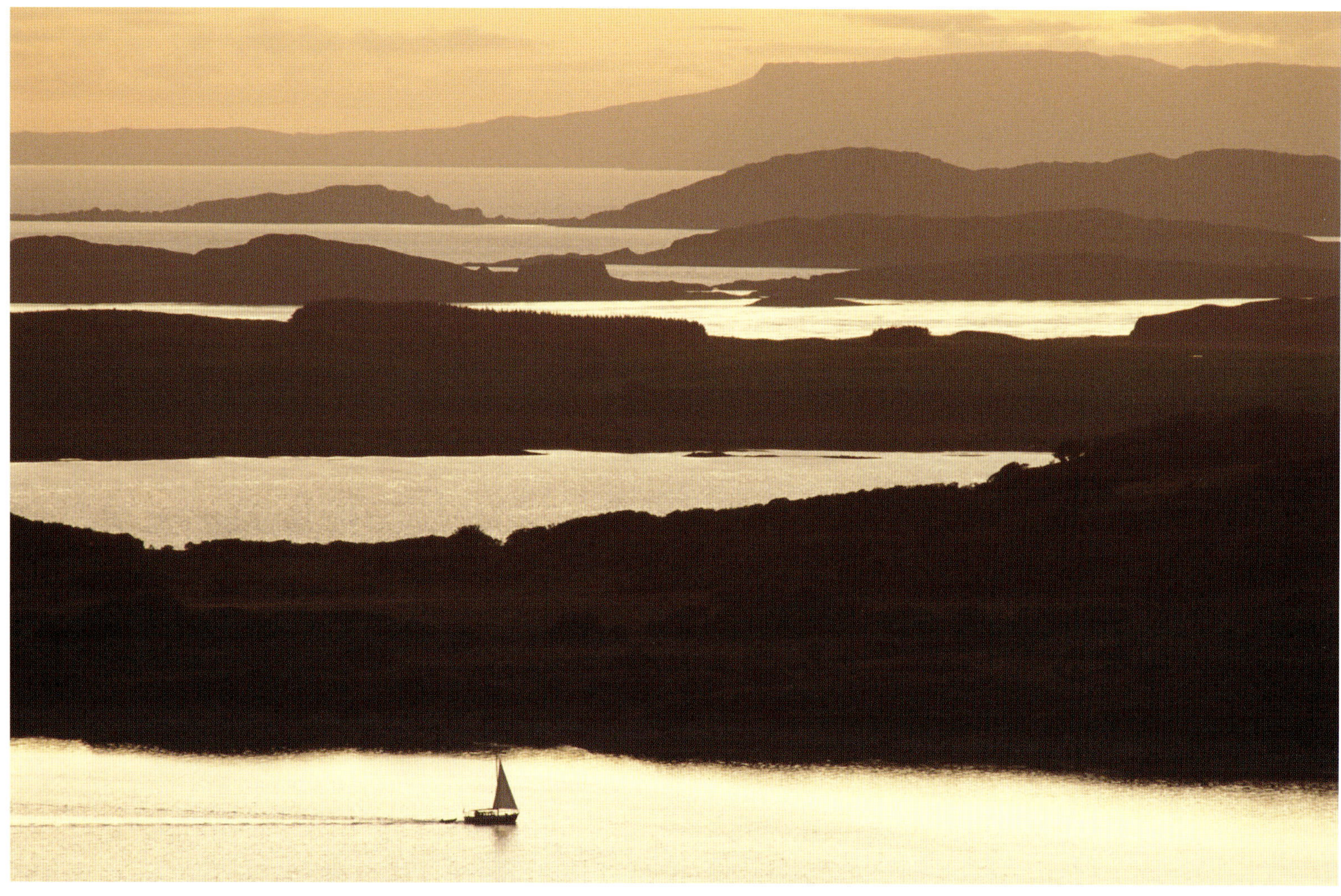

From Ardfern a mellow Firth of Lorne sunset highlights
the isles of Shuna, Luing, The Garvellachs and Mull.

Montbretia abounds on the shore of Easdale, here looking back to Ellenbeich, Isle of Seil.

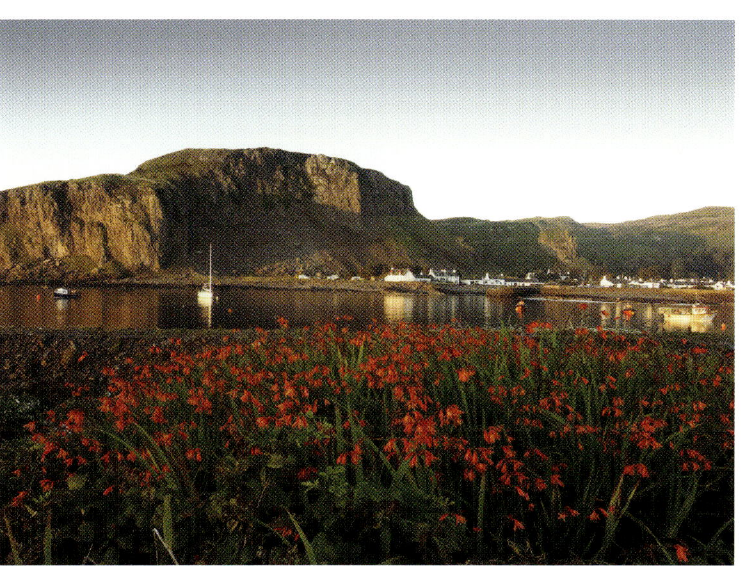

The Garvellachs Lighthouse in the Firth of Lorn, with Mull in the distance

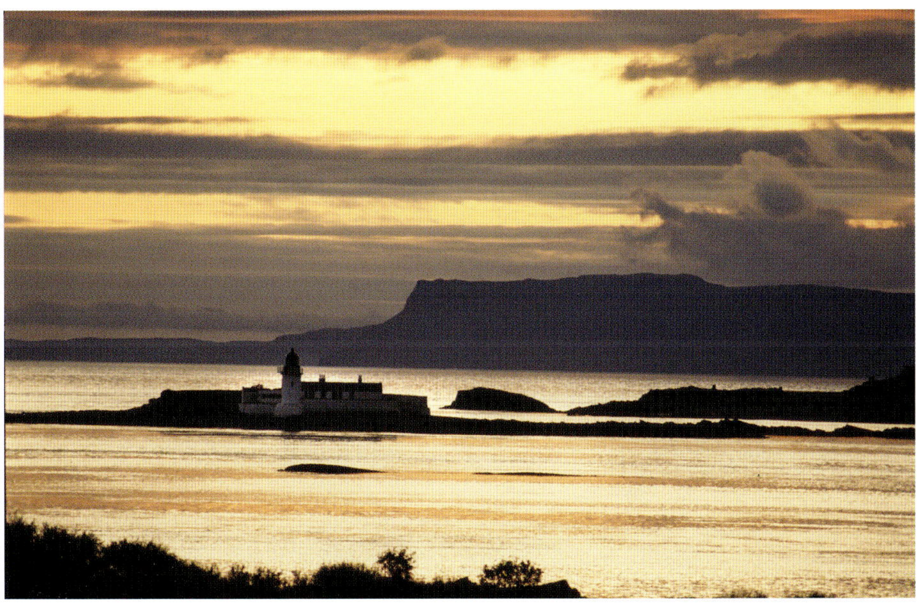

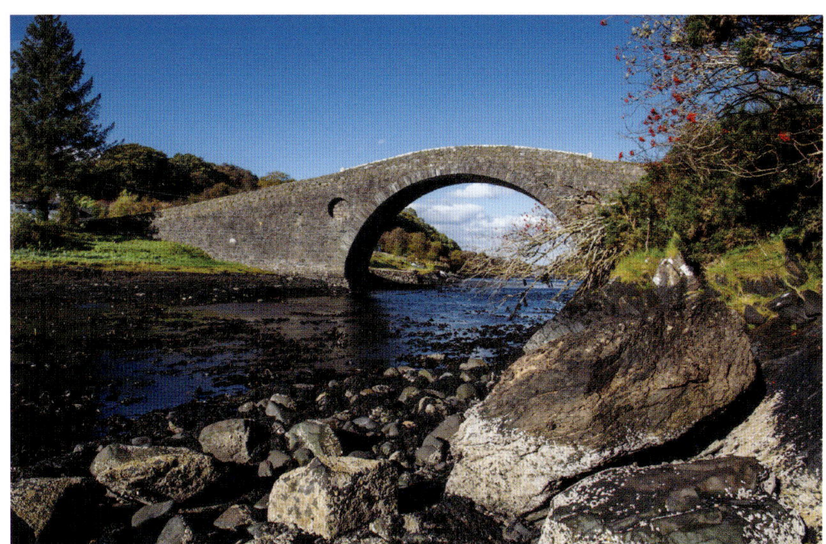

Isle of Seil barely qualifies as an island at low tide, however its iconic bridge savours the pseudonym, Bridge over the Atlantic.

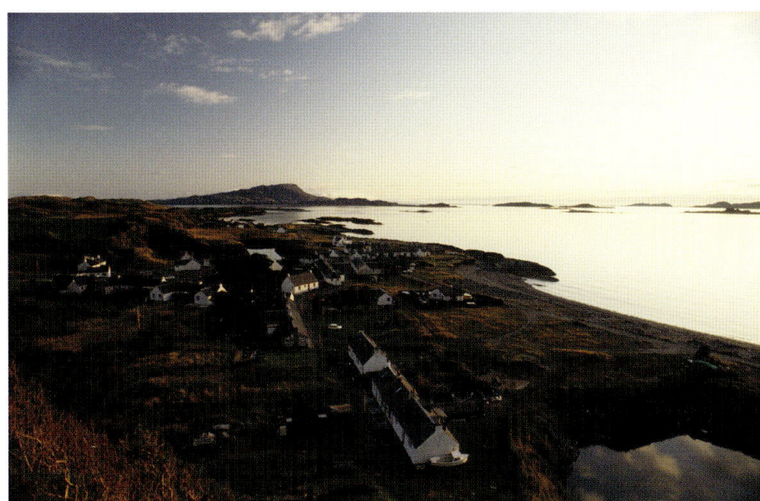

Cullipool has heritage as a former slate quarry

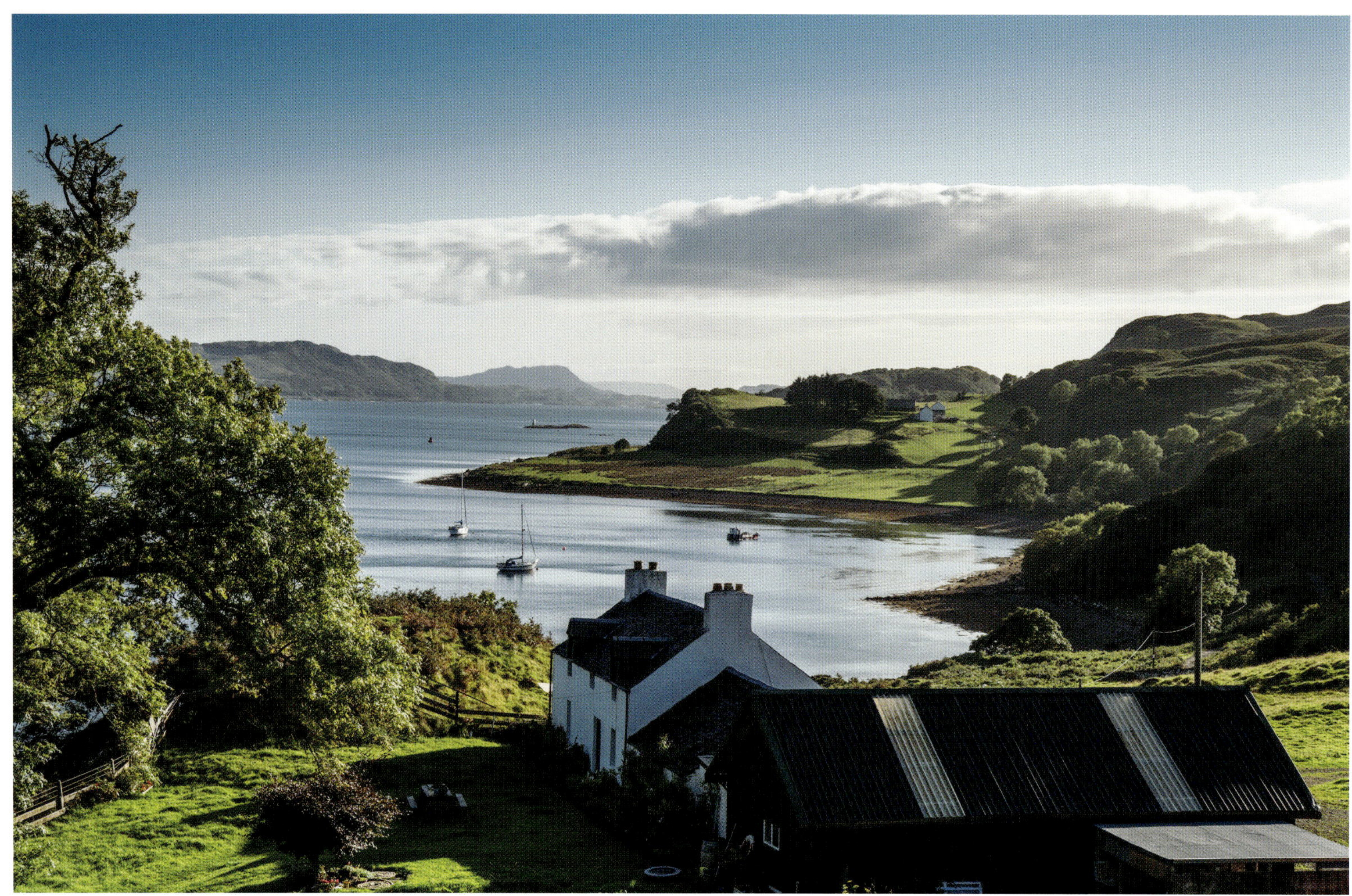

Sitting just a short hop from Oban, Kerrera makes for a perfect day trip.

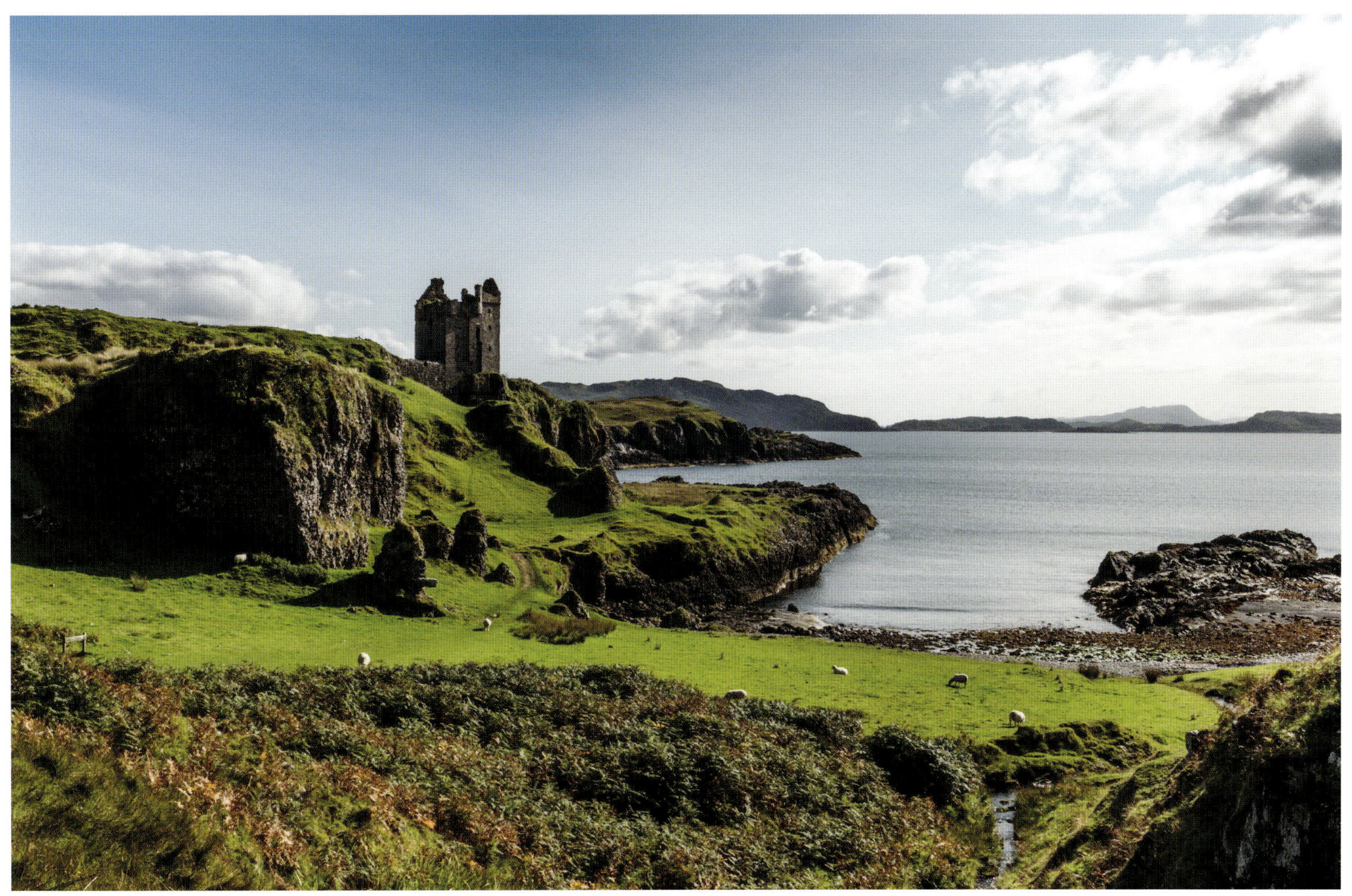

Gylen Castle, a former tower house, commands the south coast of the island along the Firth of Lorn.

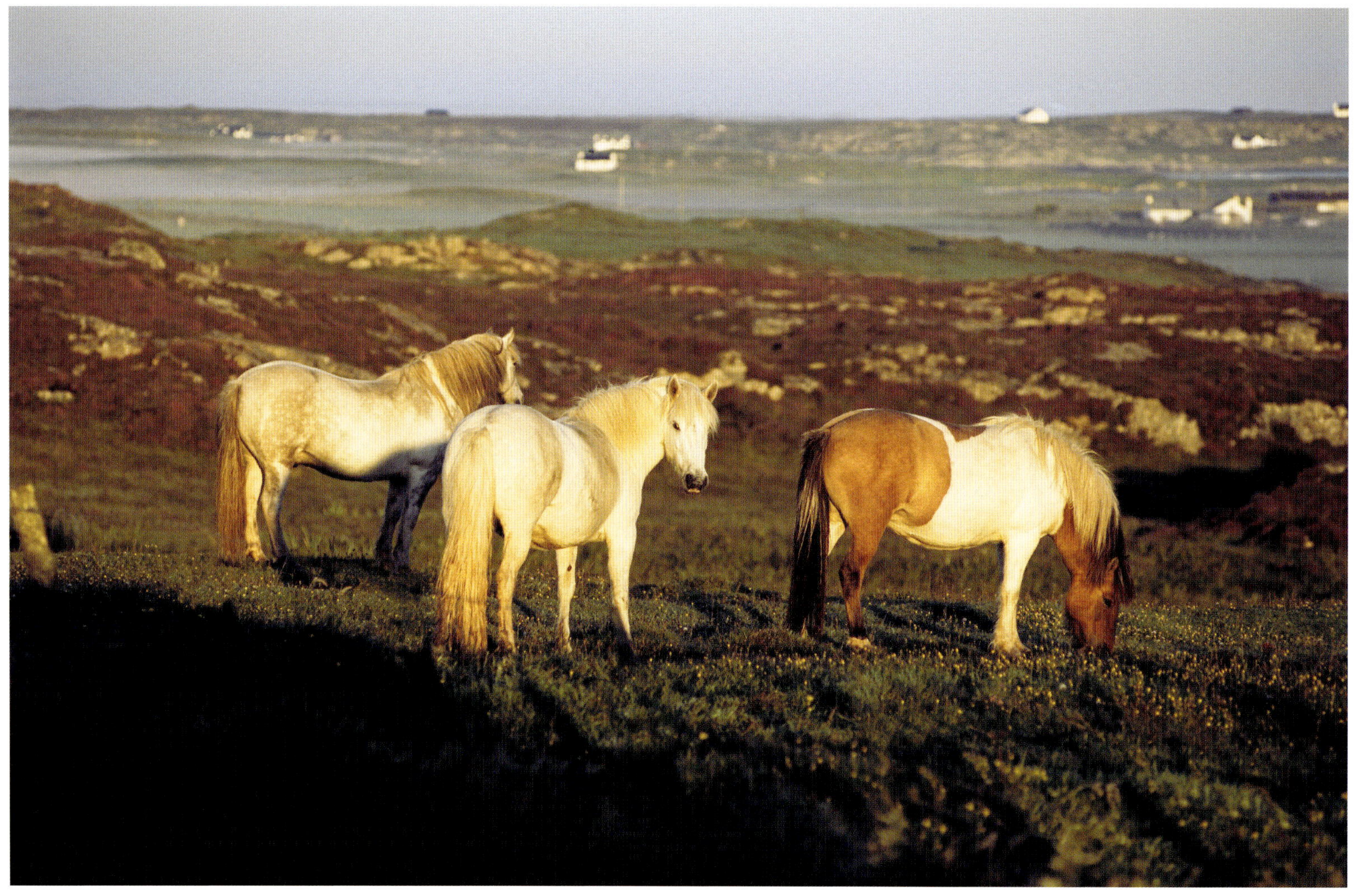

First light strikes a warm glow on this sturdy native breed, the Highland Pony.

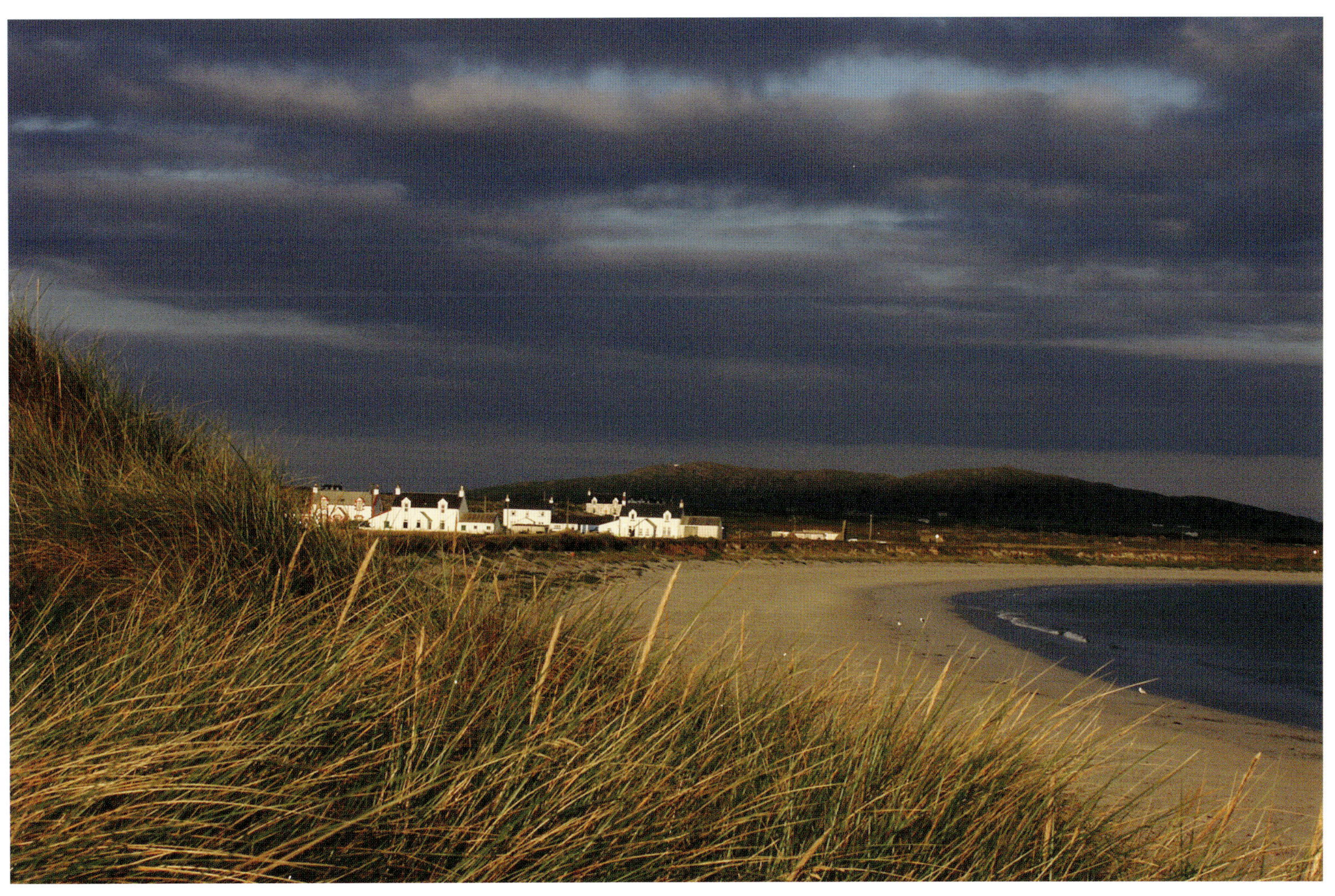

The richness of the Hebridean light is fleeting at Balephuil.

Washed up upon the beach at Hynish

A traditional cottage in Balevullin

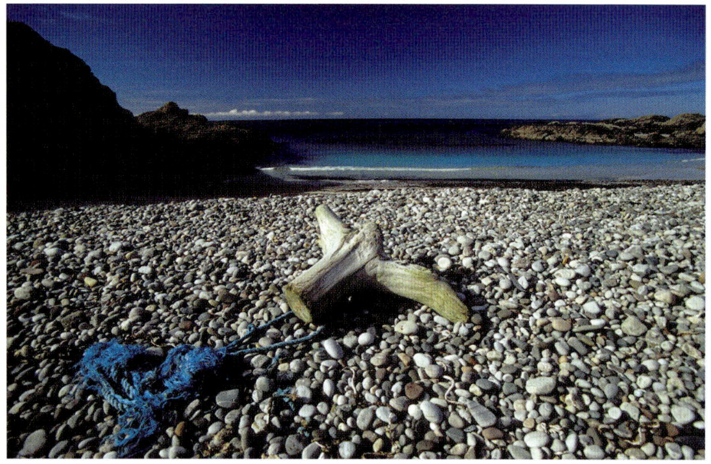

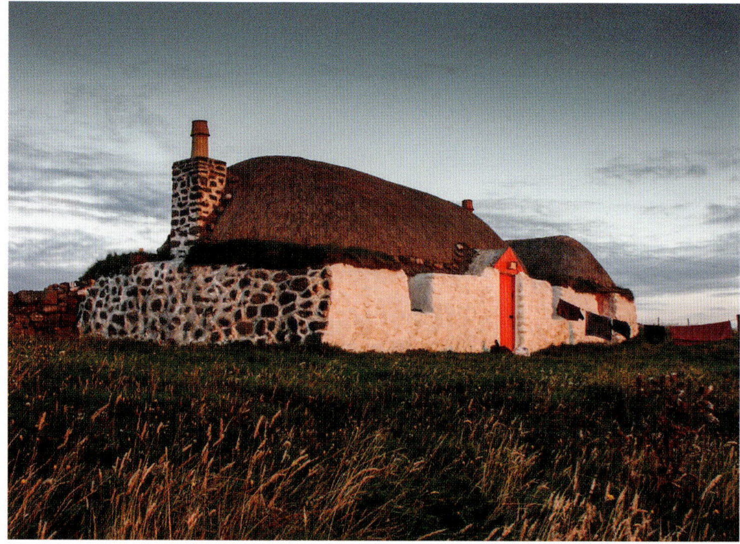

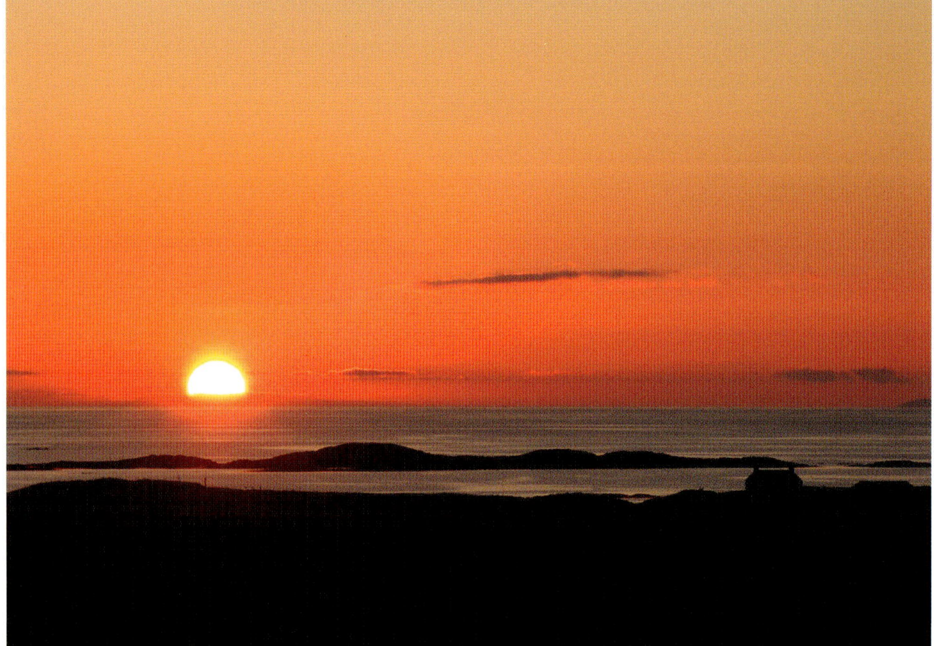

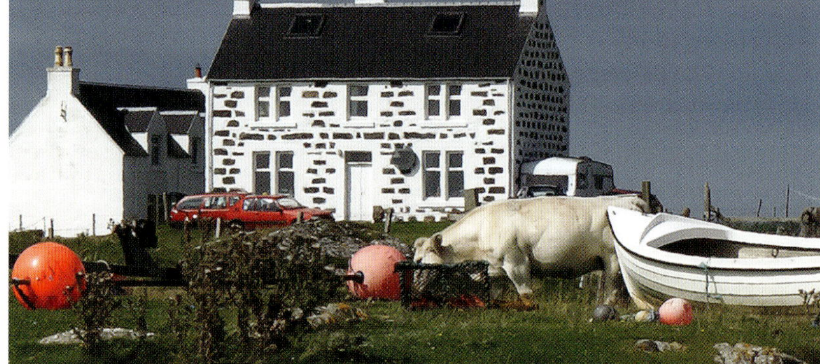

Crofting is still a way of life for islanders.

Sunset at Sandaig

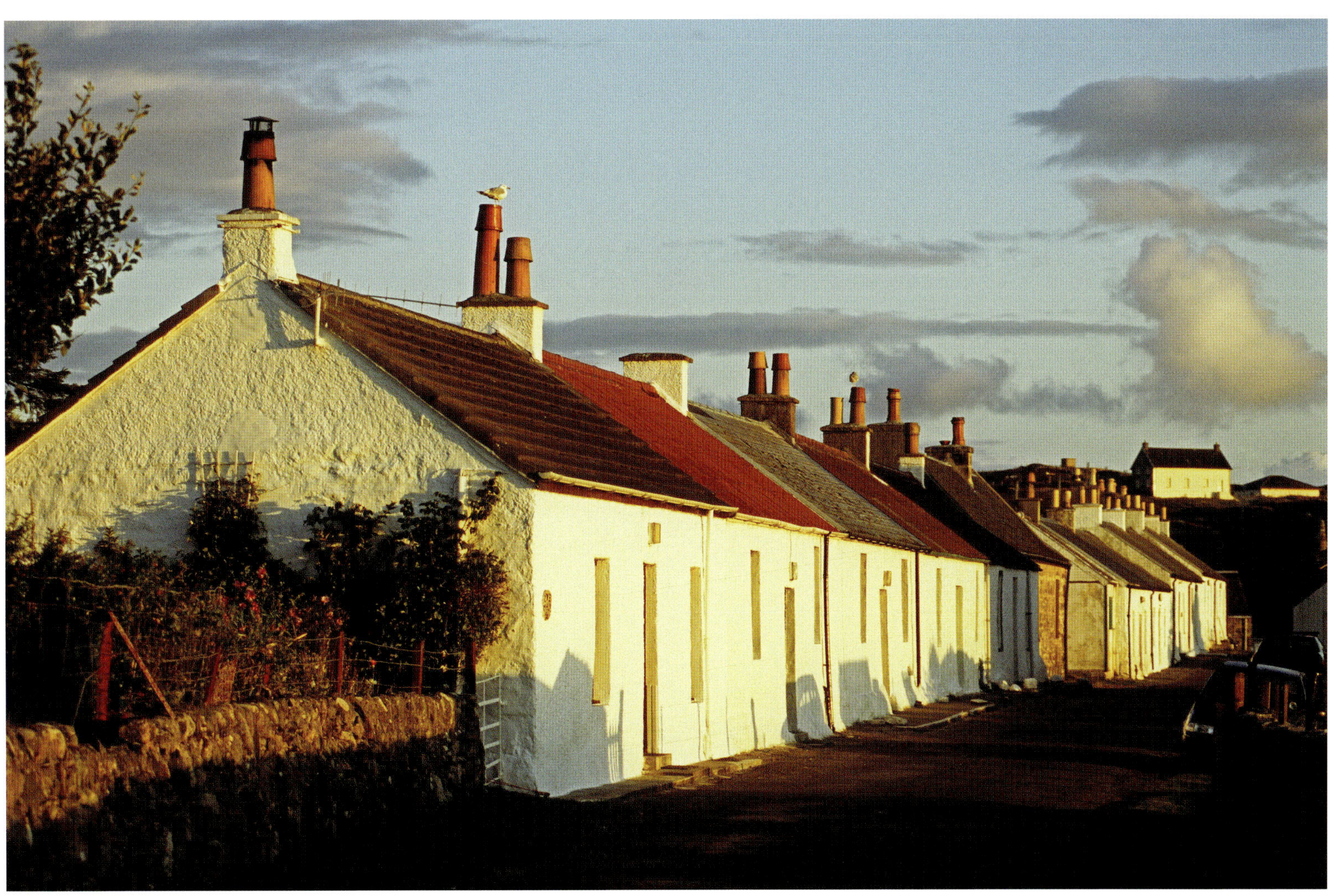

Terraced cottages catching the dawn light in Arinagour main street.

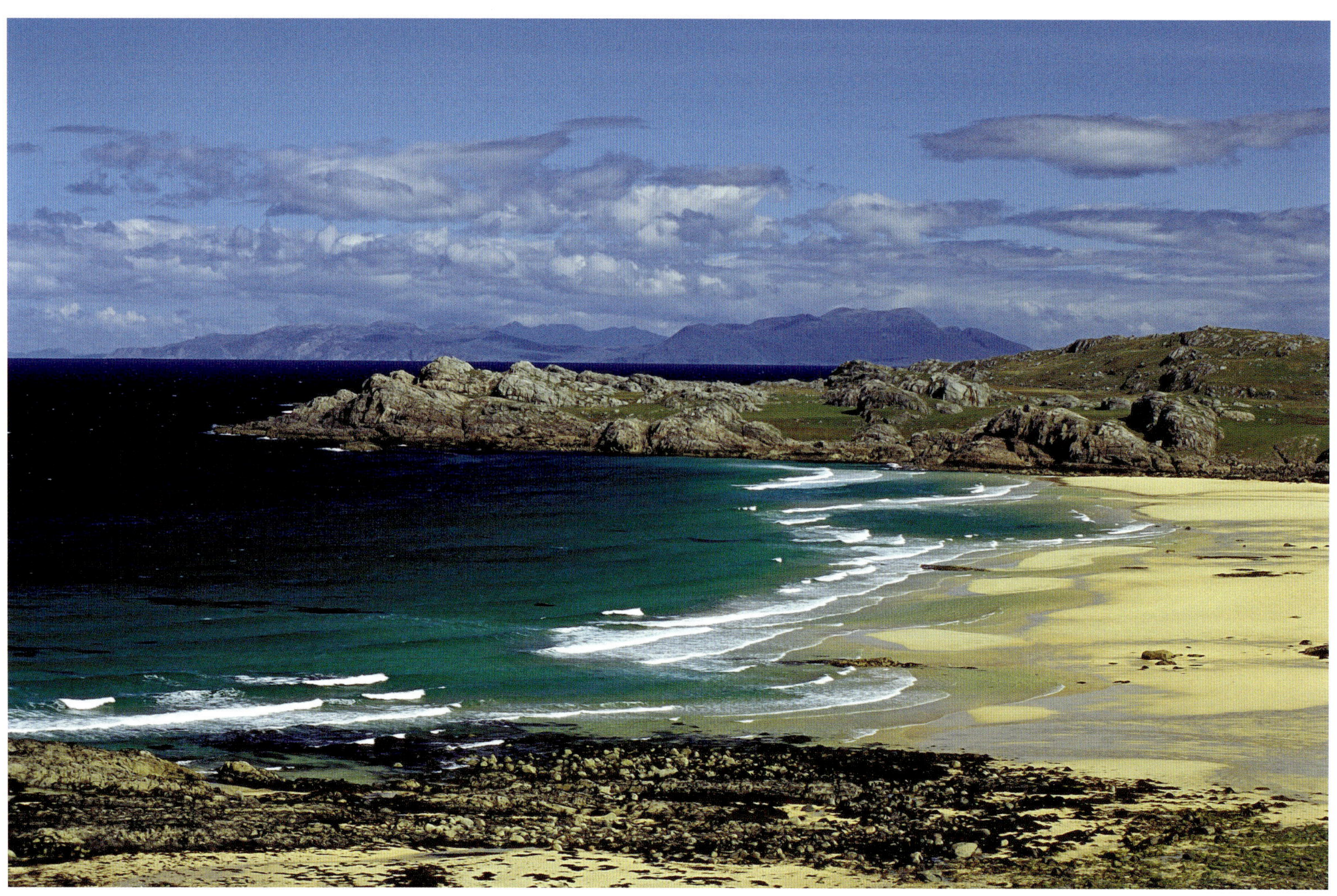

The splendour of Hogh Bay with Rum and Skye as a backdrop

Breachacha Castle, the 15th century tower house built by the McLean clan in 1431

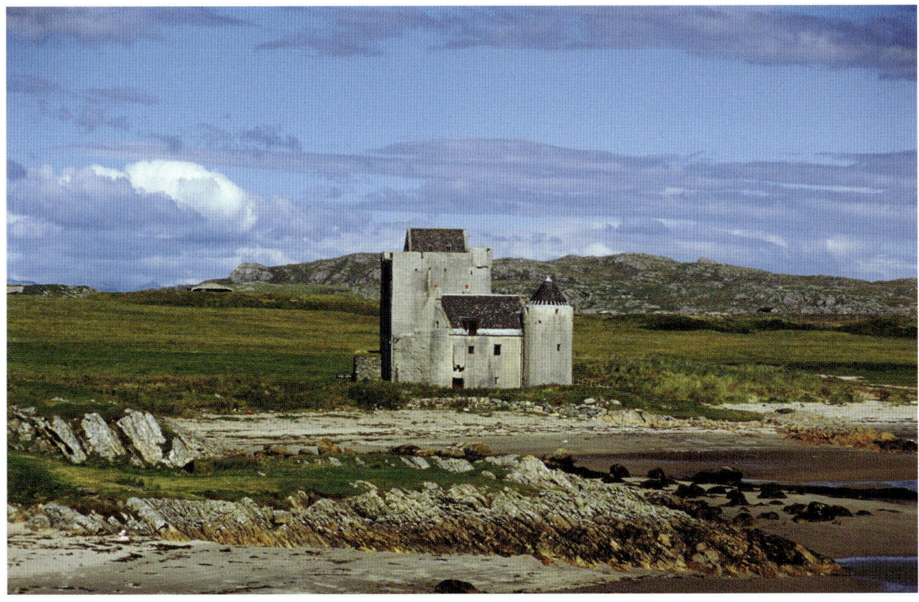

North west point, by Sorisdale

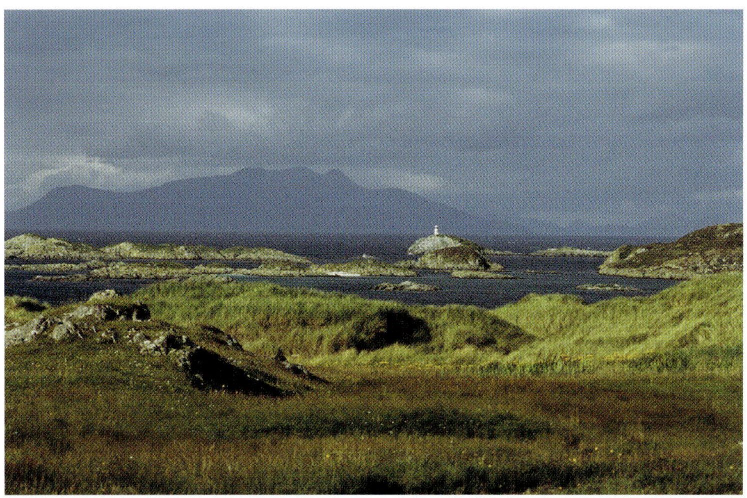

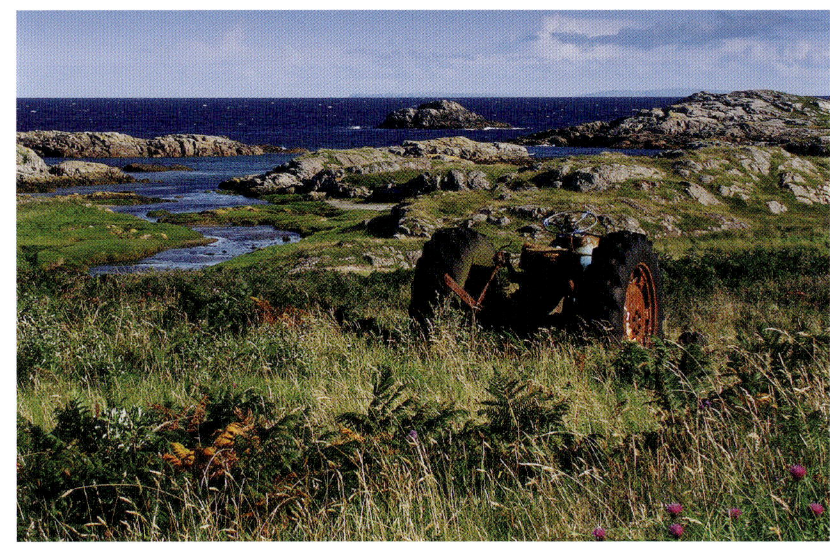

A crofting workhorse in Grishipoll

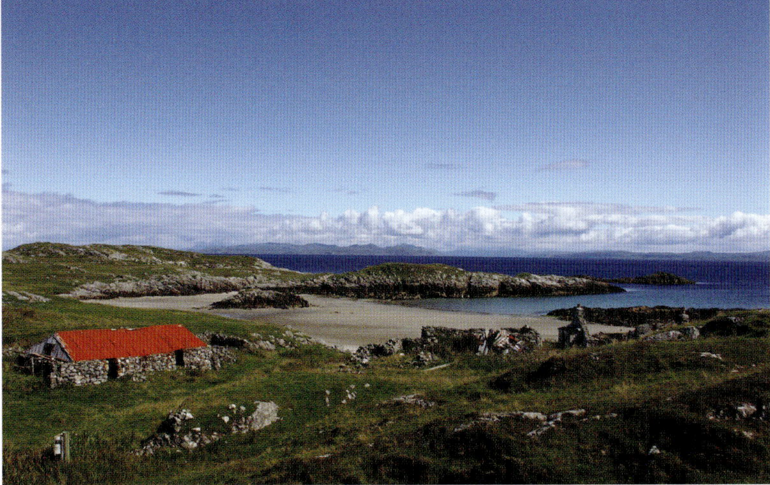

Beach, steadings and ruin, Sorisdale

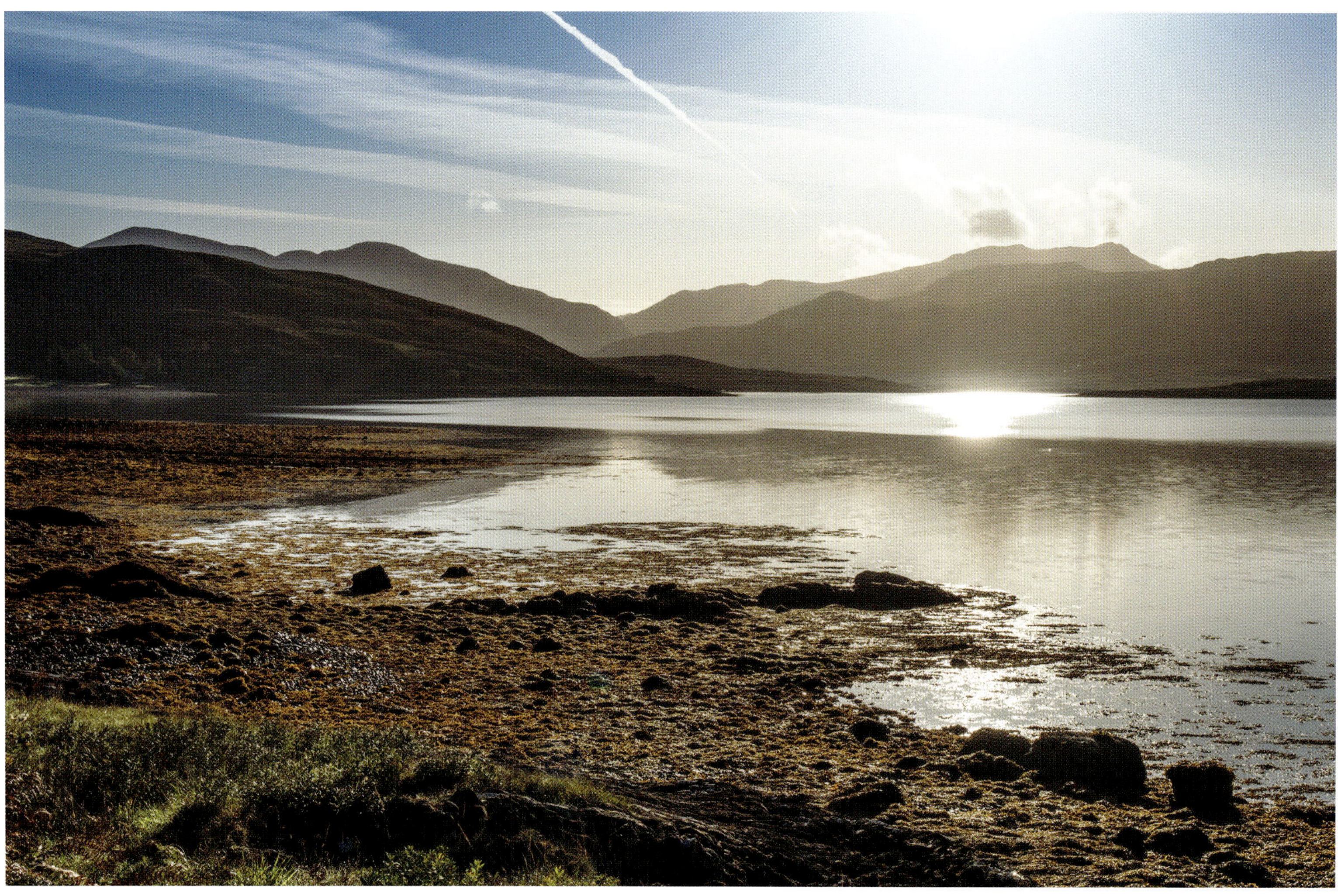

Exquisite dawn light pervades the shore of Loch na Keal at Kellan.

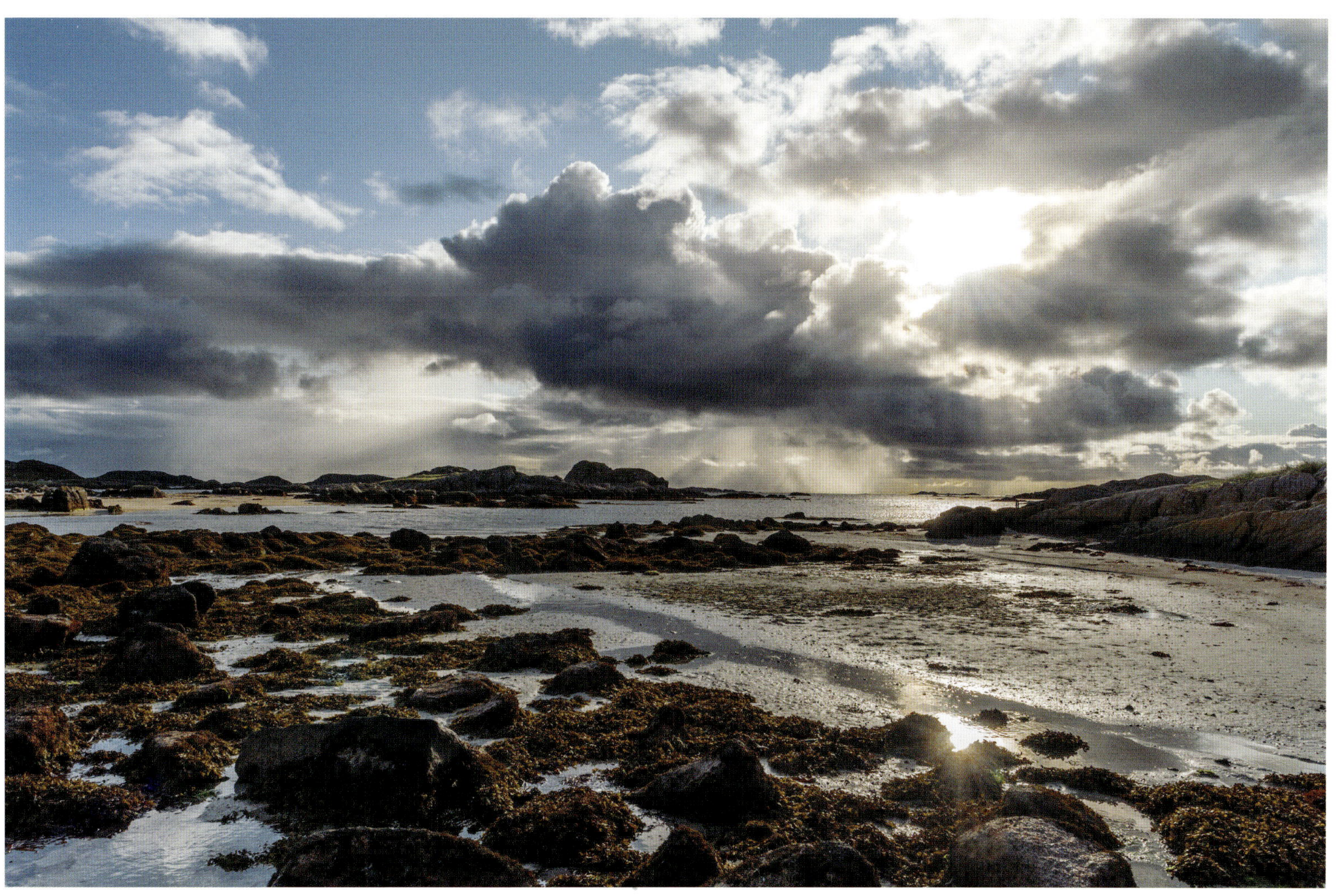

Dramatic skies highlight the beach patterns at Fidden, Ross of Mull.

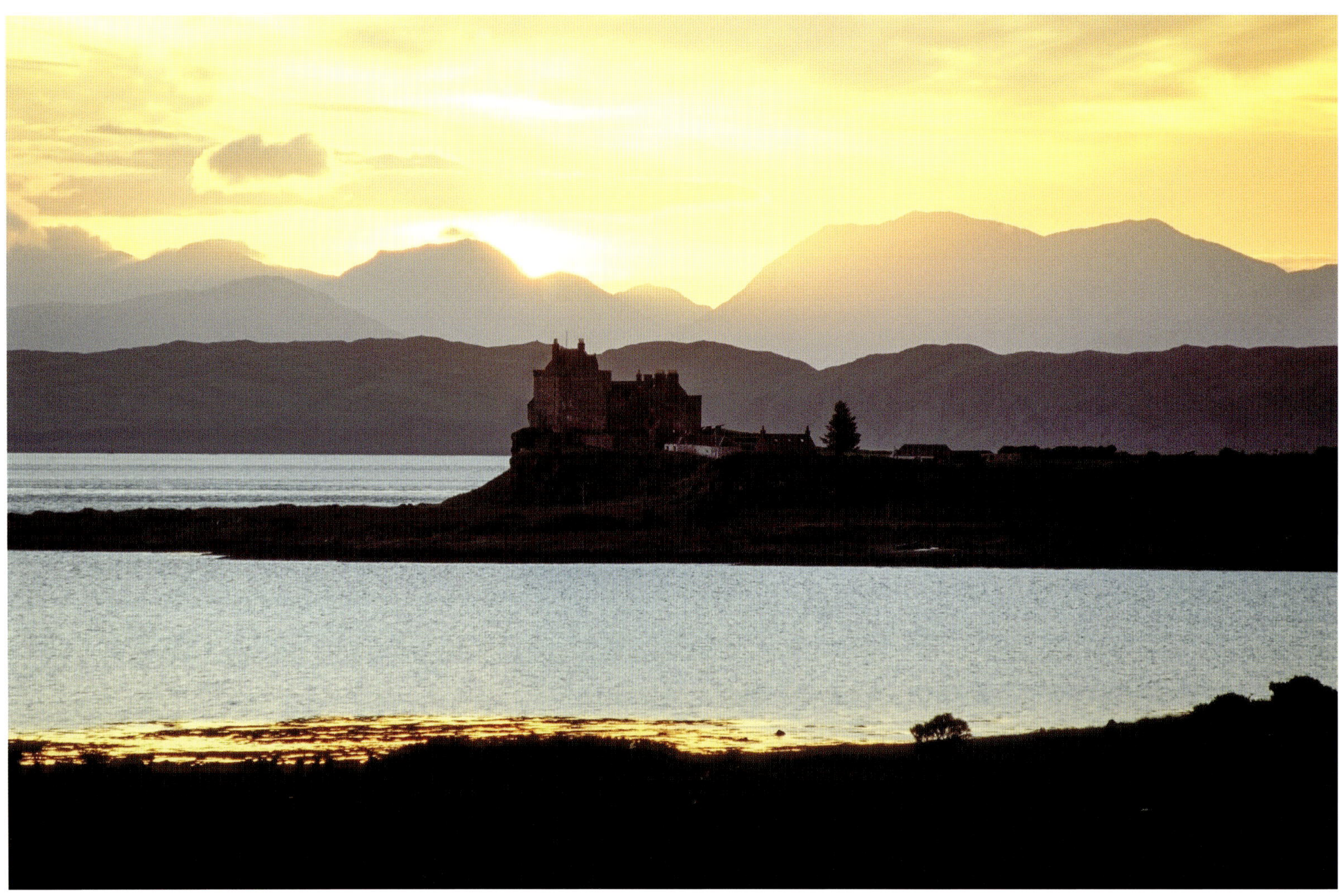

Duart Castle sunrise and the Cruachan range, Argyll

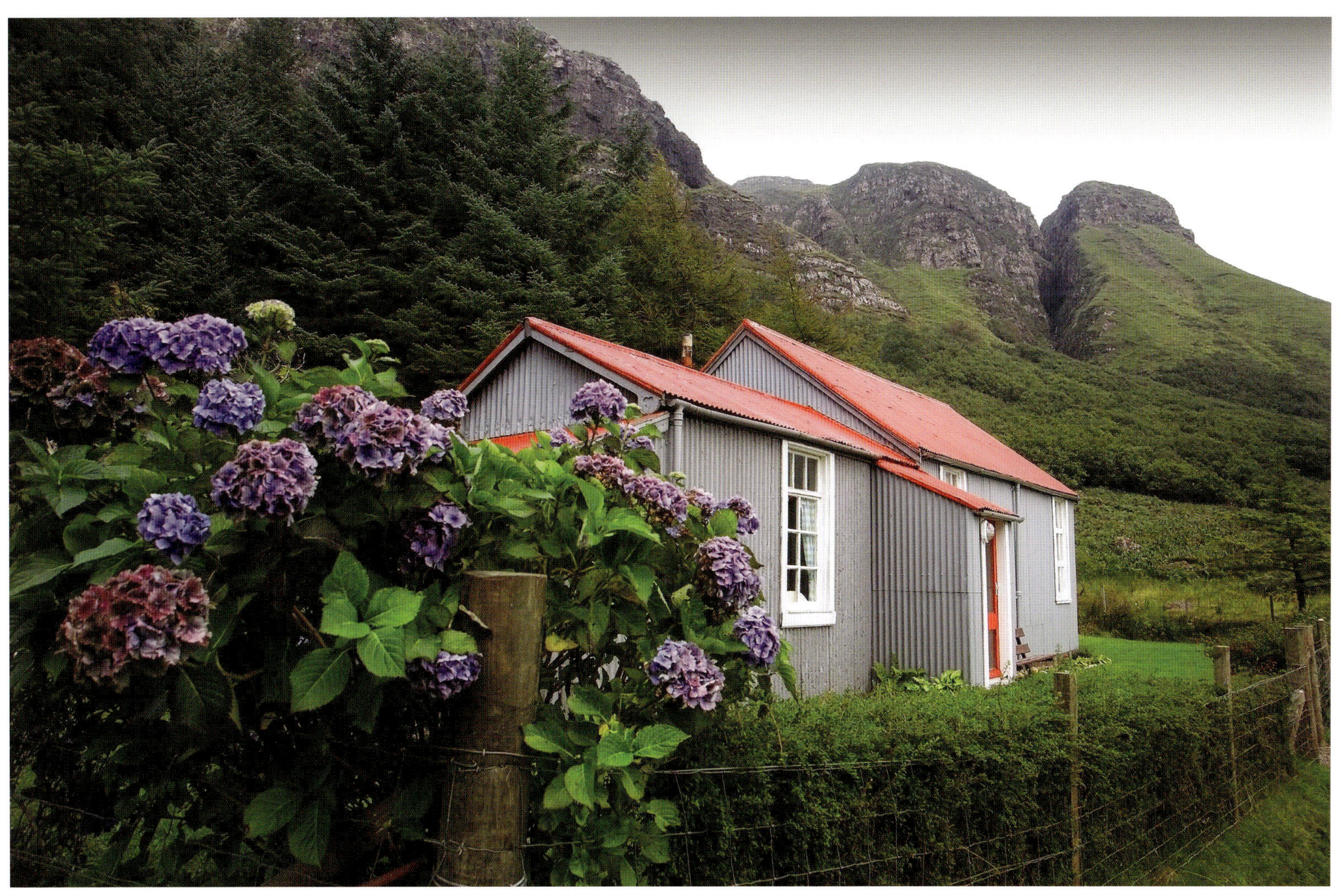

Summer sheiling, Balnahard, Mull

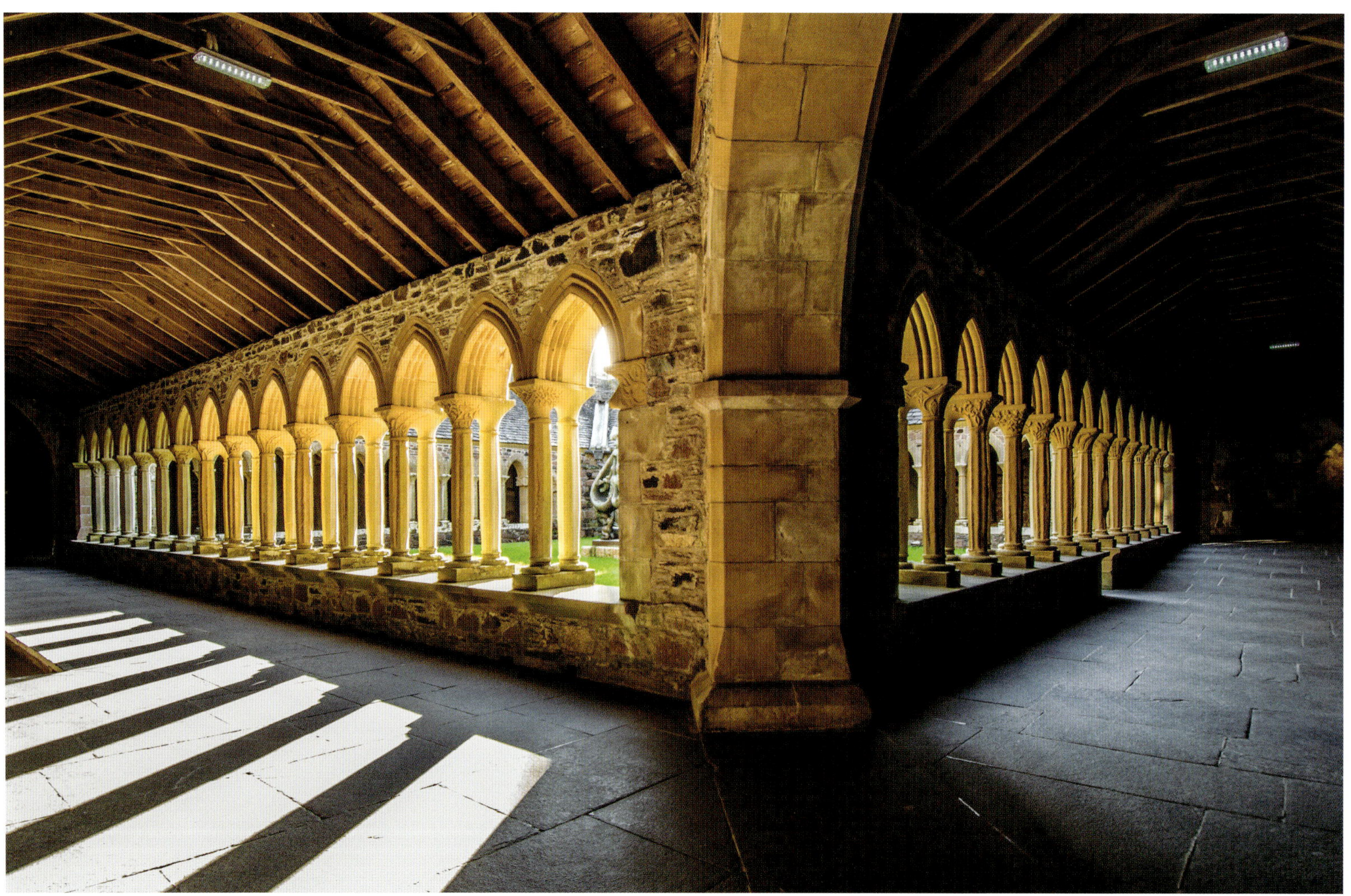

The ancient and atmospheric cloisters at Iona Abbey

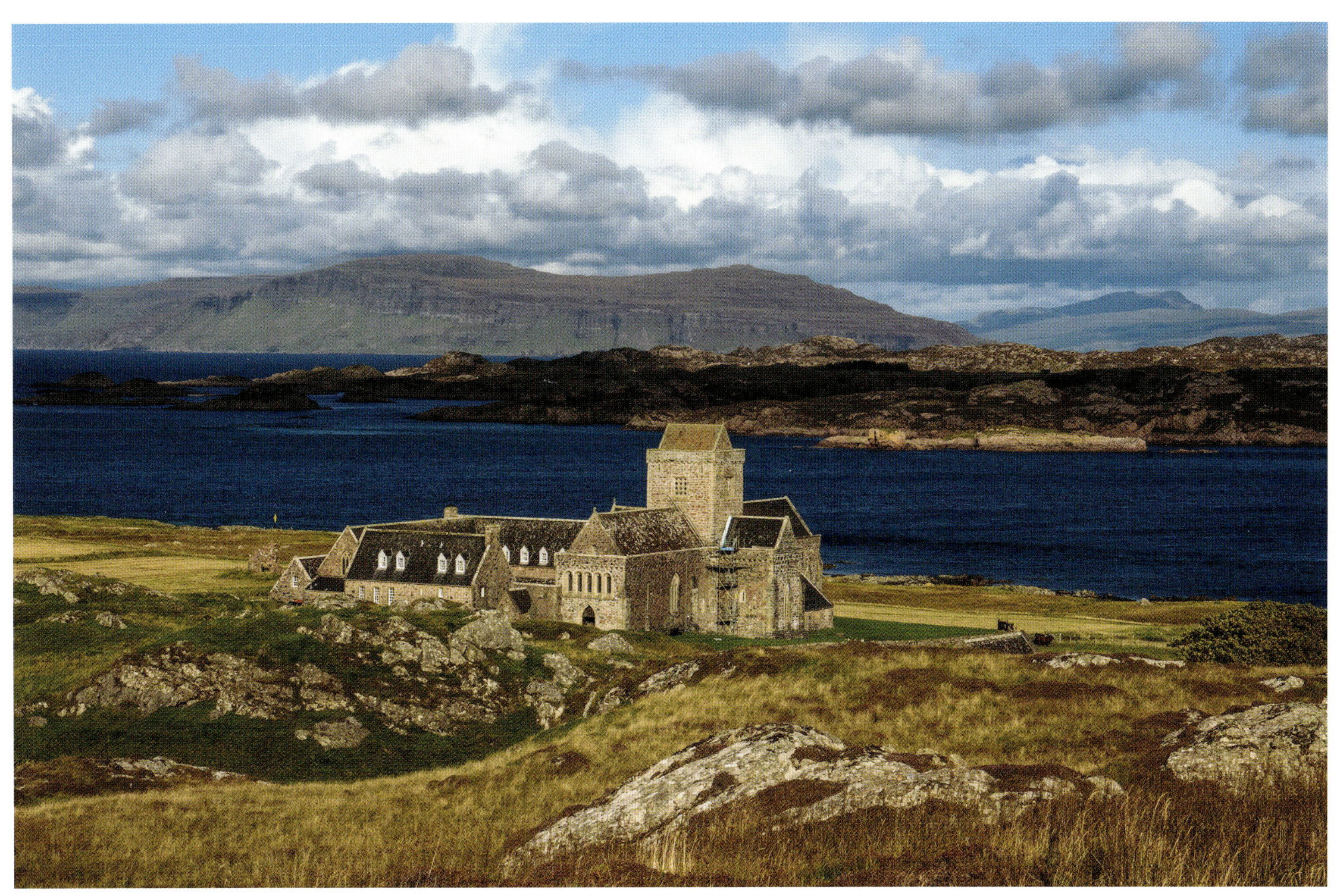

Iona Abbey, founded by St Columba in 563AD, remains
a significant place of pilgrimage for Christians today.

Rich Hebridean light shines on the western shoreline of Iona.

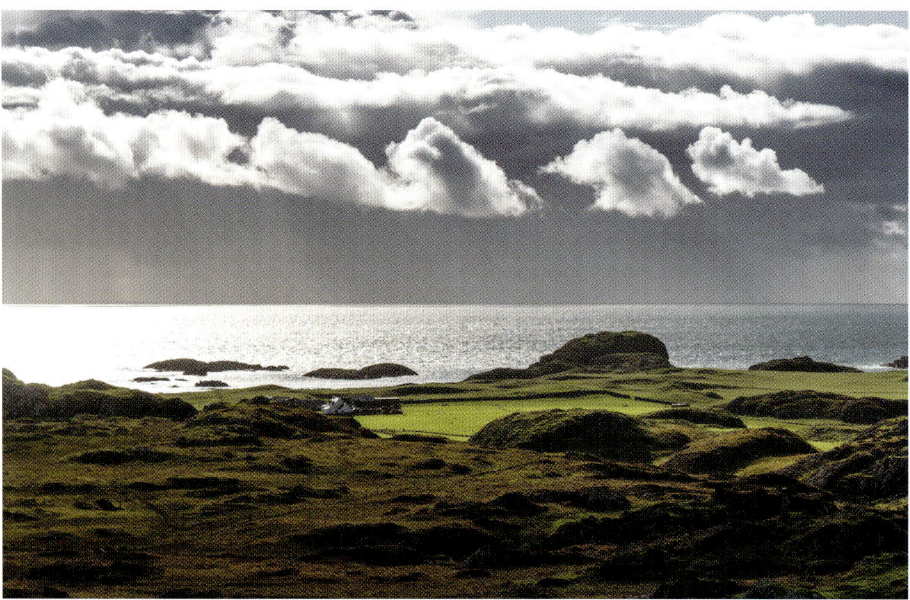

Feral goats on the Carsaig Arches trail

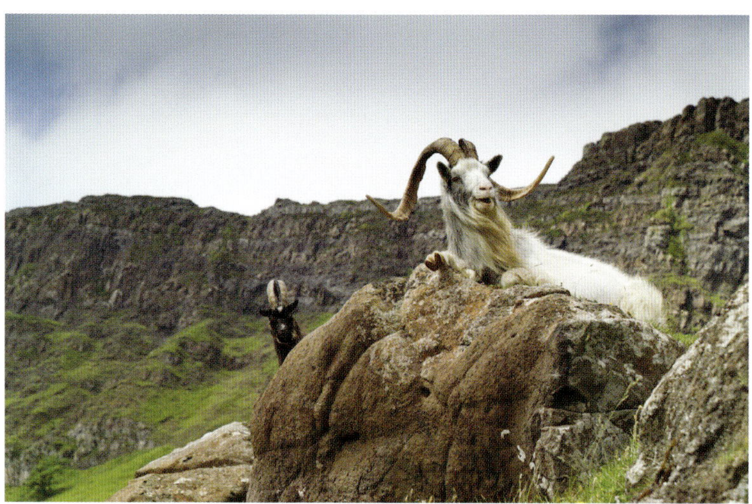

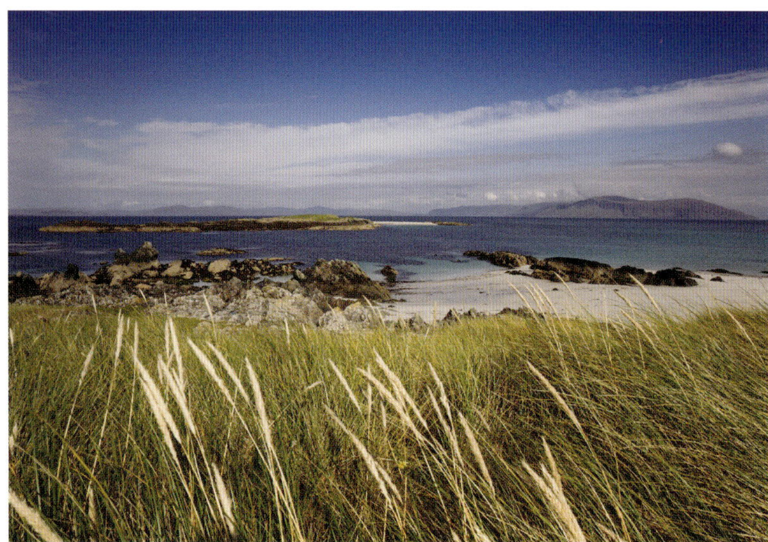

The beach at Iona's north shore is sublime.

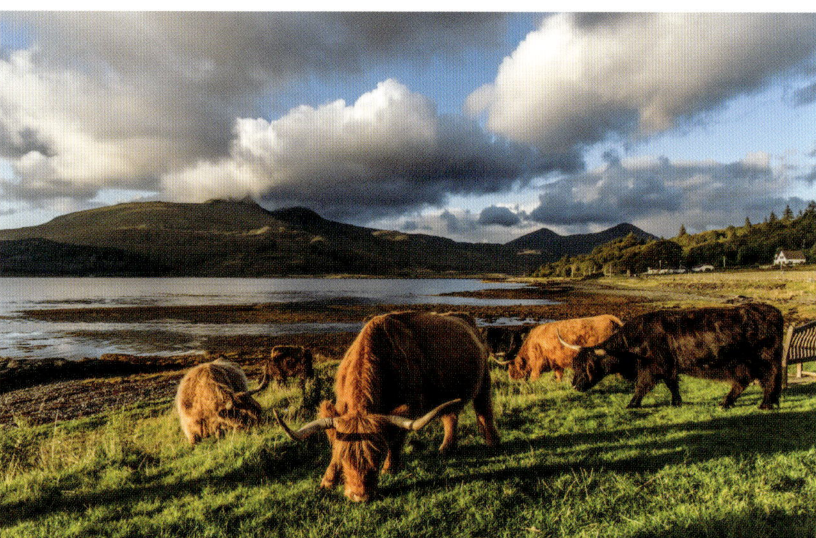

Easy pasture by Pennyghael.

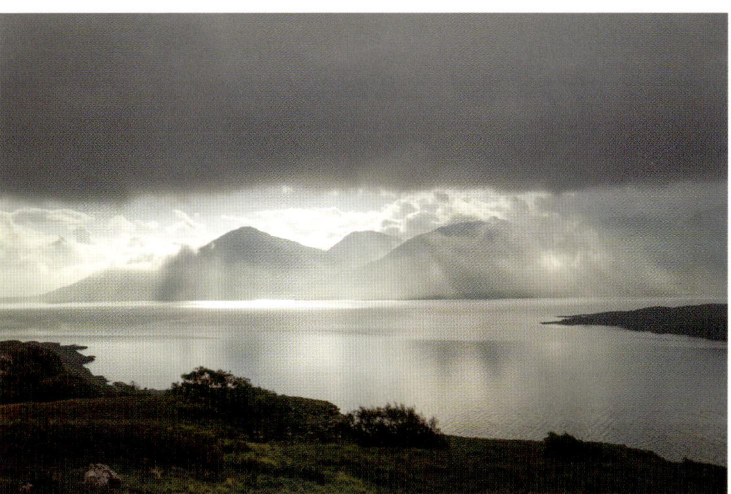

First light above Ben More range, Loch na Keal

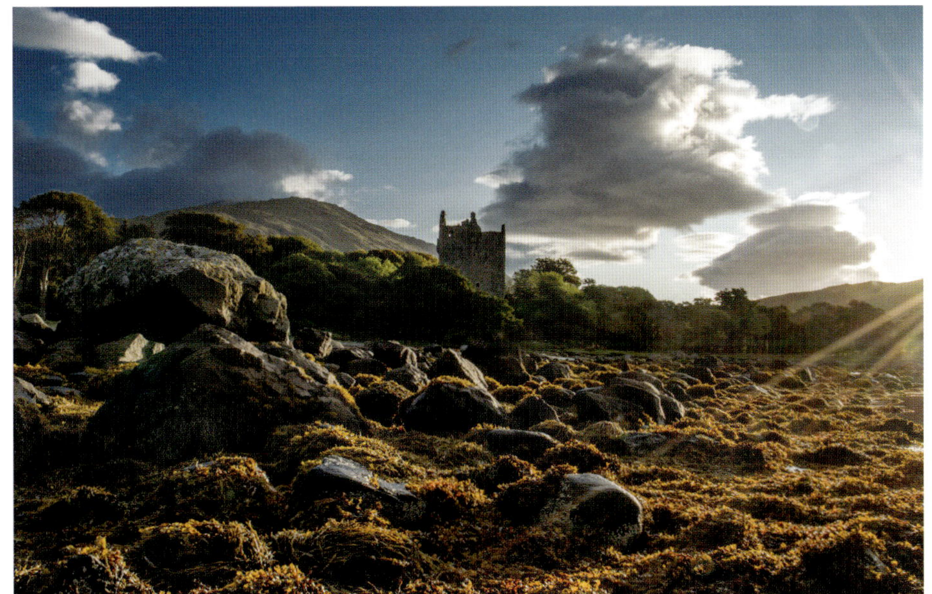

Moy Castle, Loch Buie

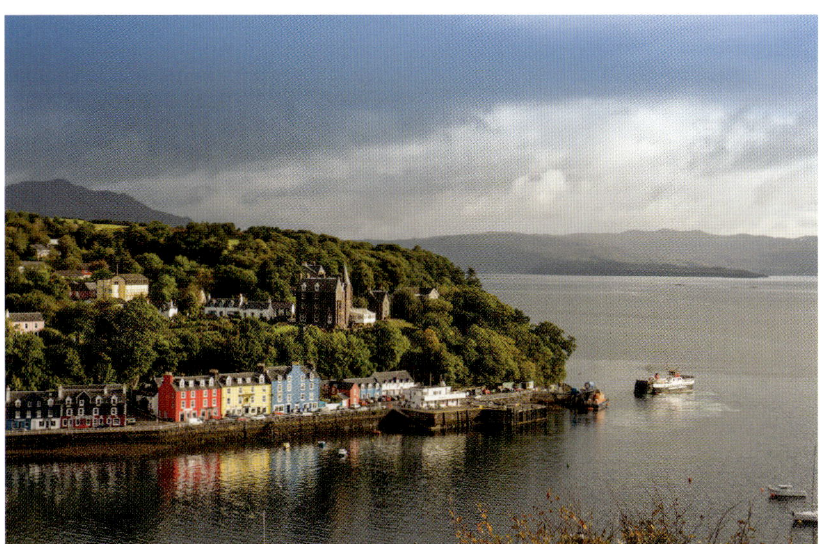

Stunning Tobermory

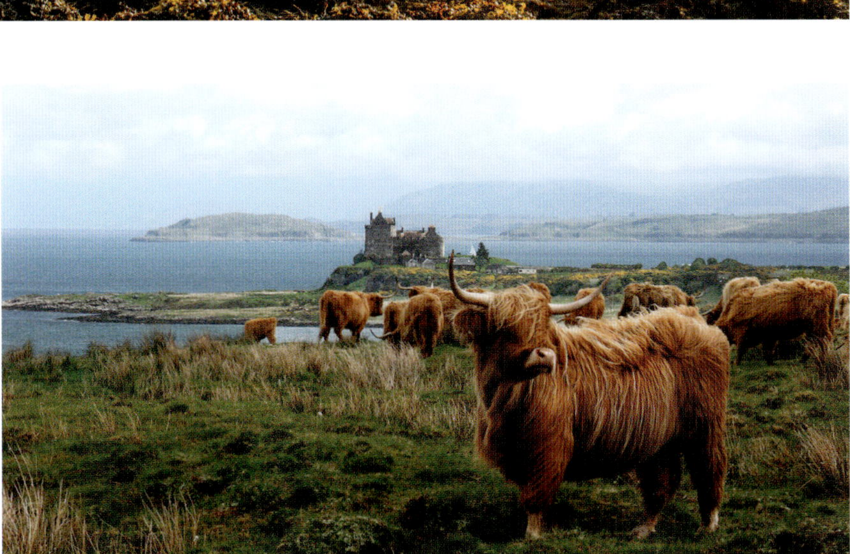

A noble Highlander takes centre stage by iconic Duart Castle.

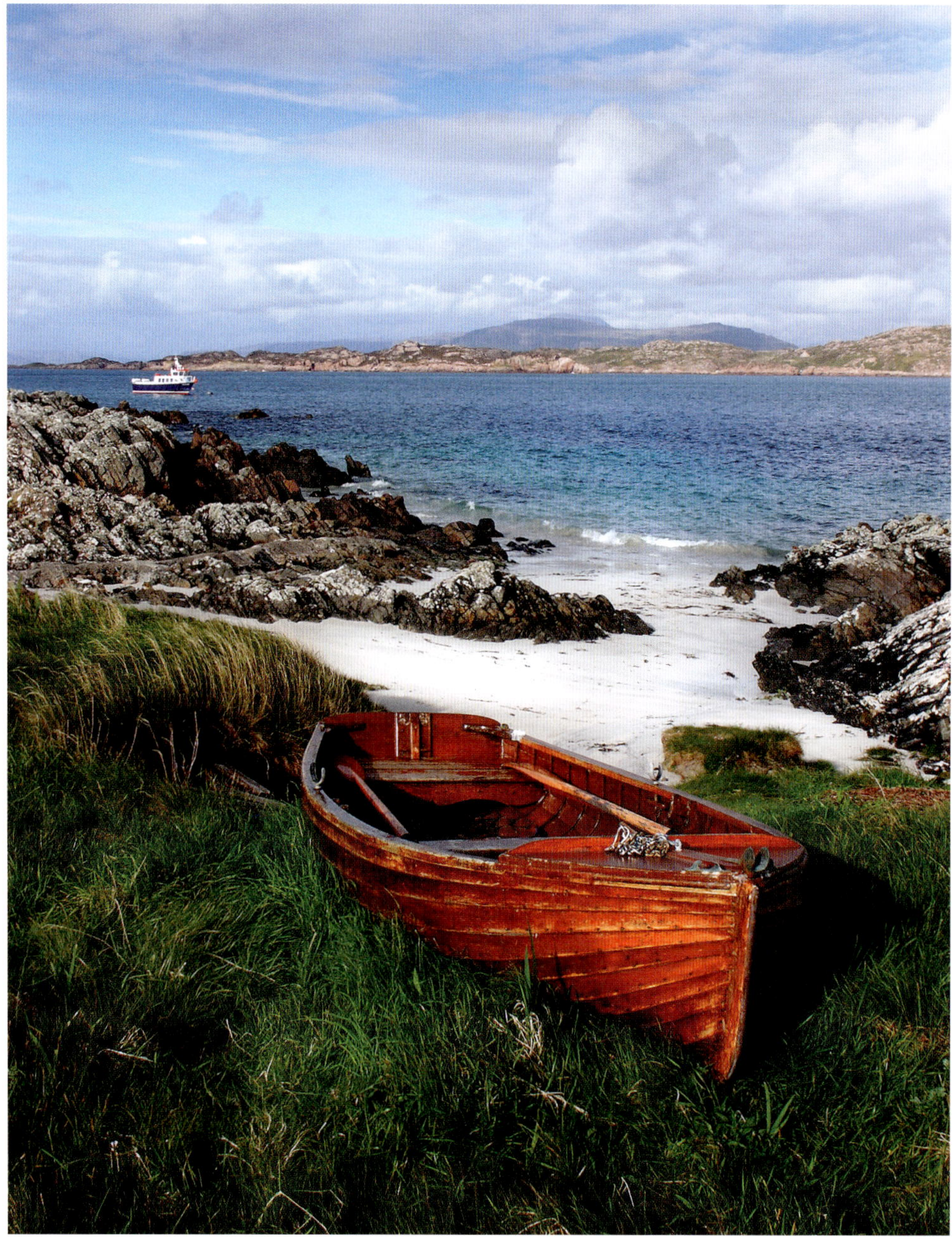

Clinker built, St Ronans, Iona

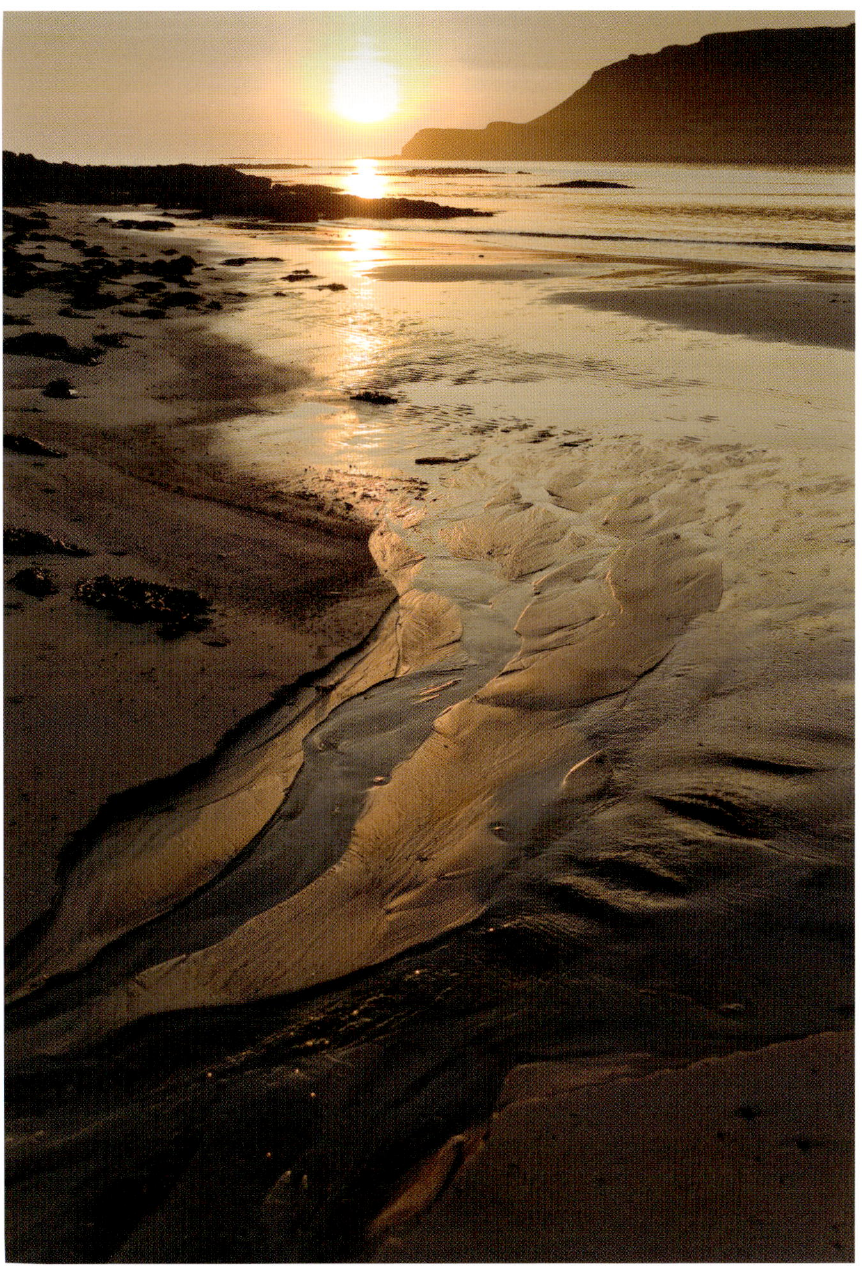

A rivulet at Calgary Bay

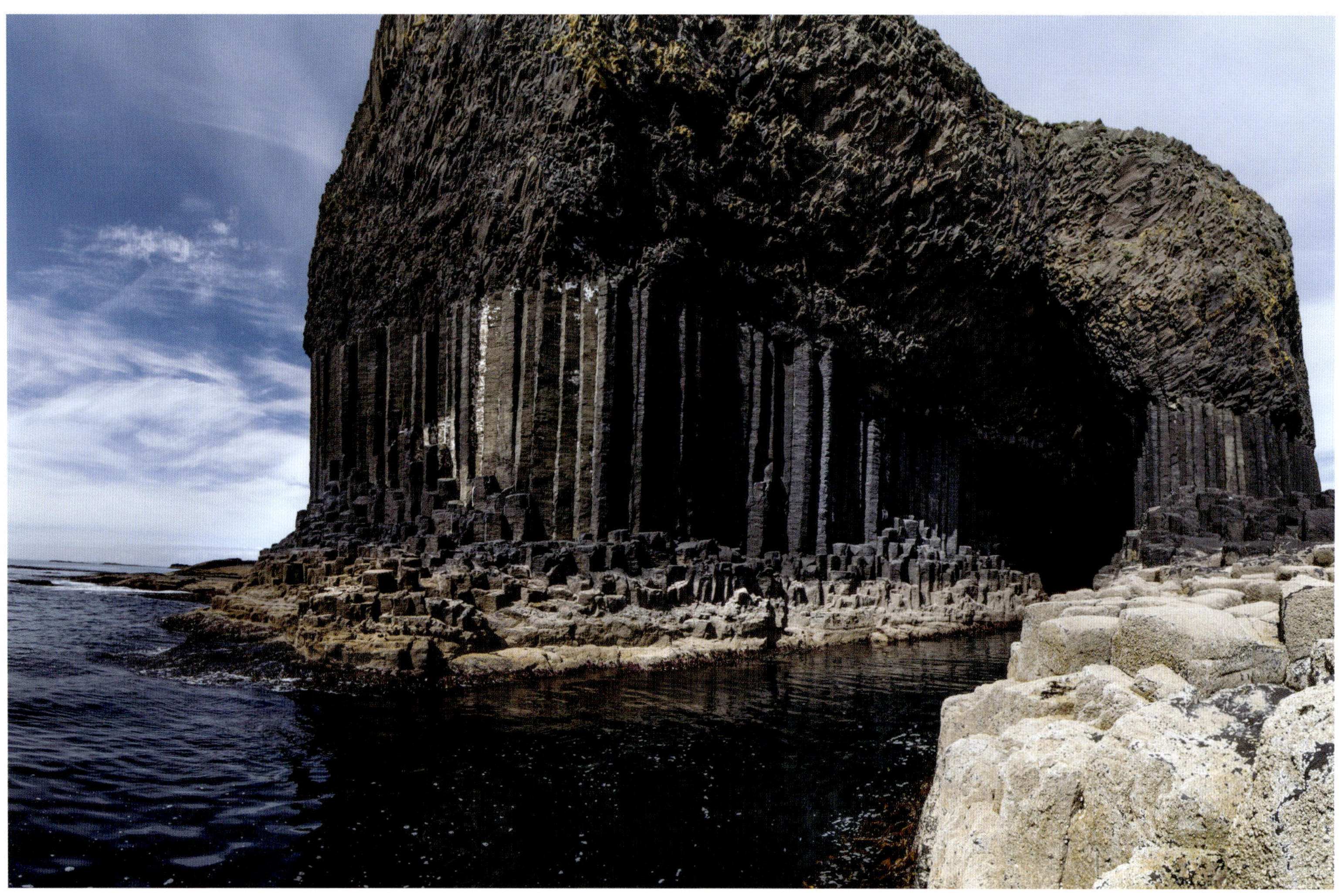

The extraordinary columnar basalt pillars at Fingal's Cave on the isle of Staffa

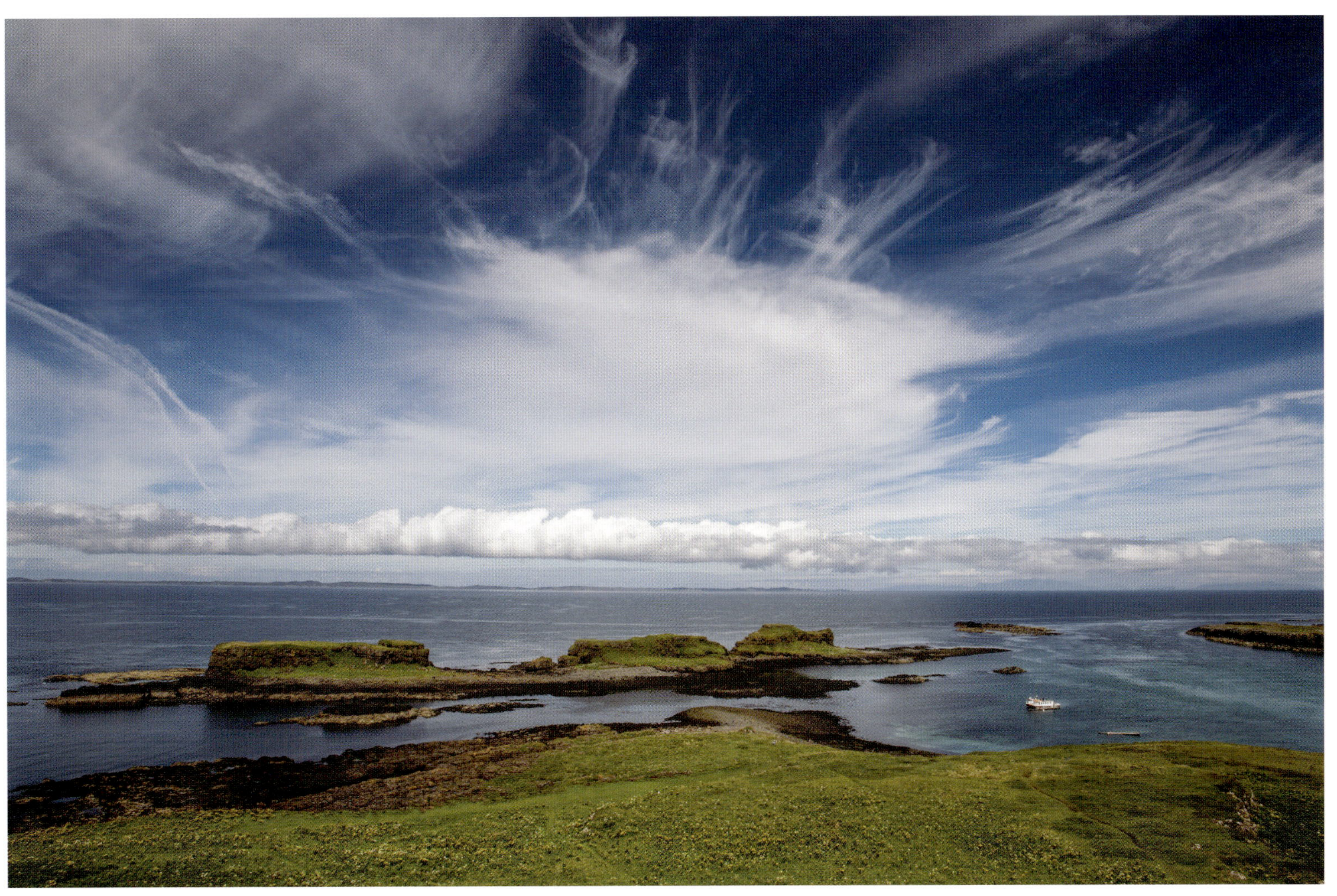

Lunga, larger of the Treshnish Isles, under a magnificent summer sky

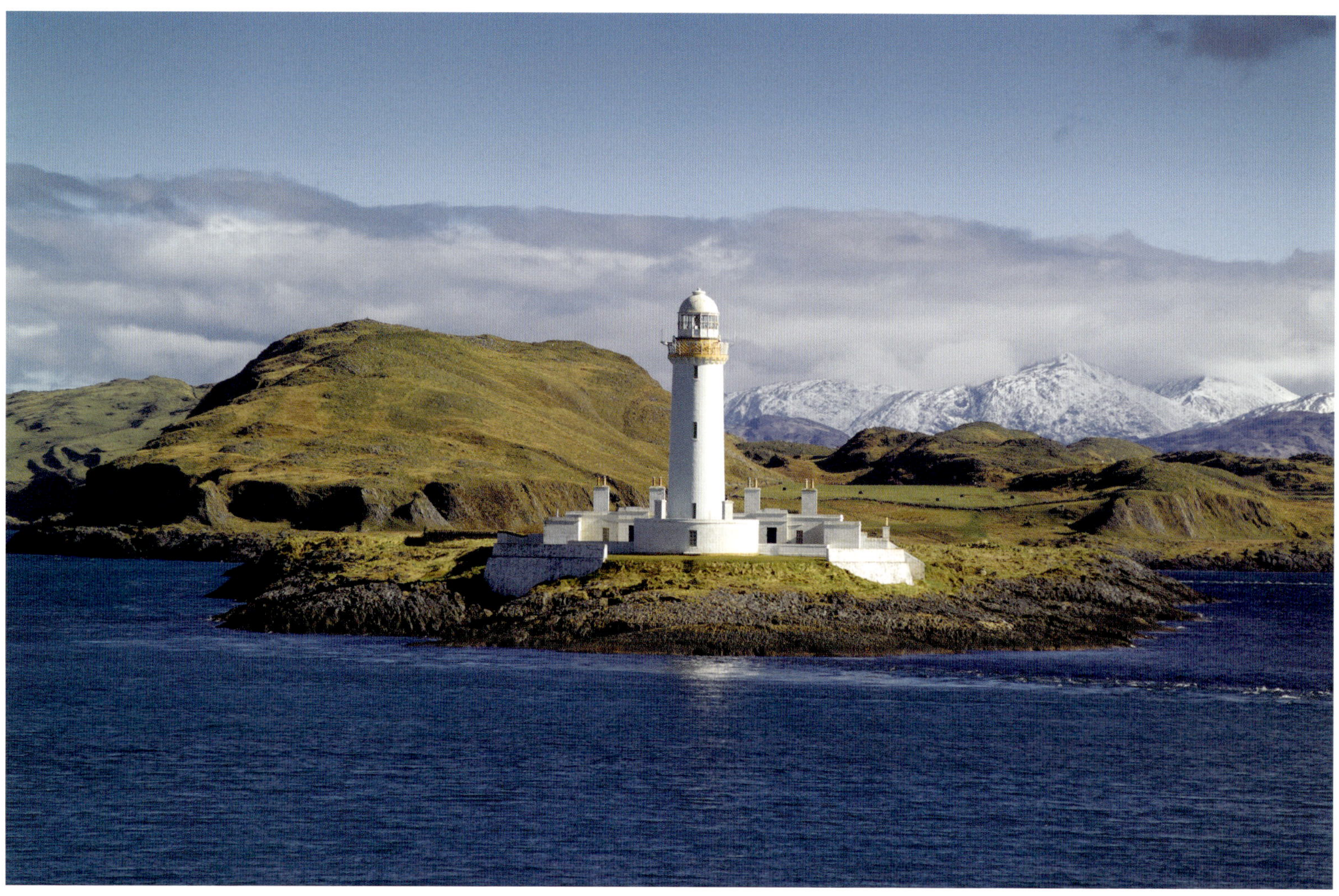

Eilean Musdile lighthouse, known as the "Lismore Light"
is etched in the memories of ferry travellers to Mull.

There's a slower pace of life on Lismore.

A Hebridean tumbledown sits sheepishly on the hillside

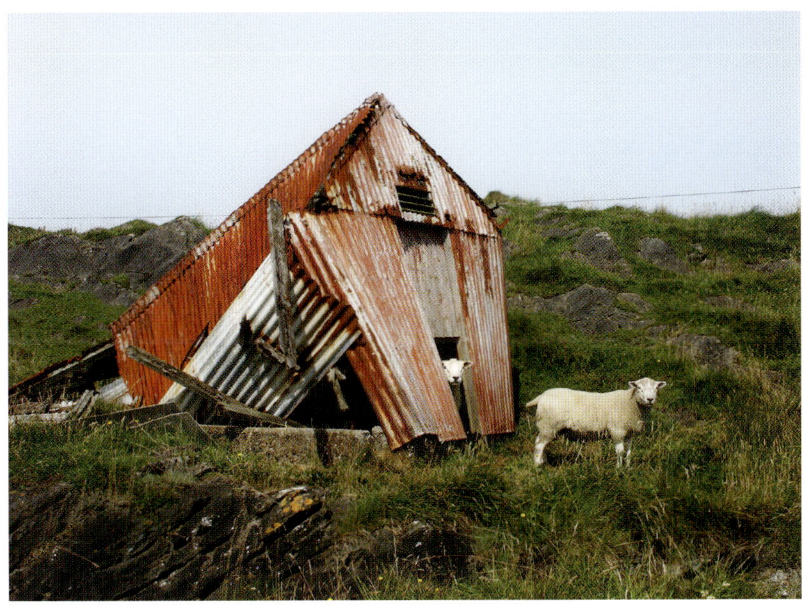

There's a slower pace of life on Lismore.

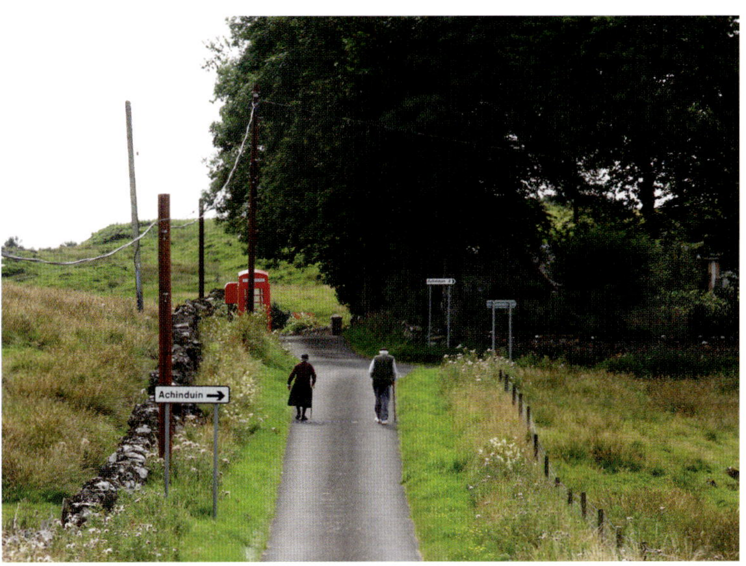

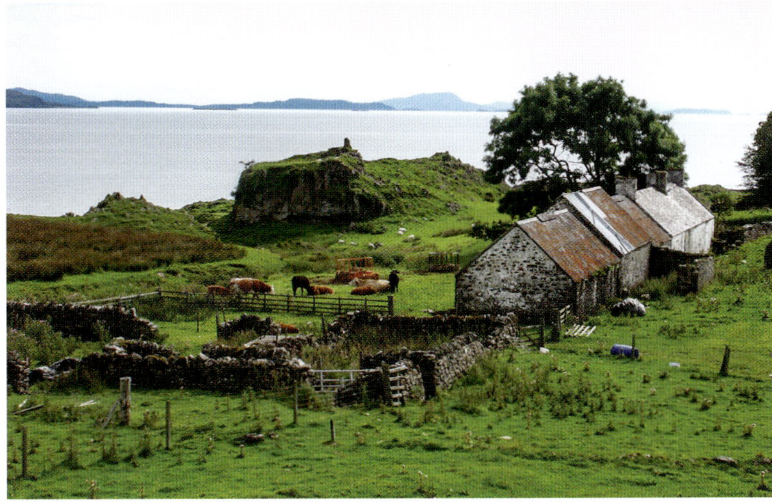

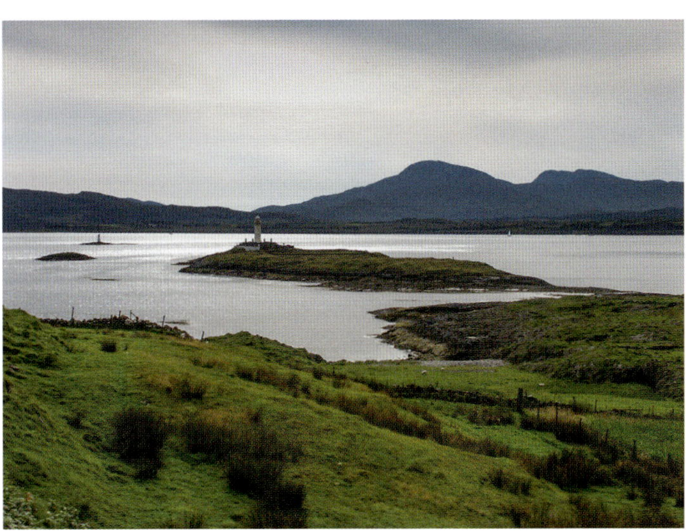

Eilean Musdile and the lighthouse

Crofting at Dalnarrow, at the south end of the island

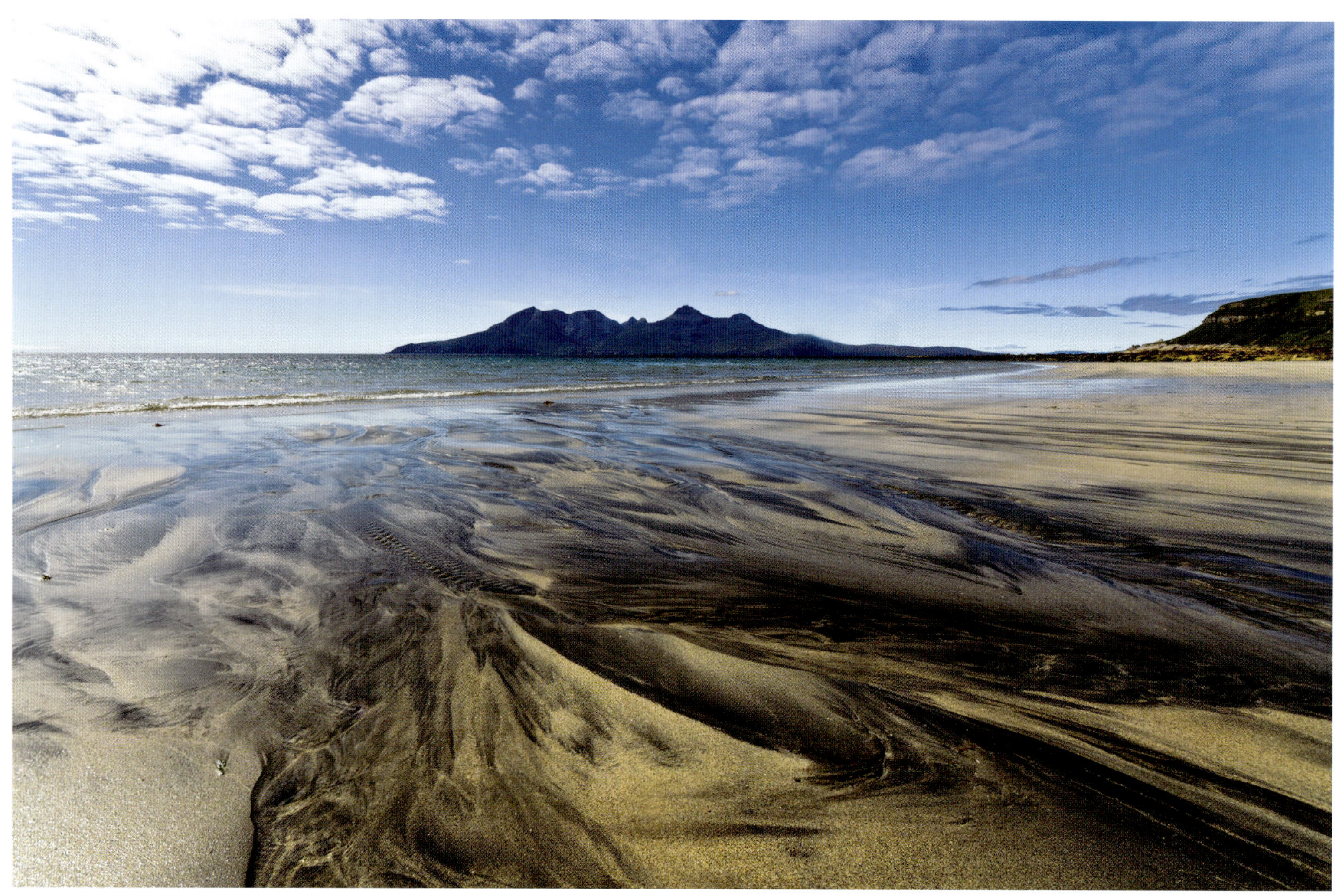

Nature is usually the best artist, as this view from Laig Bay to Rum highlights.

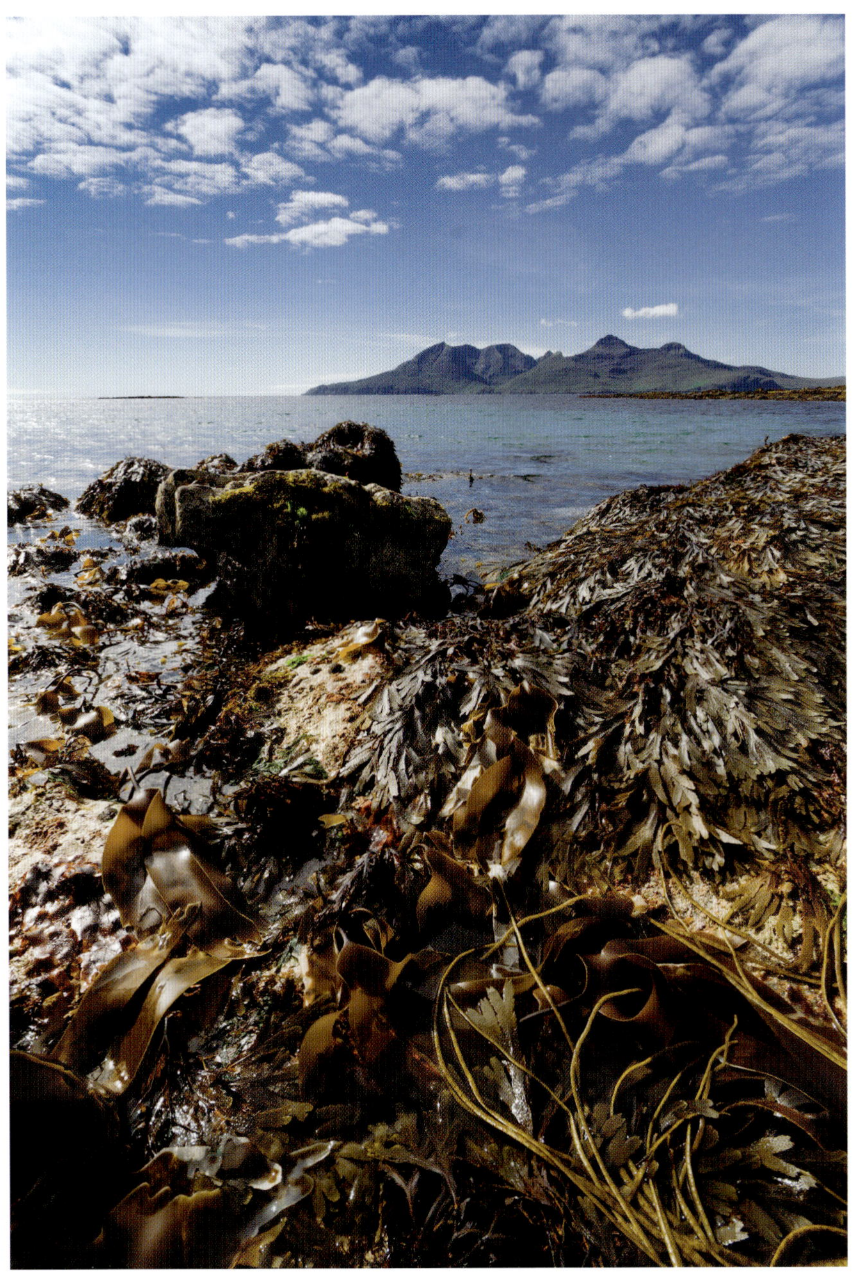

Rich kelp beds at Laig Bay point

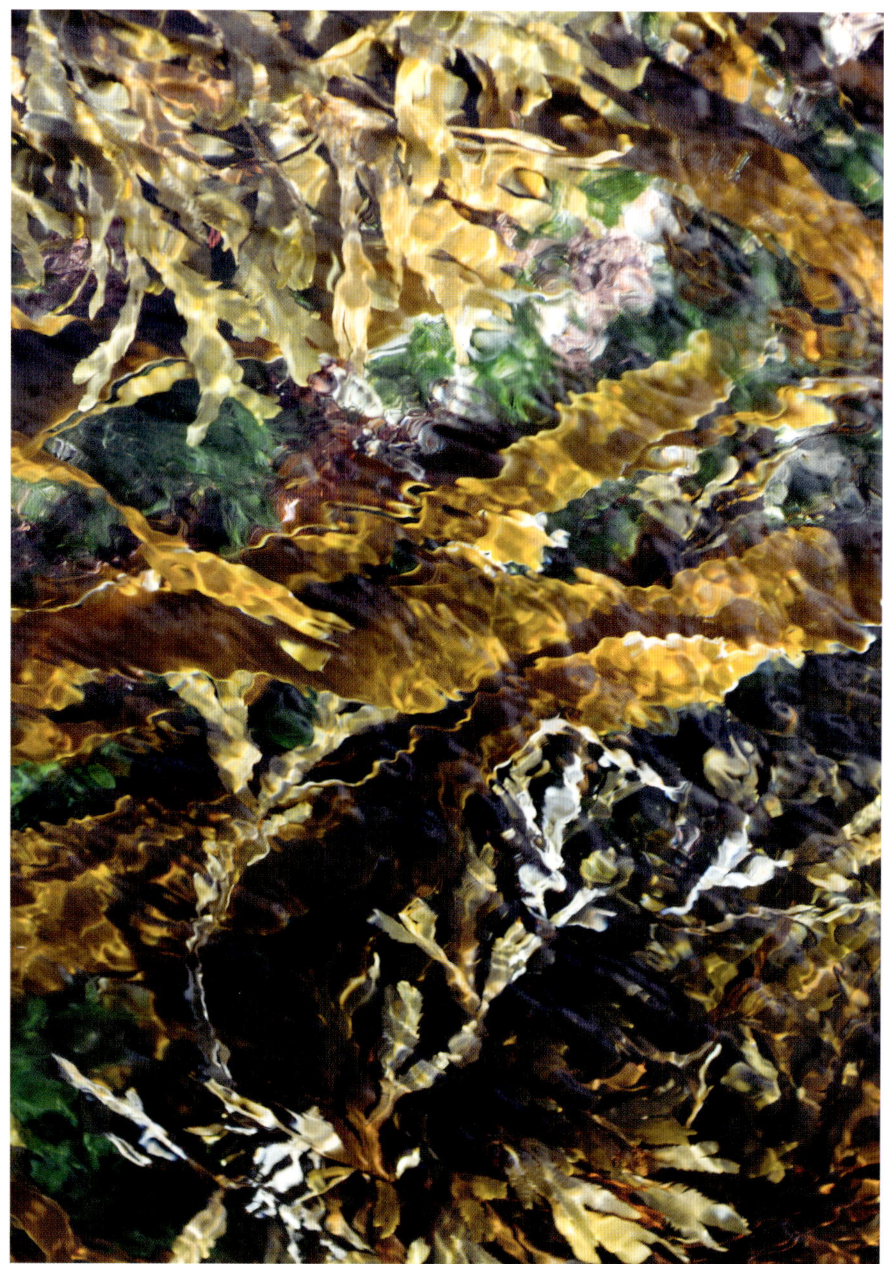

Crystal waters, sparkling light and intense colour all come together in this rock pool.

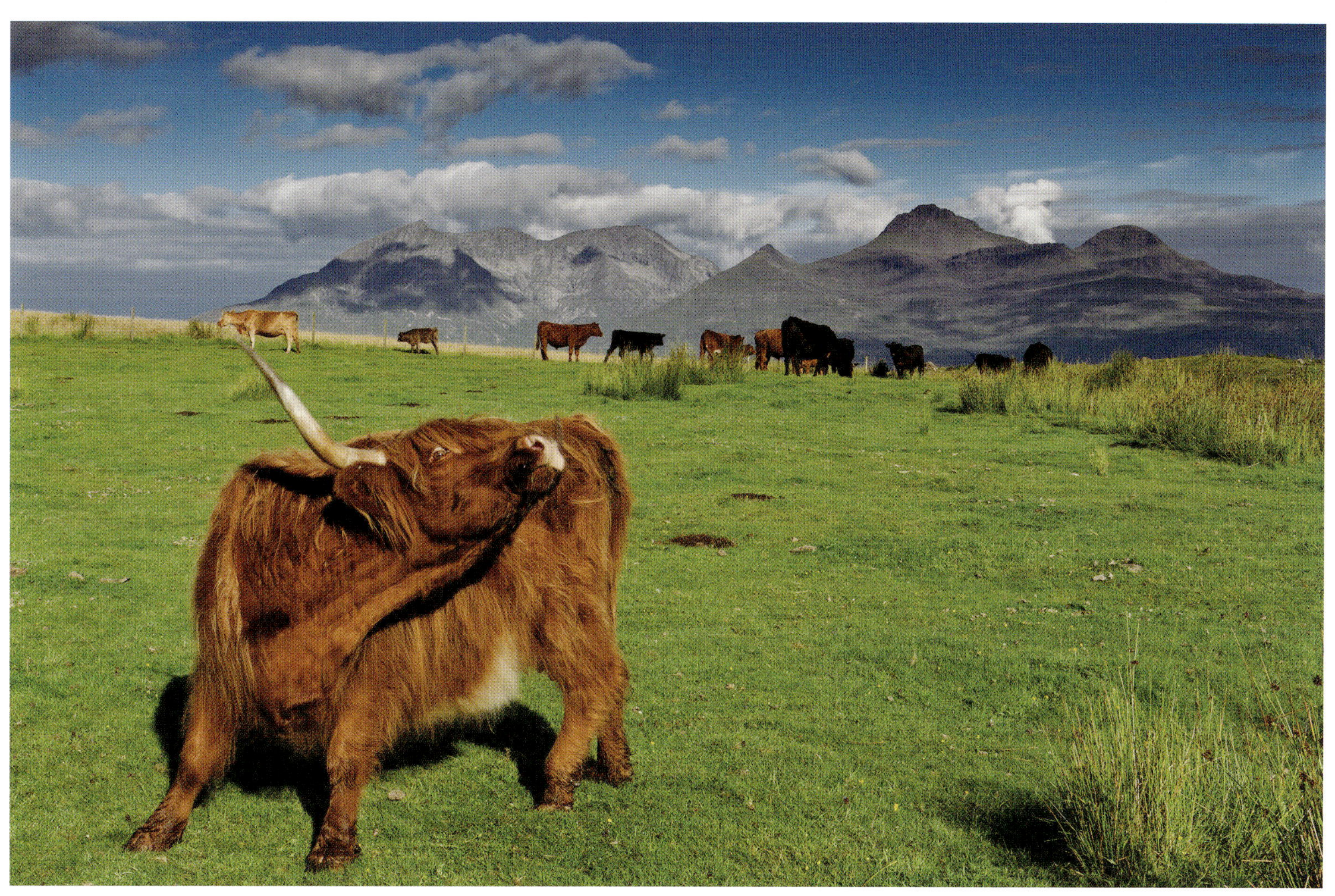

Some of Eigg's residents take views of Rum for granted.

Subsistence workhorses with stories to tell, laid to rest, their destination, archaeology.

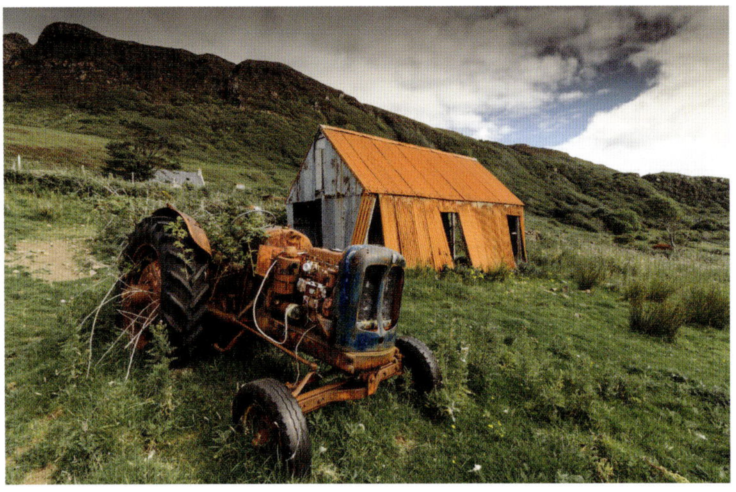

The settlement by Laig shelters beneath the island's geological backbone.

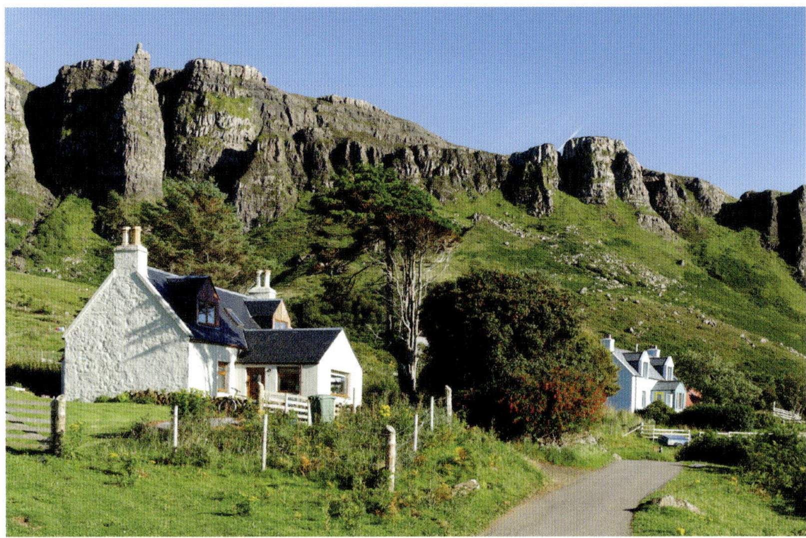

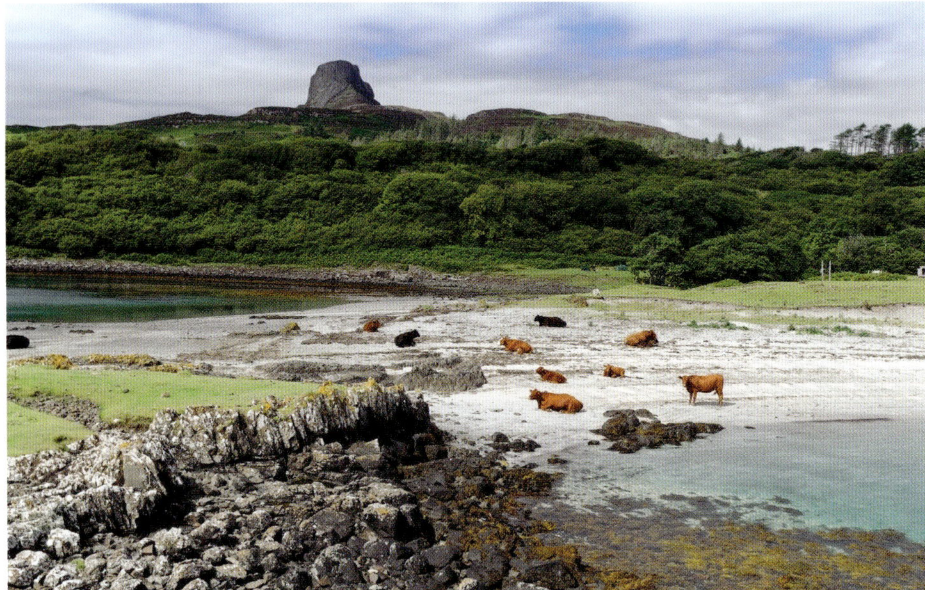

There is something particularly relaxed about the cattle on Eigg, as this scene at Kildonan beach illustrates.

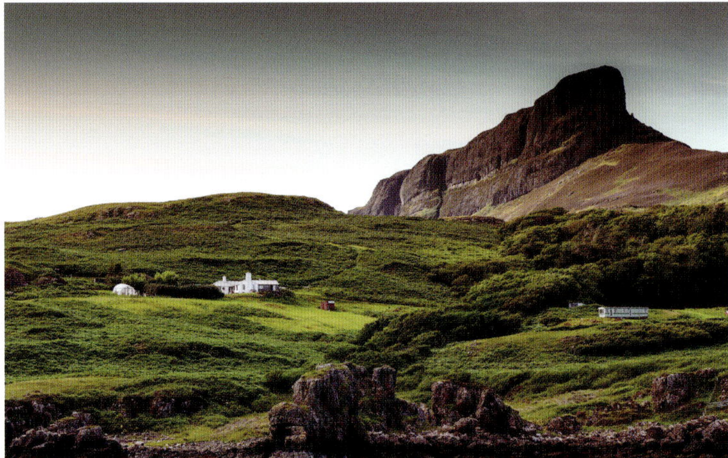

The monumental Scaur of Eigg dominates this part of the island.

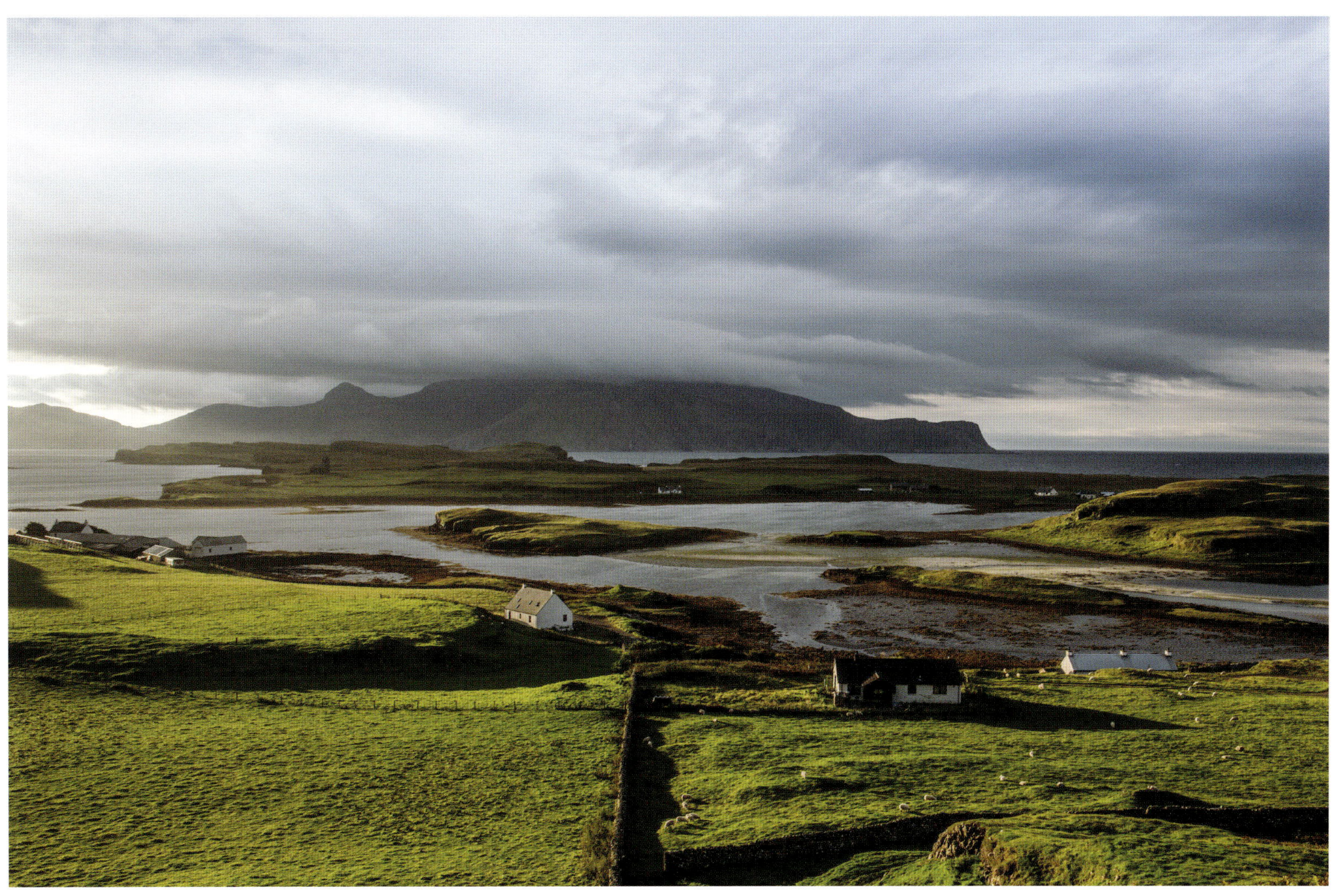

Gifted to the National Trust for Scotland, this quiet member of the Small Isles overlooks its bigger more brooding neighbour, Rum.

The interior of St Edward's Church - on Sanday.

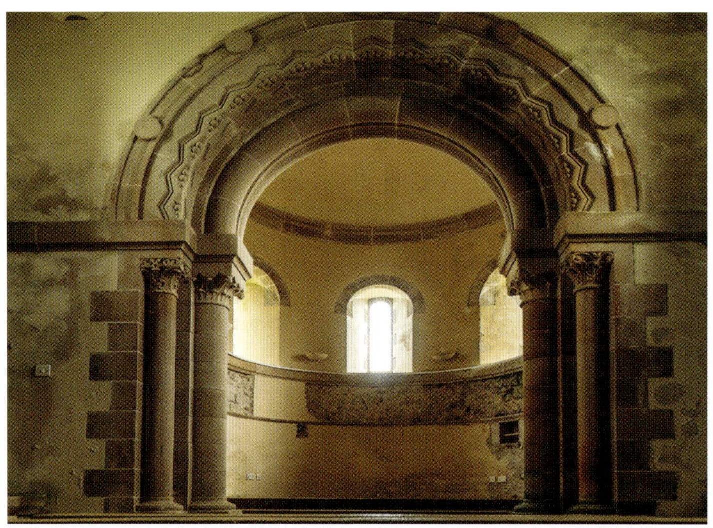

Mist rolls in across the tidal isle of Sanday

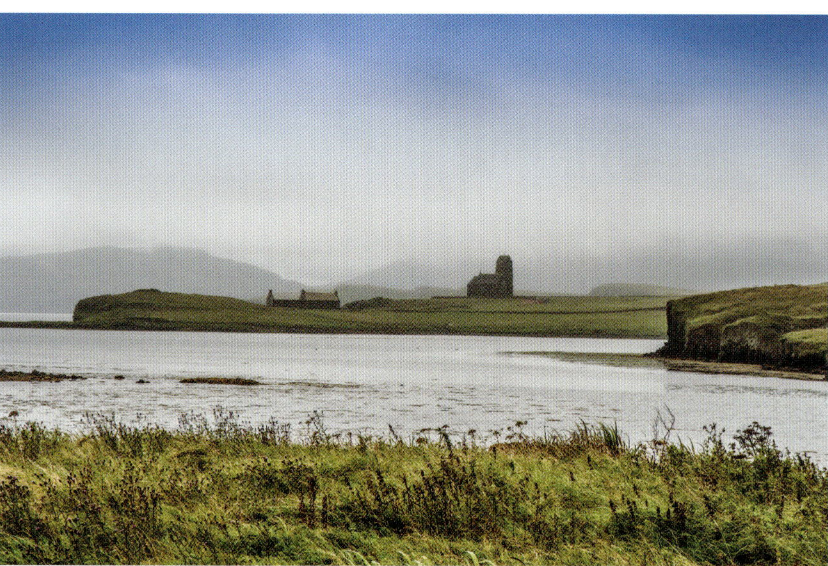

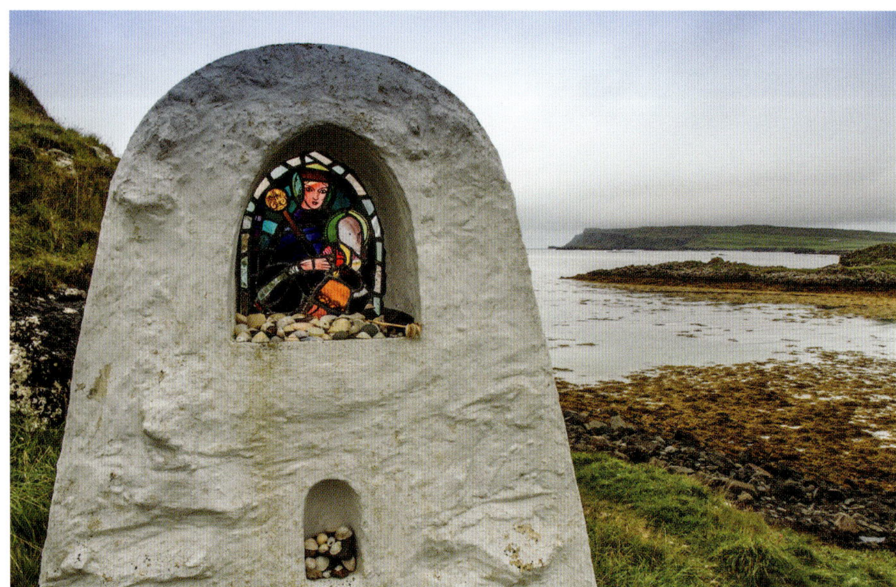

Benedictine monk, Father Routledge built this charming little shrine at the bridge to Sanday

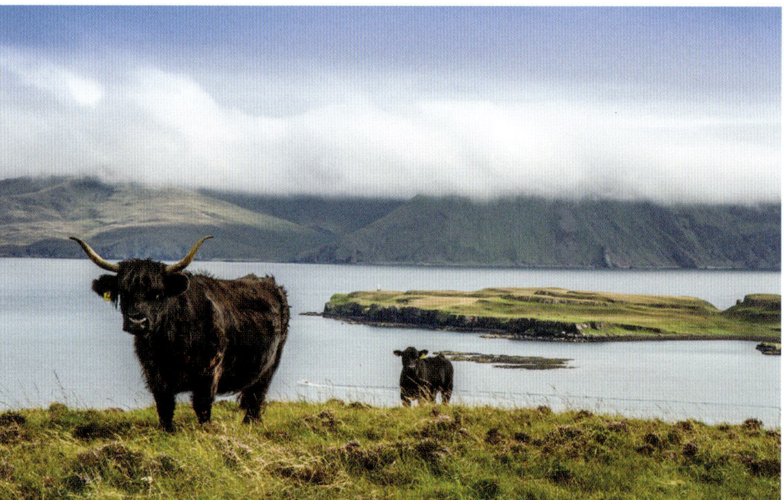

Native breeds contribute to the conservation status of the island

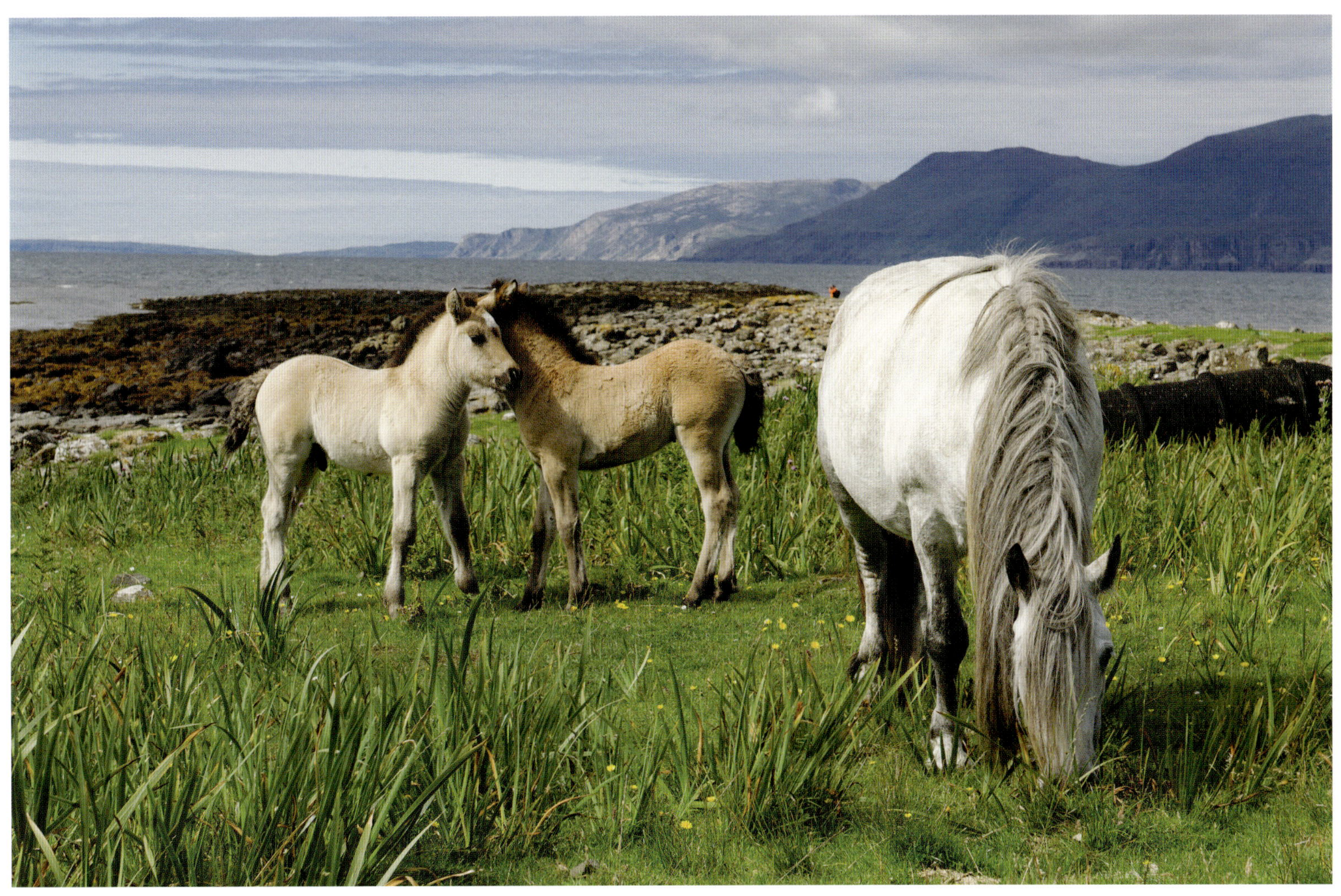

Native Highland ponies graze on the foreshore

The lush and fertile lowlands of Muck

Rusty corrugated sheds are common in the Hebridean landscape

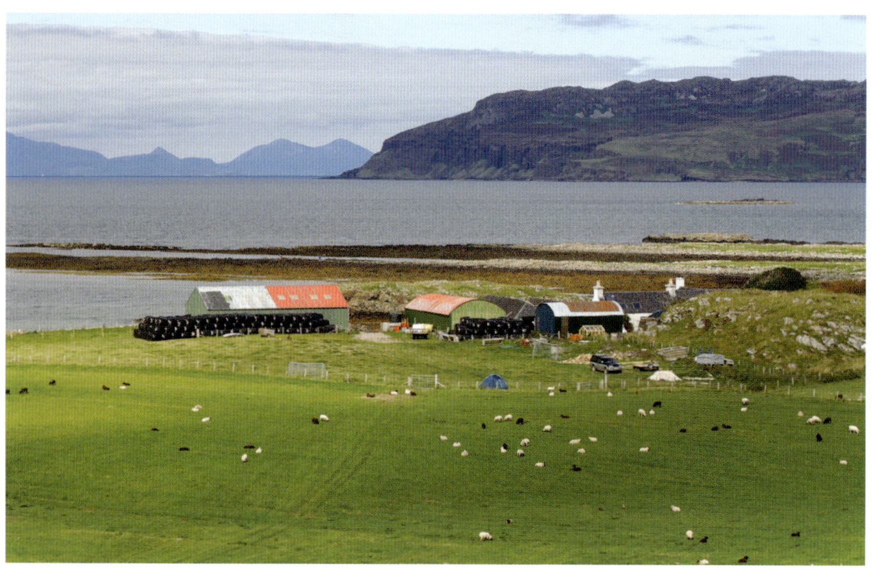

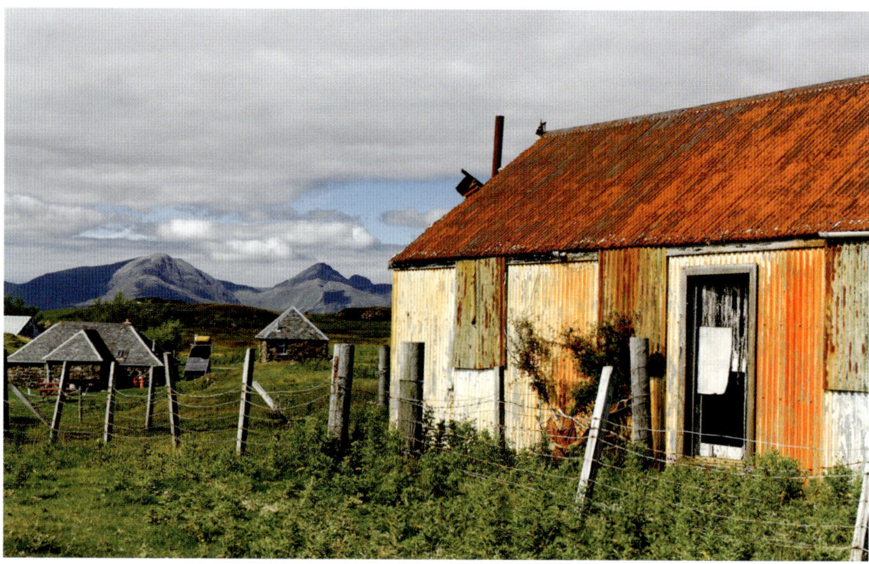

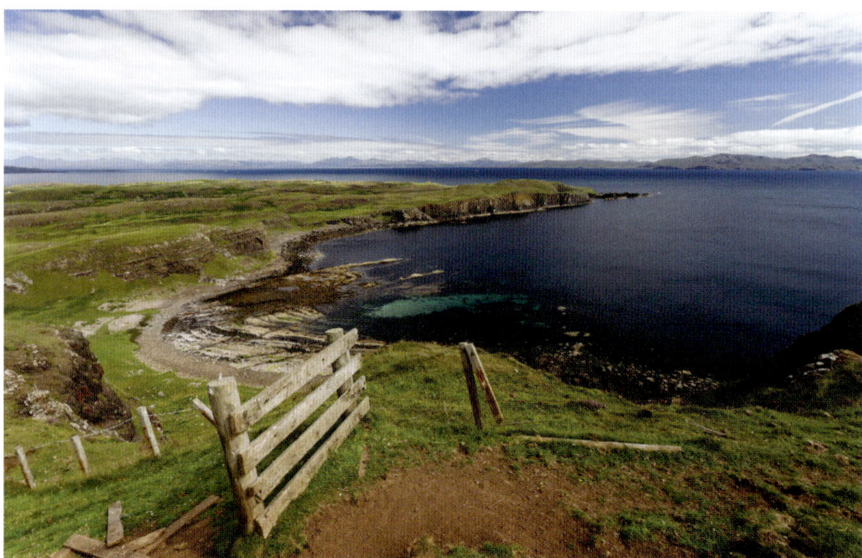

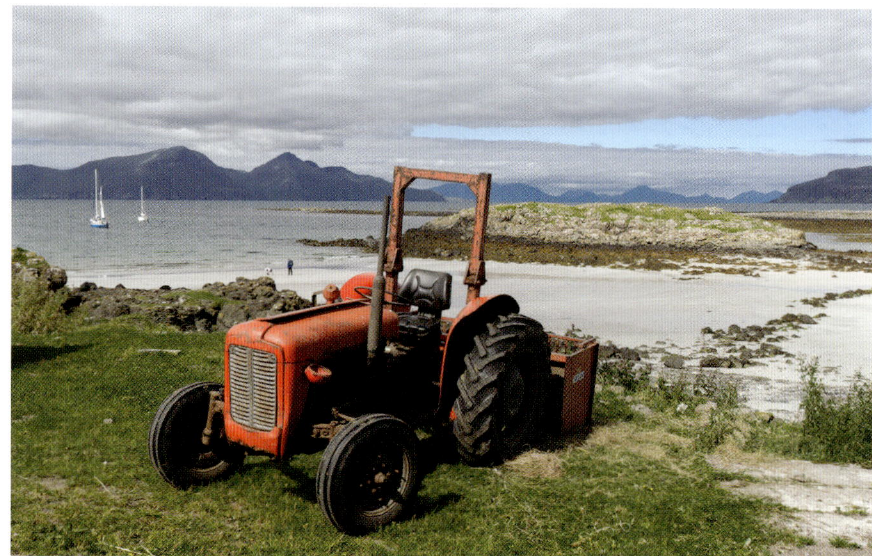

Camas Mor Bay from Glen Mairtein

A classic working Massey Ferguson 35 in good heart

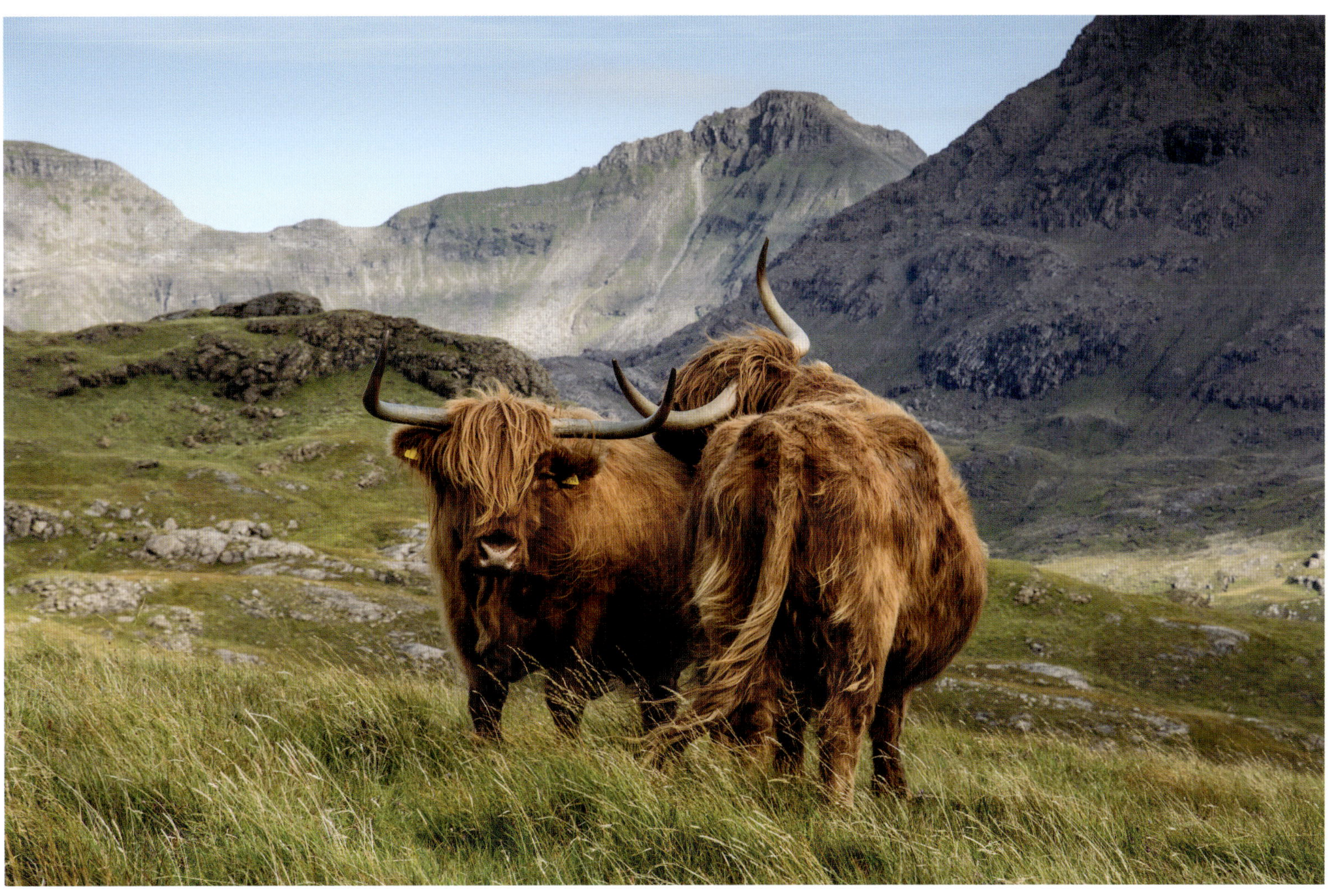
Playful Highlanders and the rugged interior beneath Barkeval

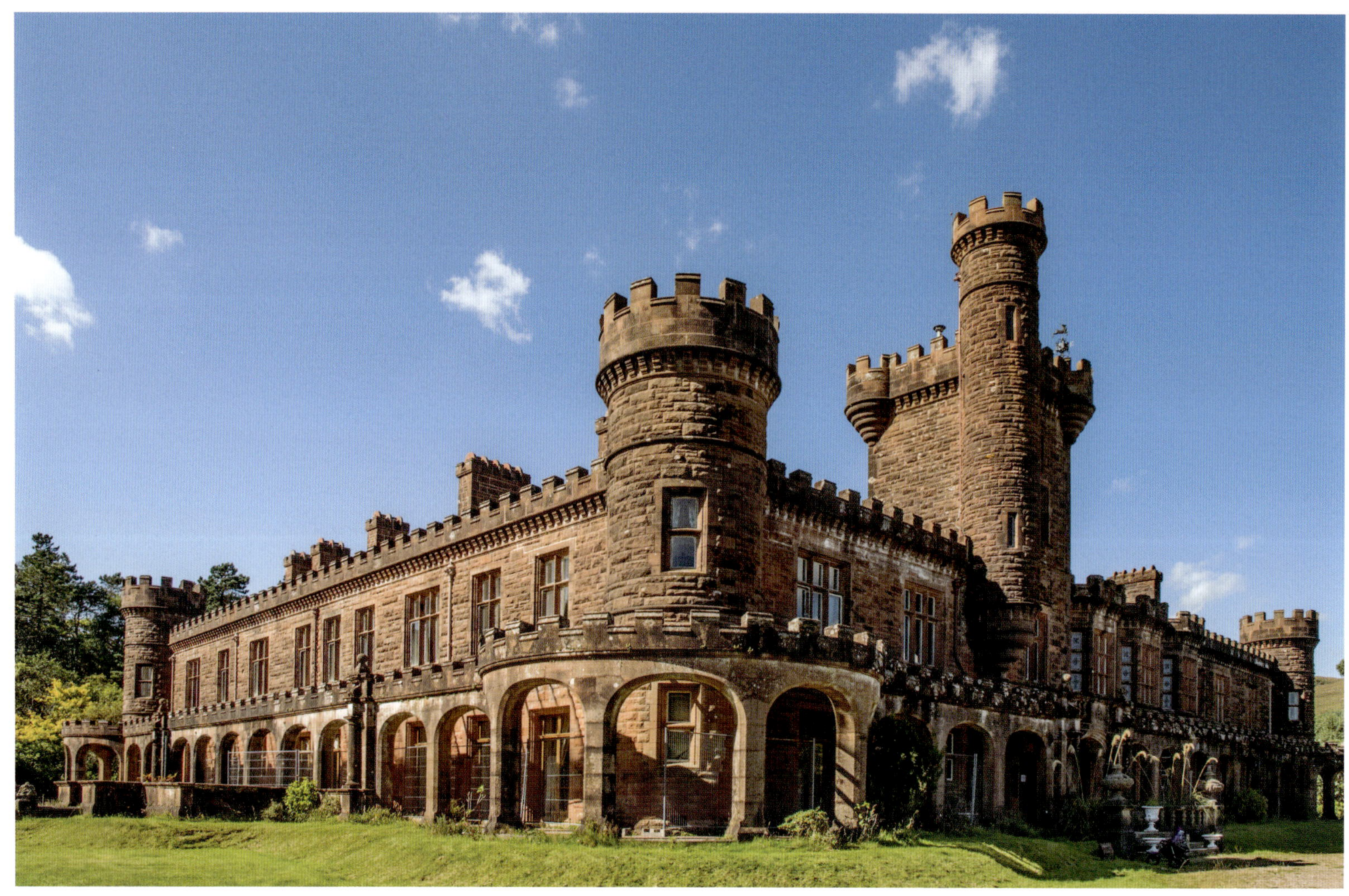

Kinloch Castle, the Victorian mansion built by textile tycoon George Bullough
for the entertainment of his wealthy companions

The trail to Harris is quite arduous but the high plateau
offers stunning views to Askival, Hallival and Barkeval

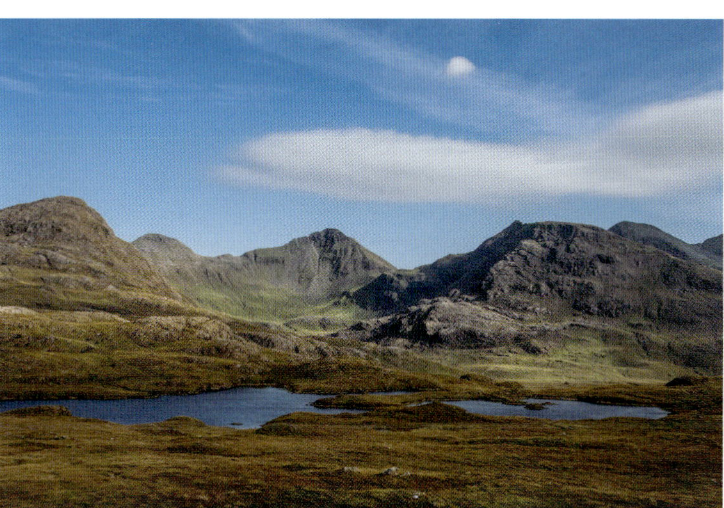

An elegant archway at Kinloch.

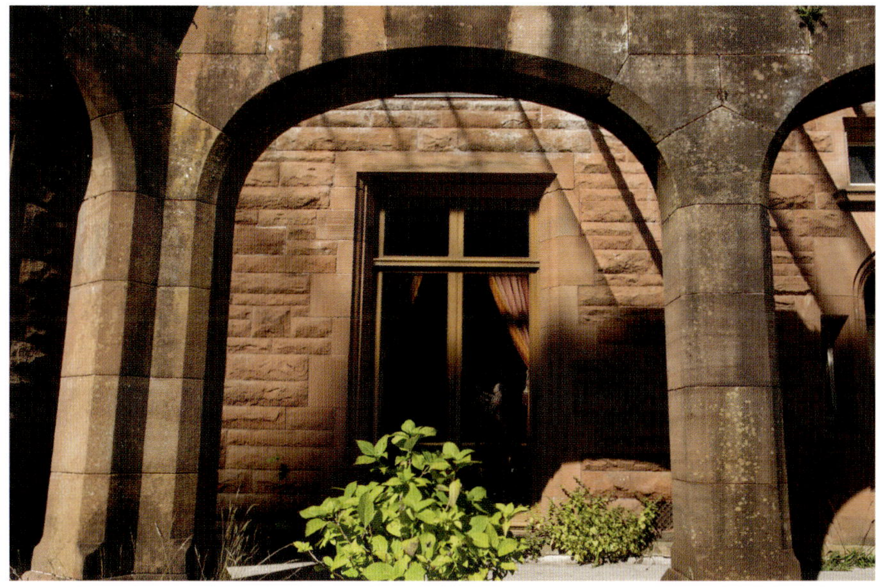

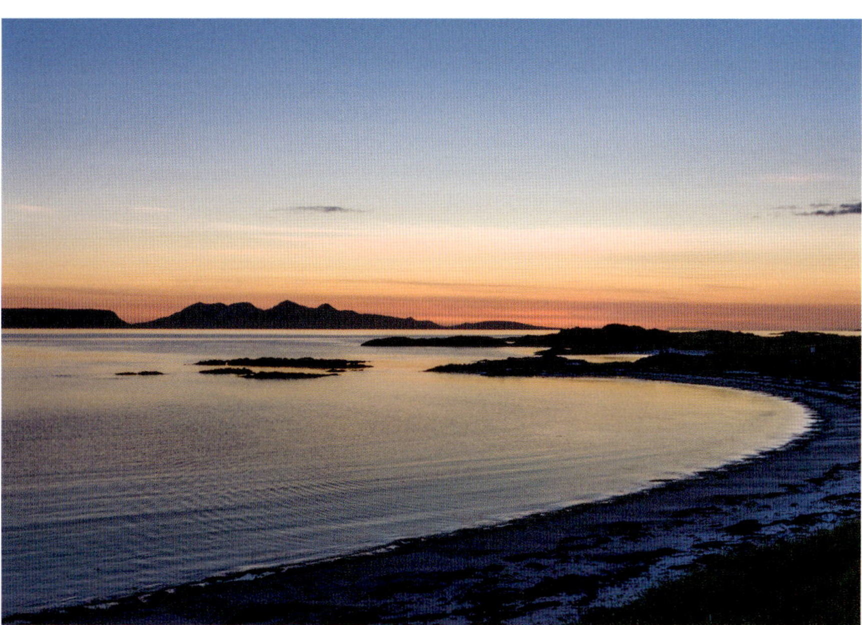

Rum features prominently on the horizon from countless locations around the Lochaber coast,
including here at Arisaig

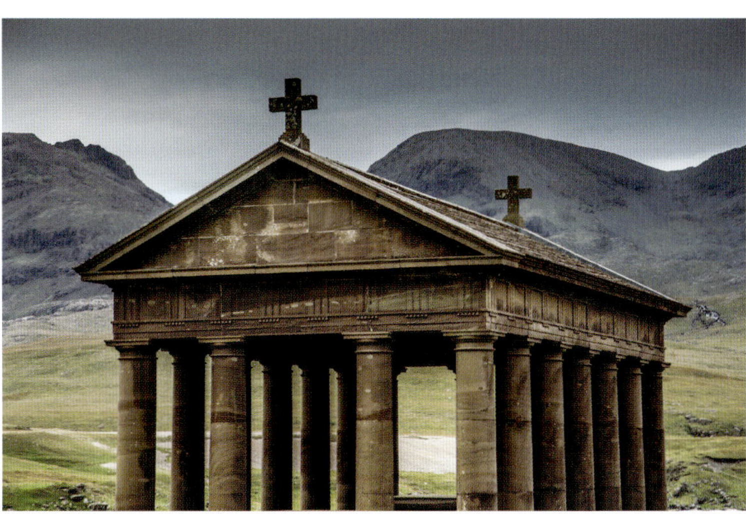

The Bullough Mausoleum at Harris is a bold statement

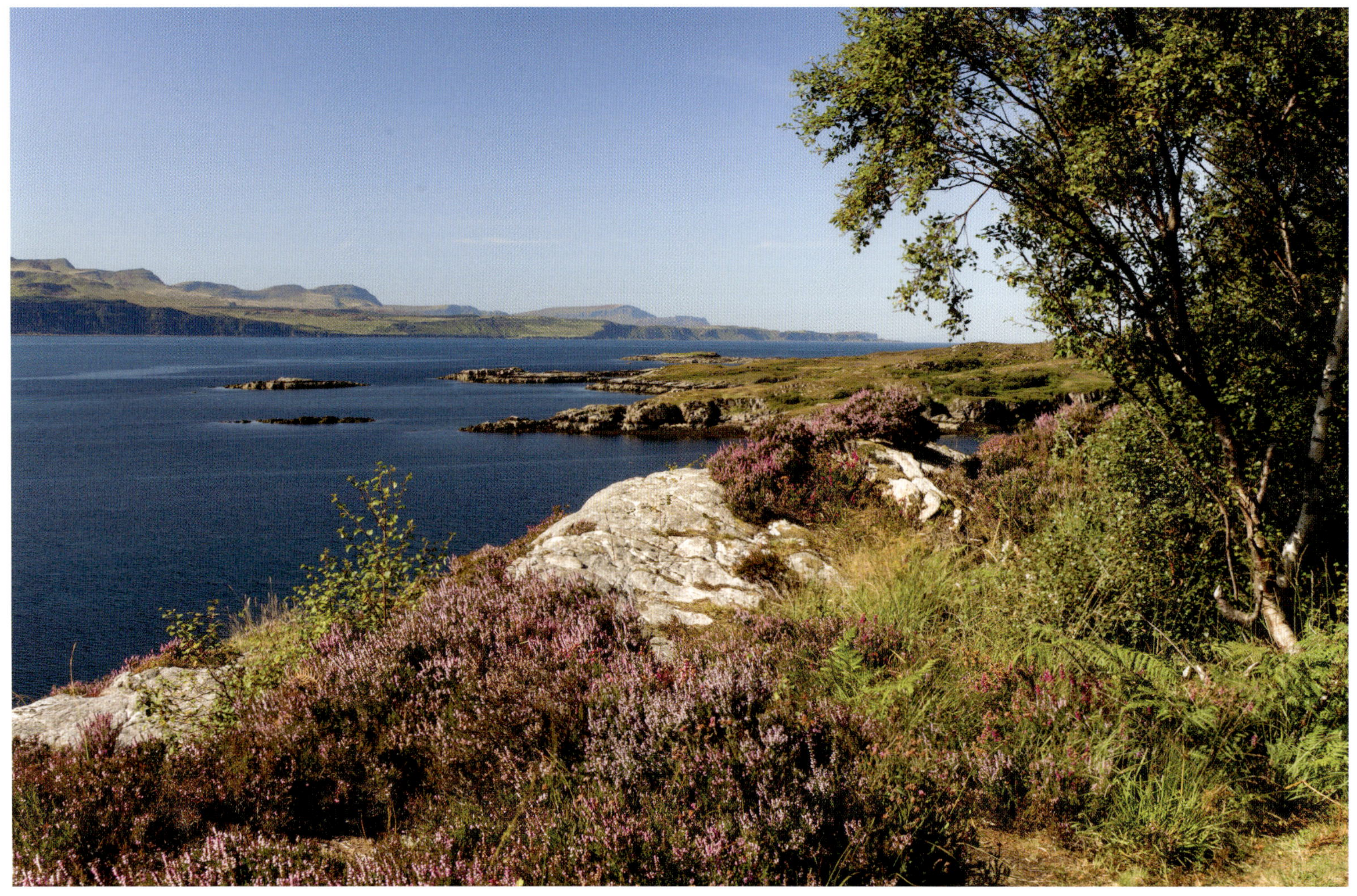

The colours of the high summer at Arnish, with views
to Eilean Fladday and Trotternish on Skye

The story of Callum's Road has become Hebridean legend. Crofter Callum McLeod almost single-handedly built the 1.75 mile road from Brochel to Arnish with only a wheelbarrow, pick and shovel

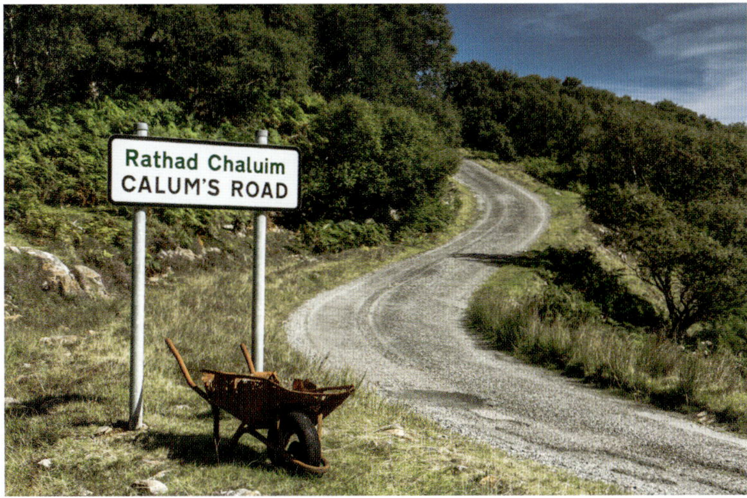

Raasay is only a short ferry hop from Sconser on Skye

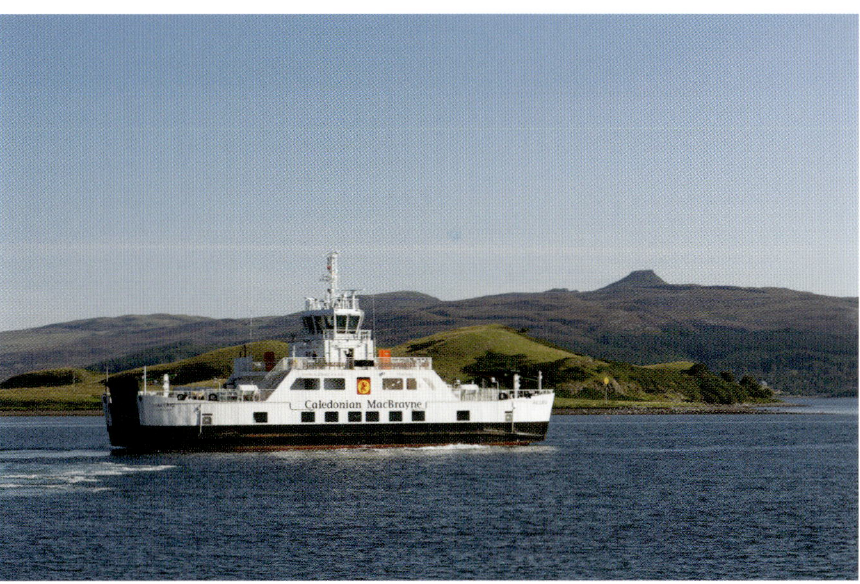

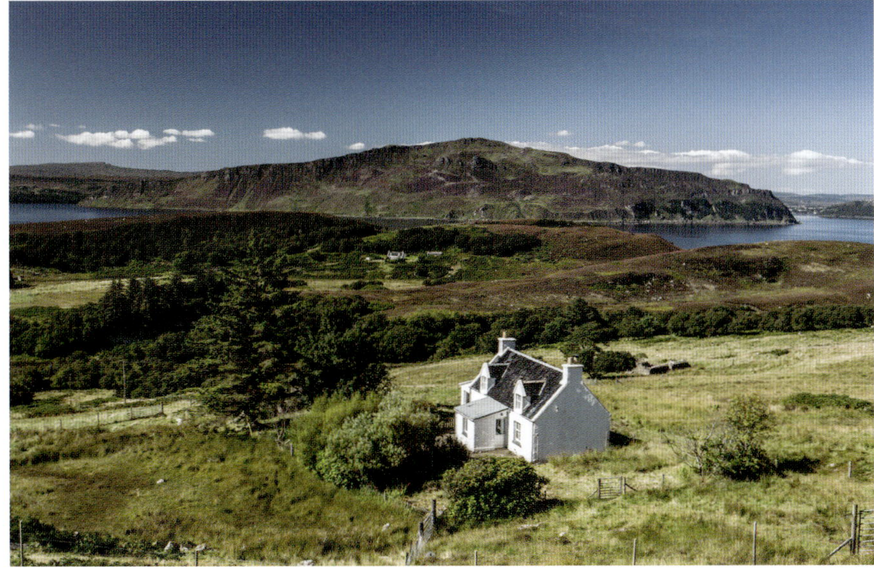

Looking west from Balmeanach Cottage to Skye.

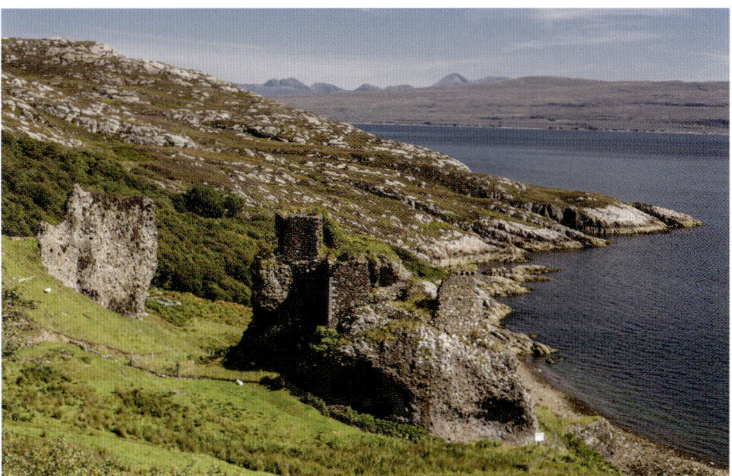

Brochel Castle, built by a McLeod chieftain in sixteenth century, lies close to the end of the road at Arnish

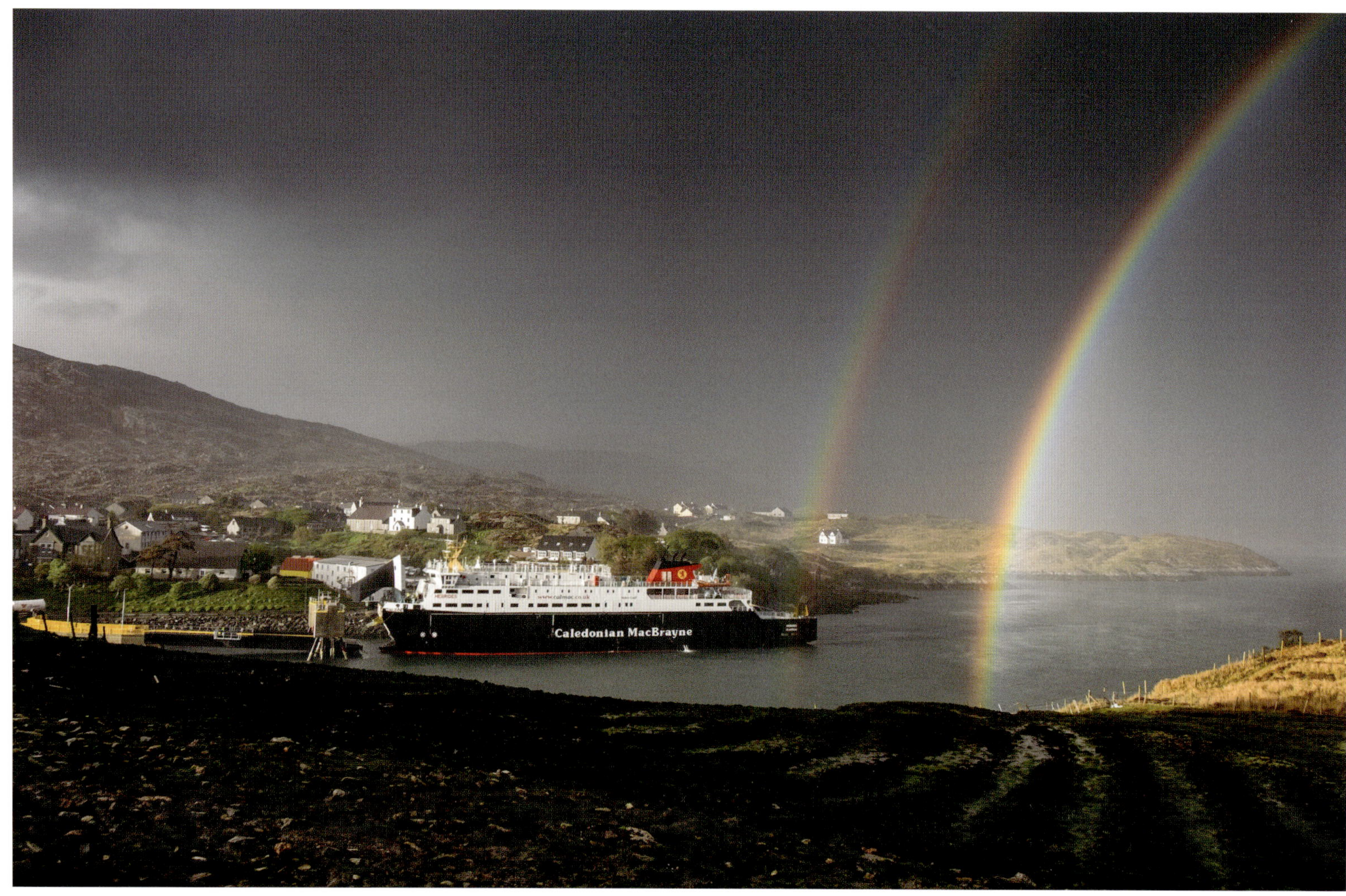

A double rainbow and the familiar red funnel of the CalMac ferry at Tarbert.

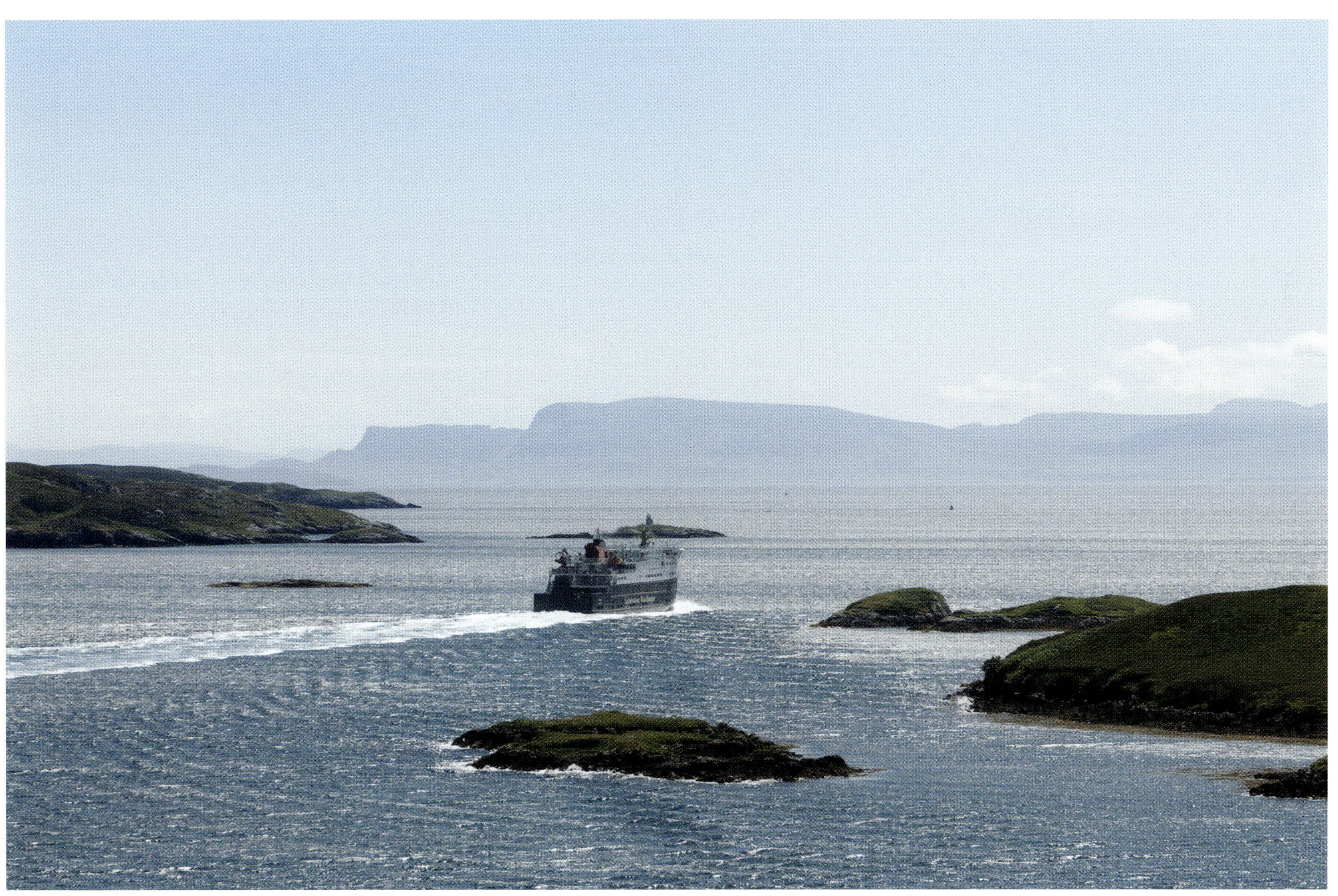

MV *Hebrides* sails down east Loch Tarbert past Scalpay.

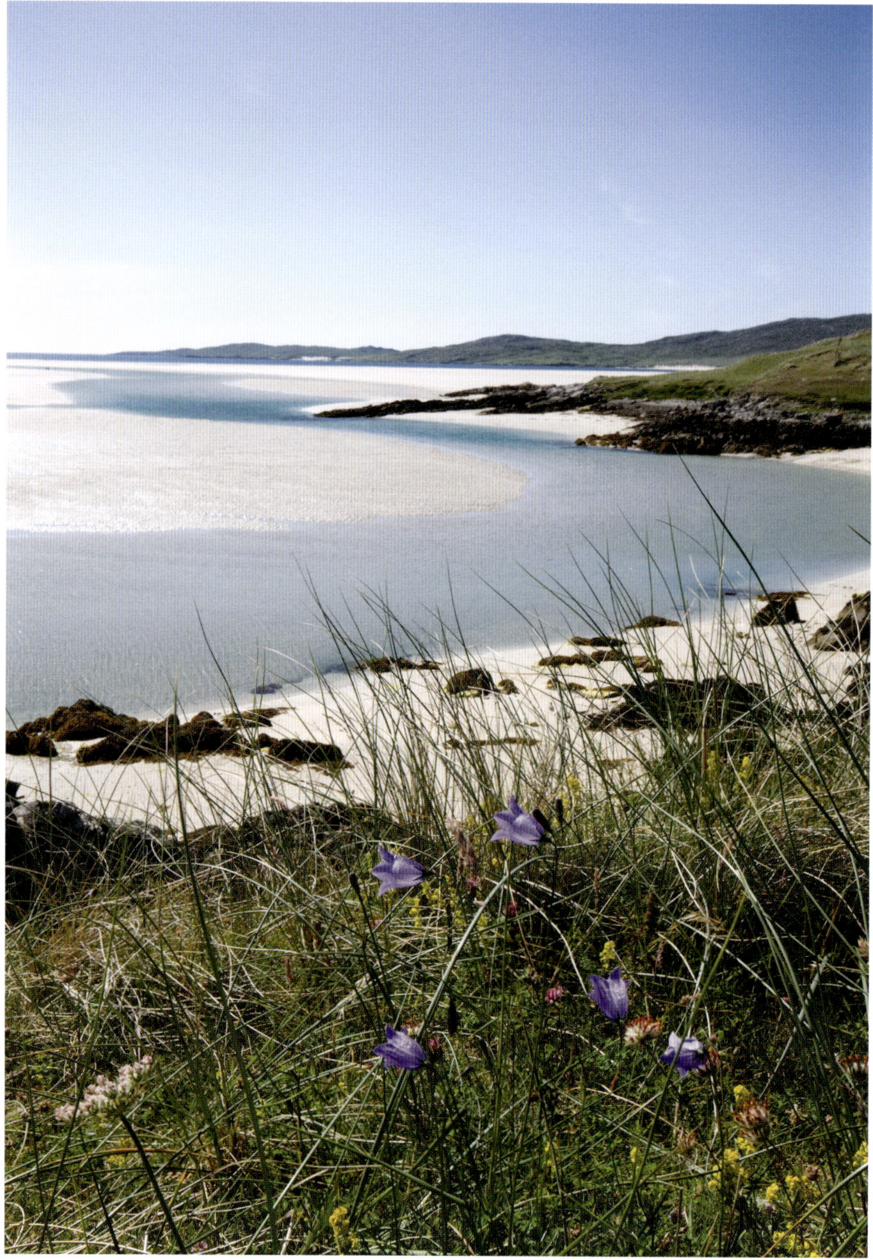

Harebells, the original Scottish Bluebell, enhance the dreamscape that is Luskentyre beach.

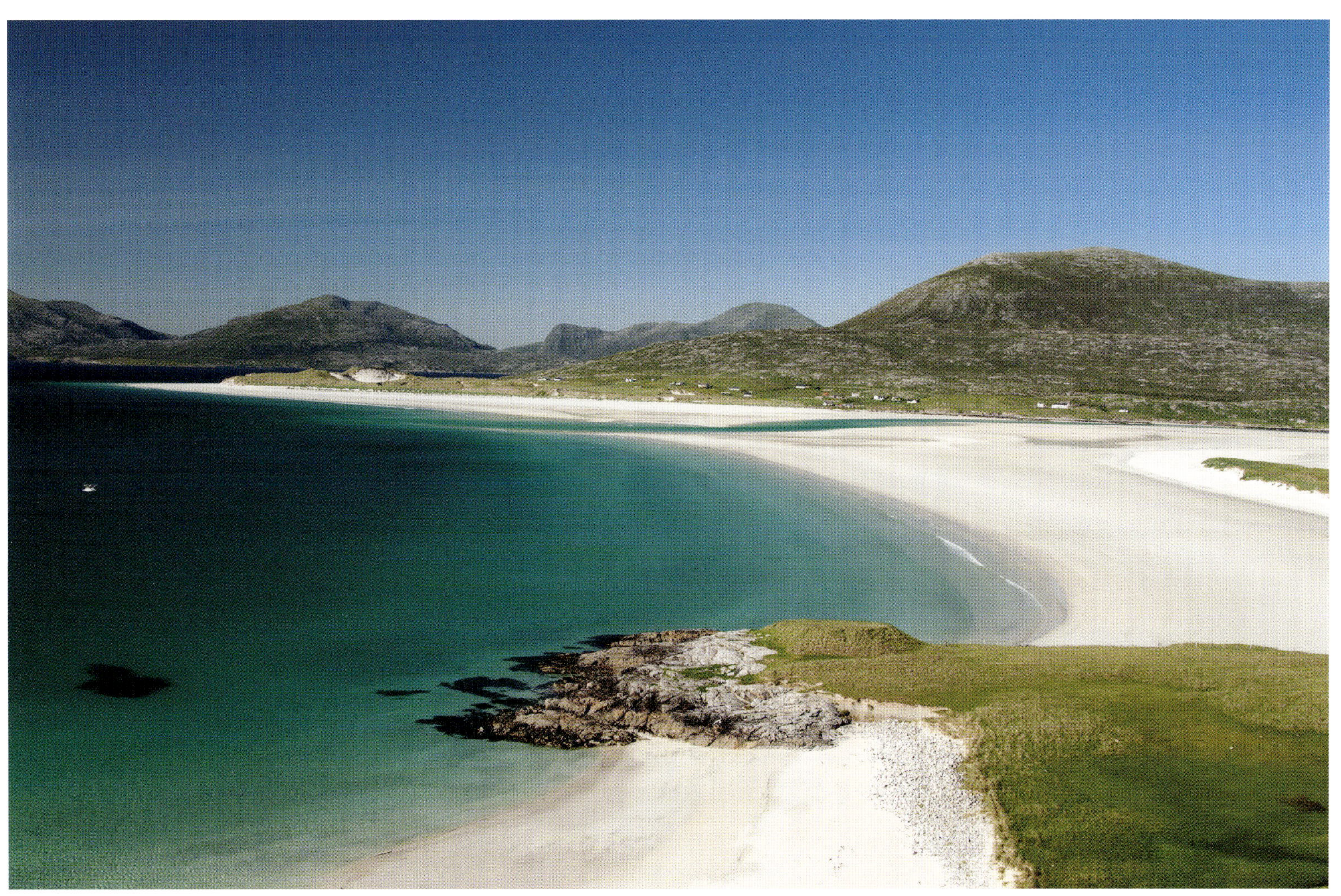

Caribbean sands? No, Lusekentyre from Seilebost

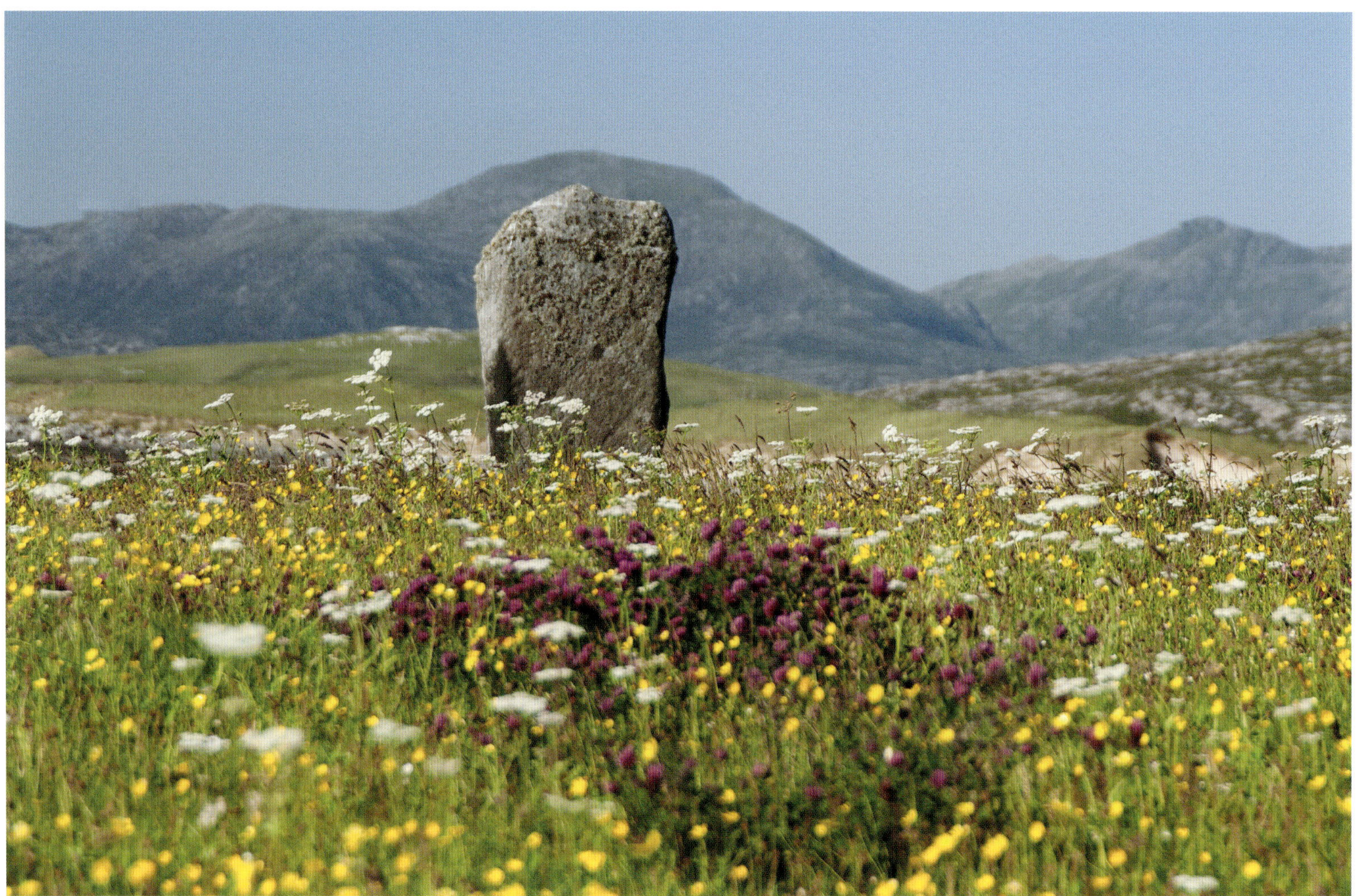

The McLeod standing stone at Horgabost emerges from the rich machair.

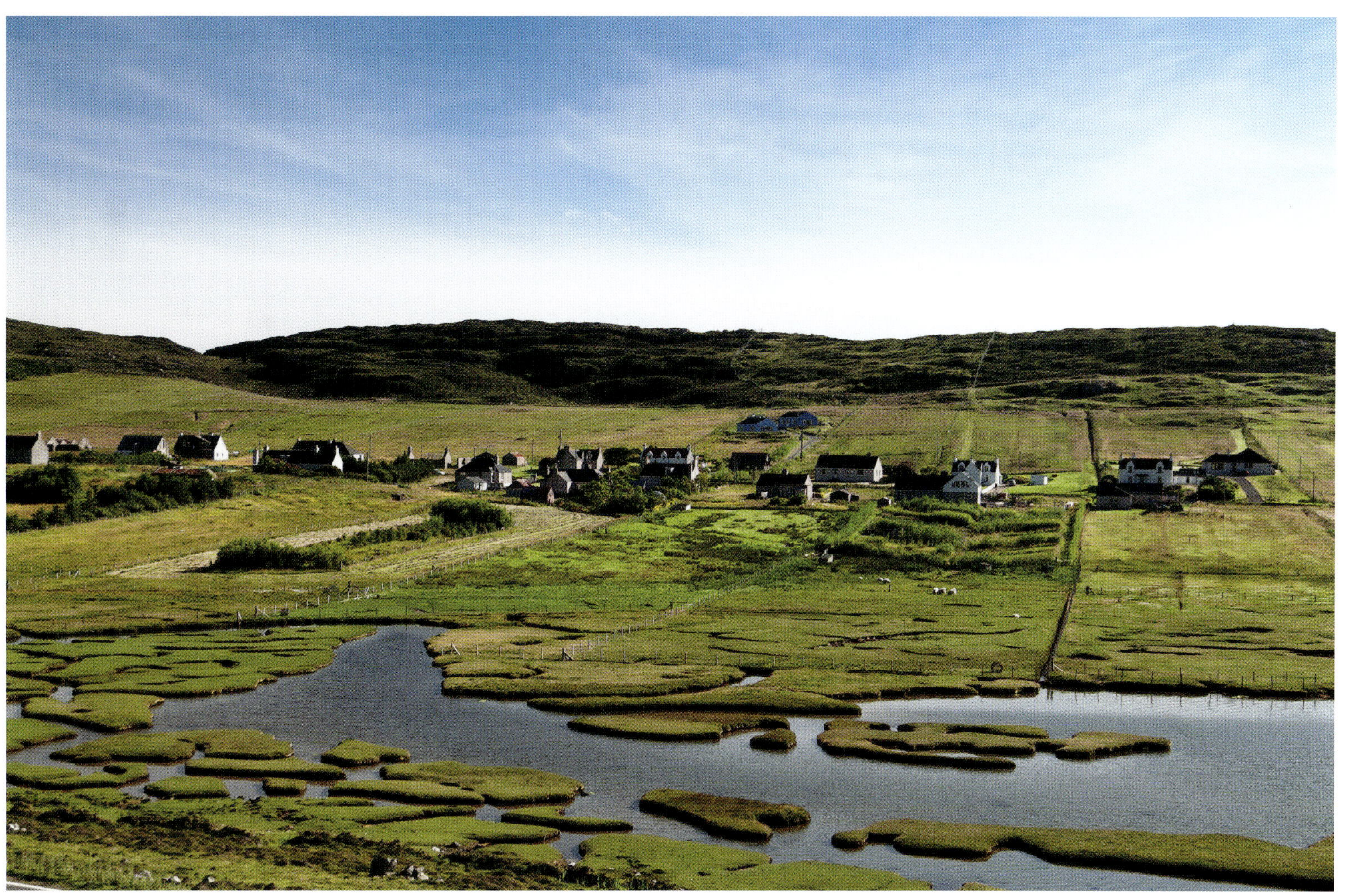

Relics of the traditional runrig crofting system at Northton, by Leverburgh

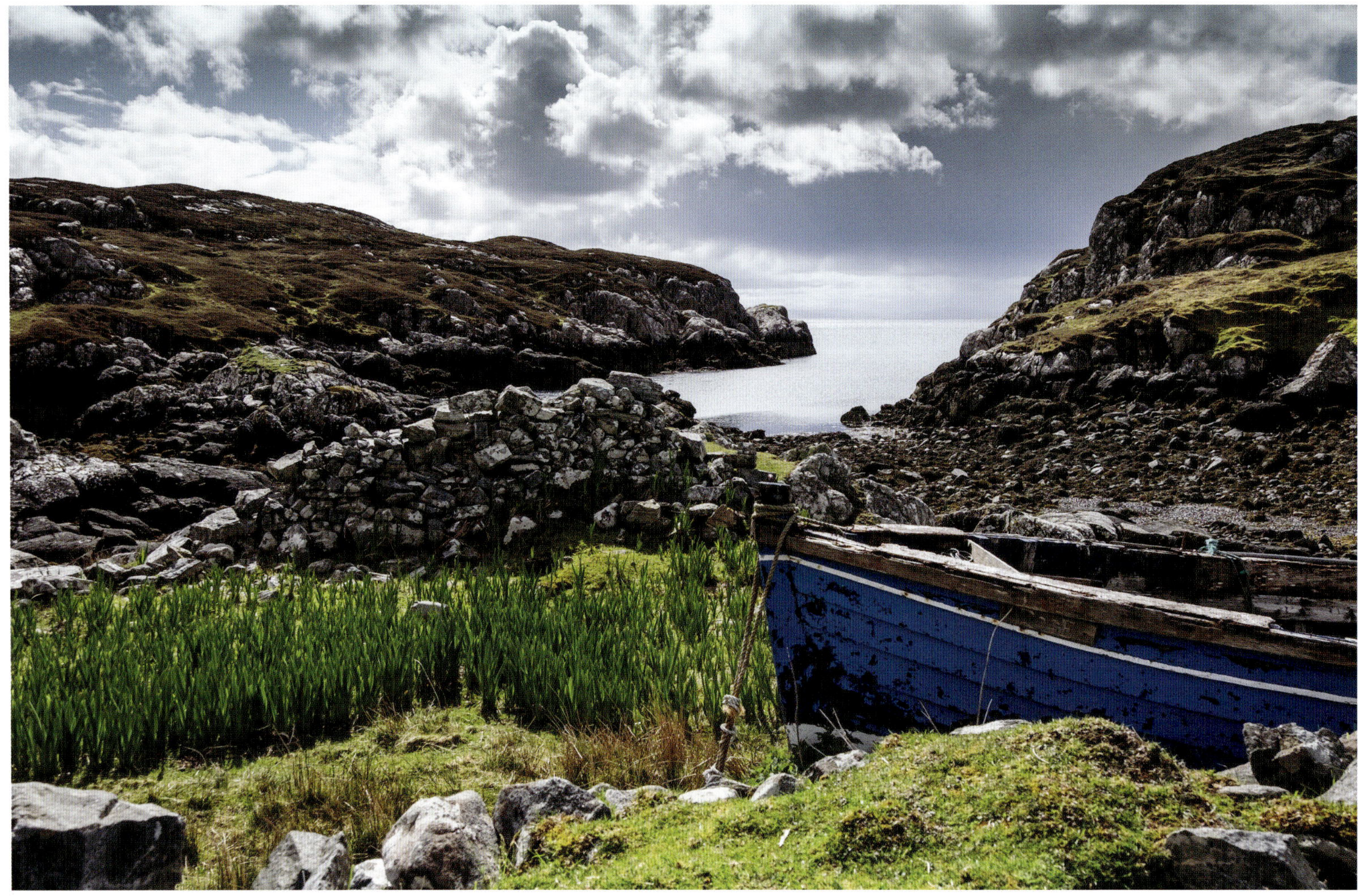

Clinker-built at Lingerbay

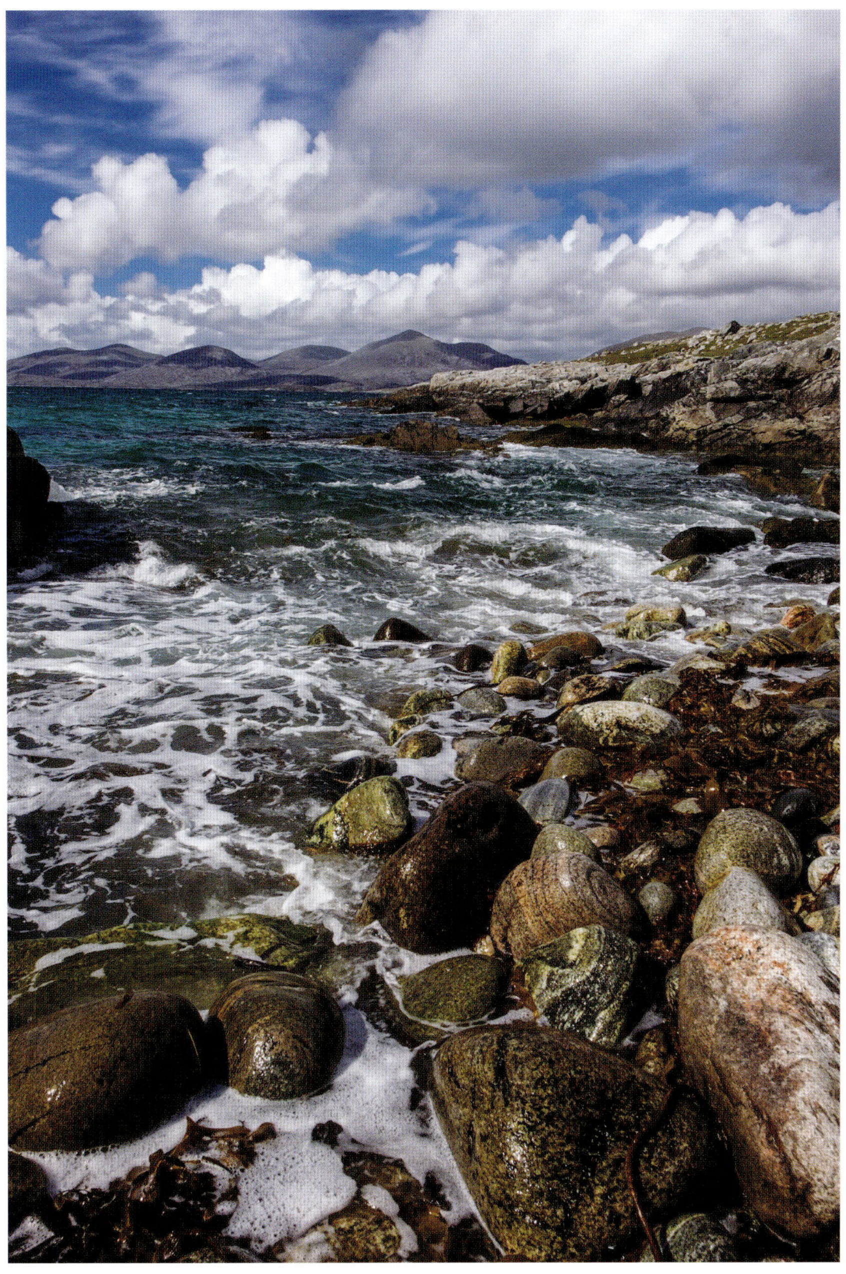

Shoreline detail, just north of Luskentyre

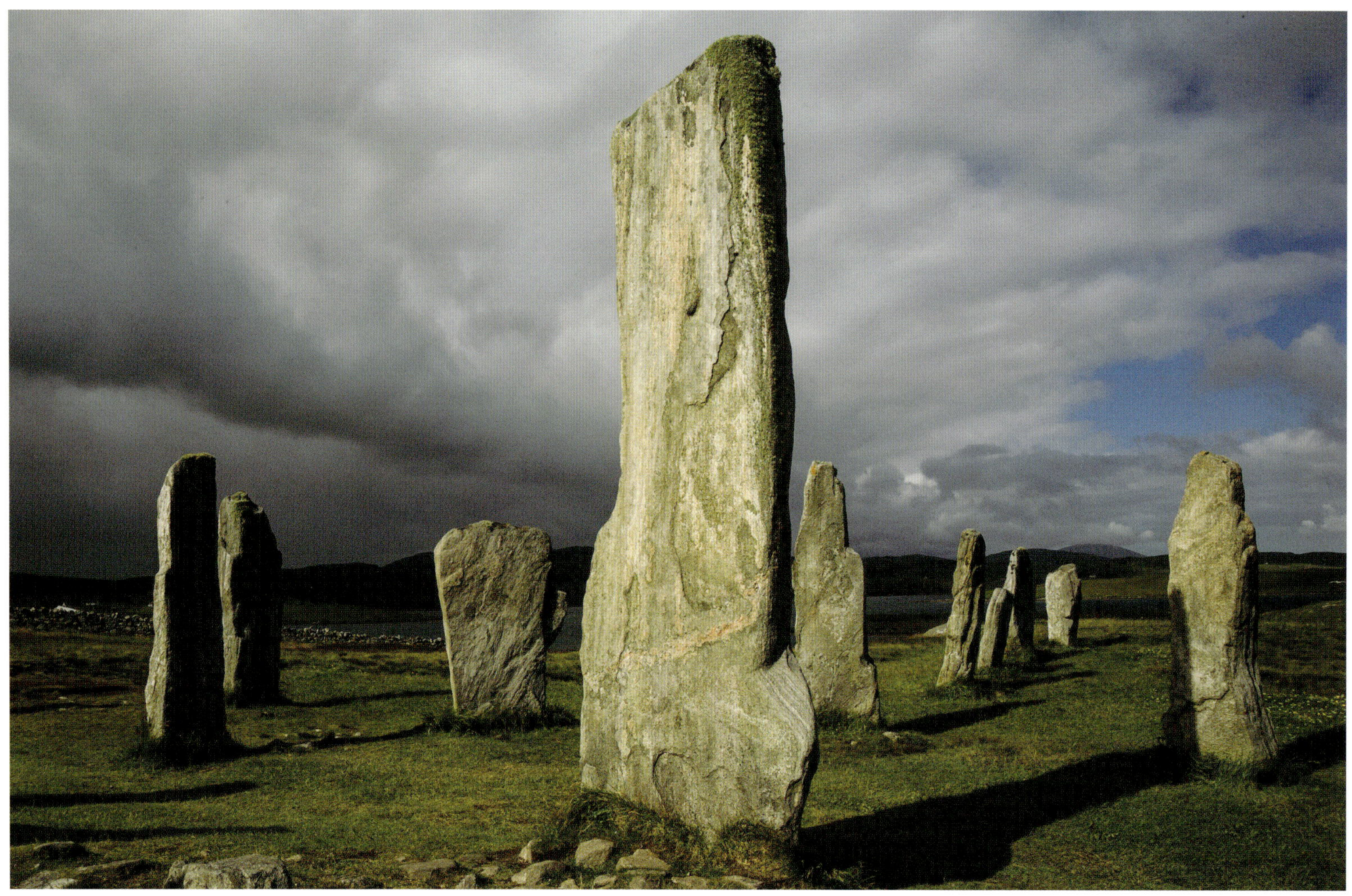

The Neolithic Callanish Stones remain an enigma.

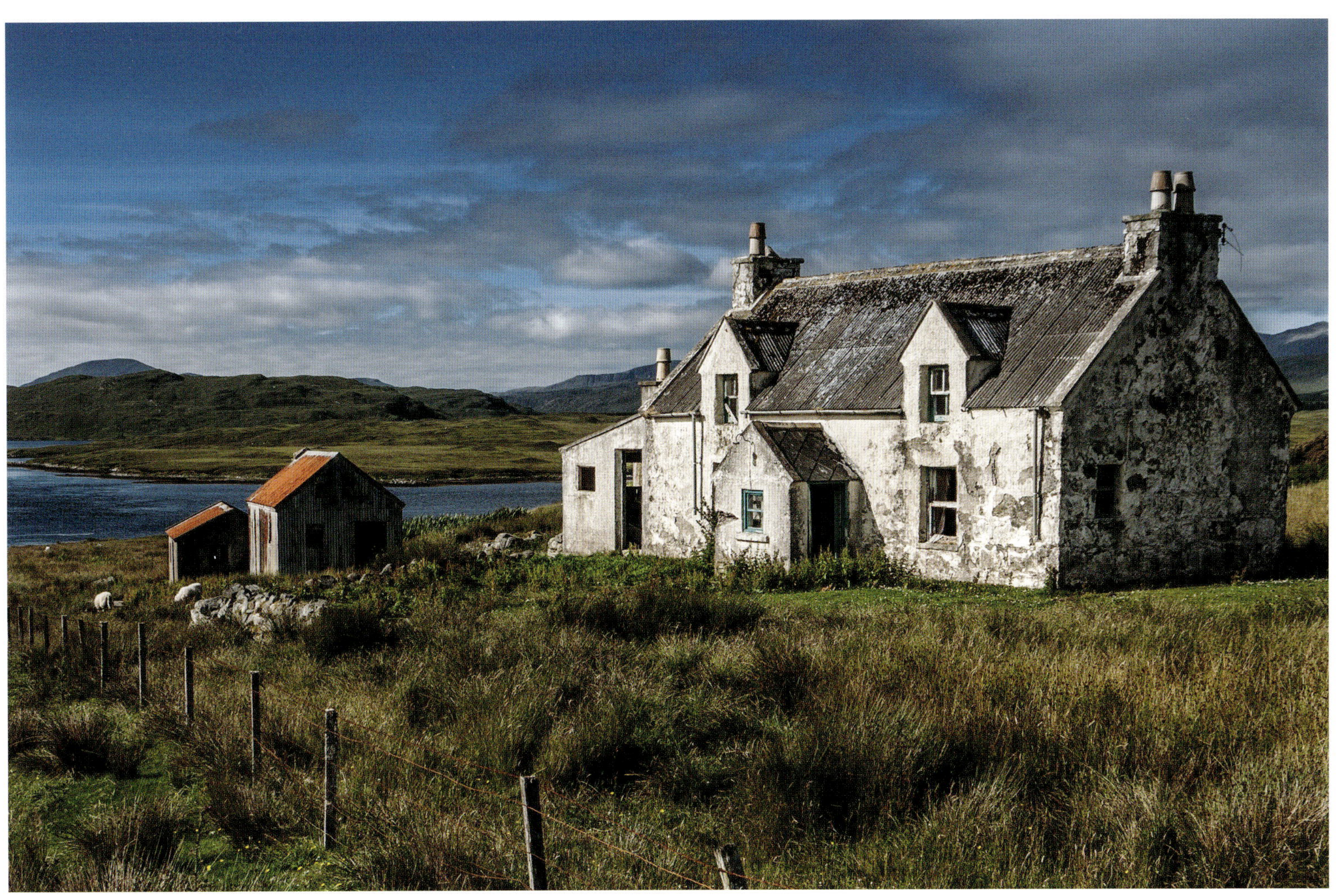

This traditional stone croft house has seen better days.

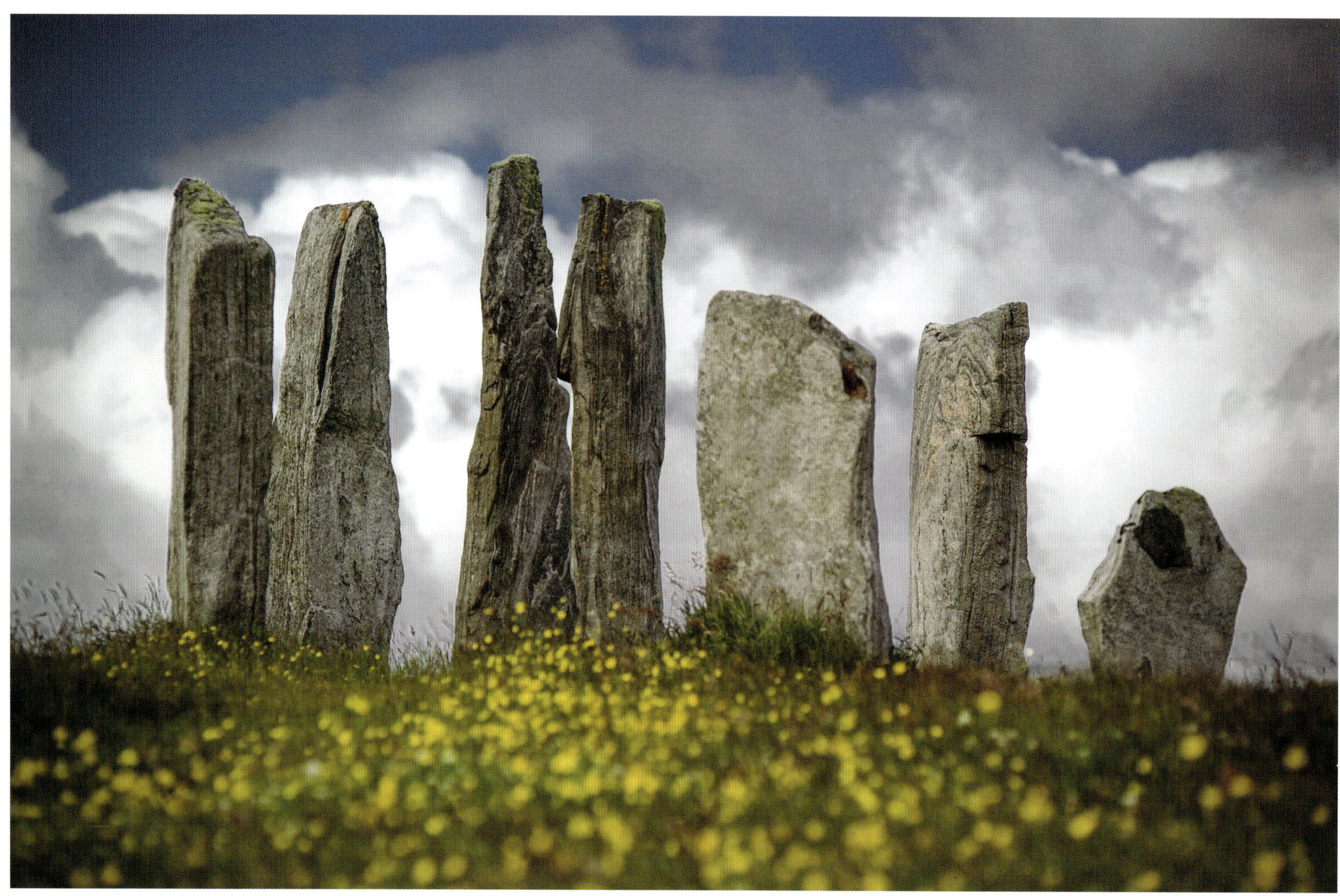

The Callanish Stones always fuel the imagination.

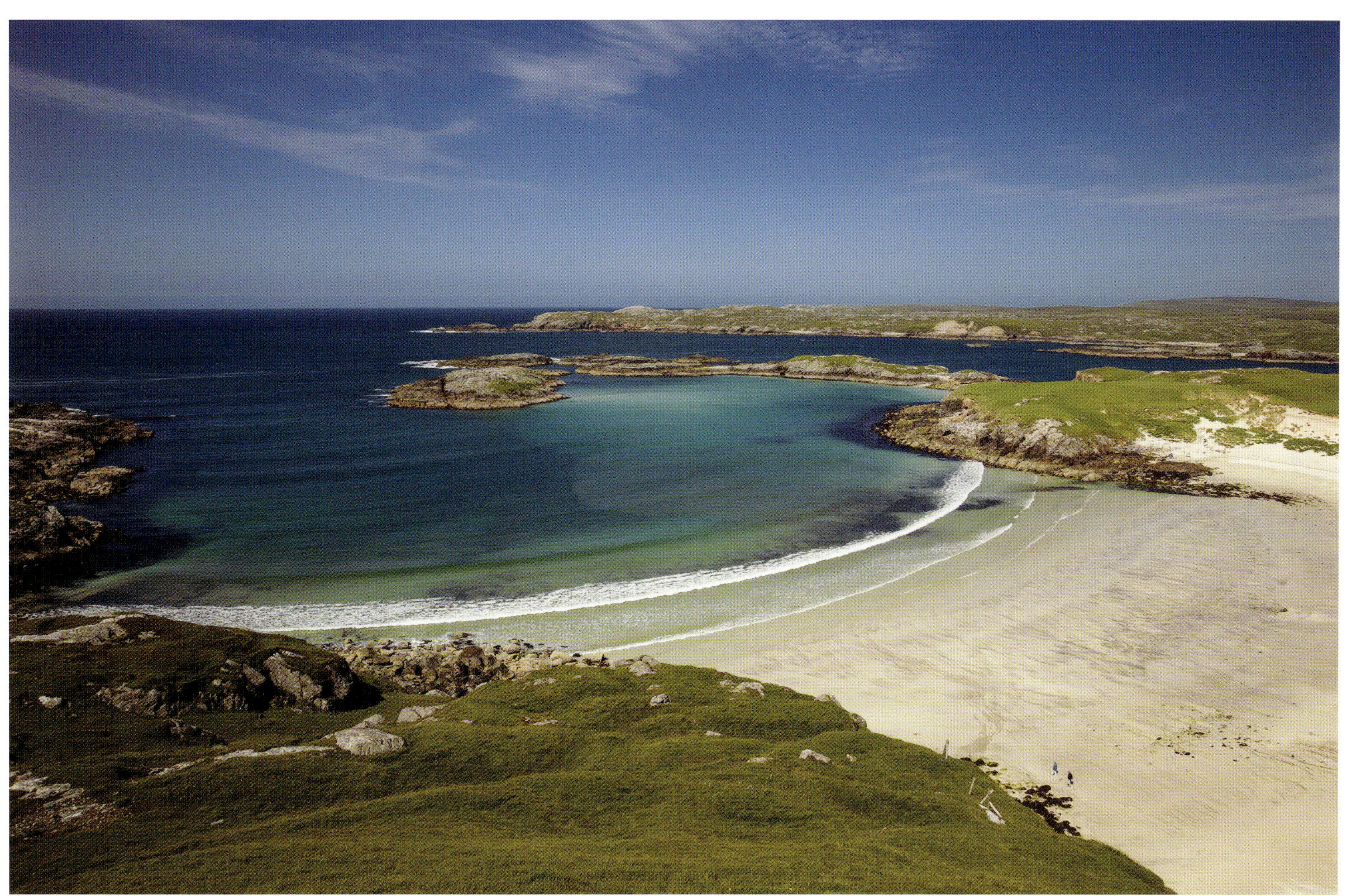

The aquamarine of Uig Beach

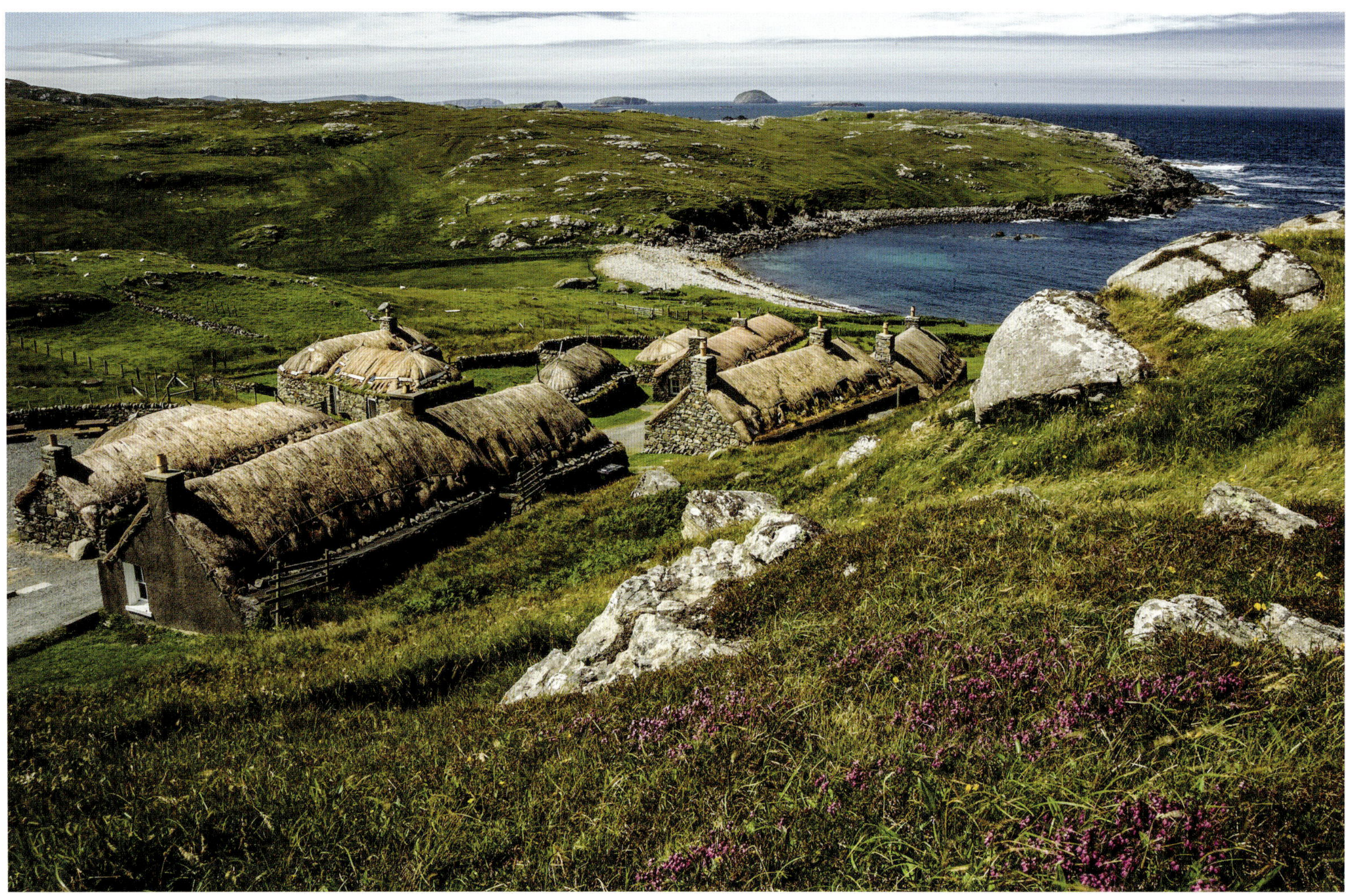

The restored Gearrannan Black House settlement offers a step back in time.

The replica Iron Age House at Bostadh, Great Bernera

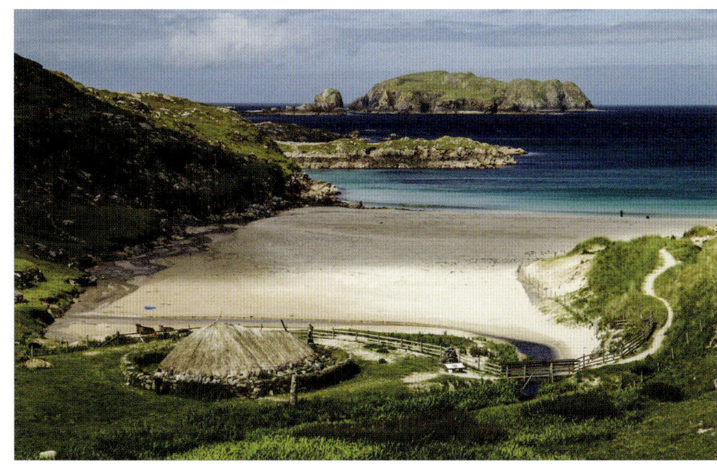

Shetlanders on Lewis

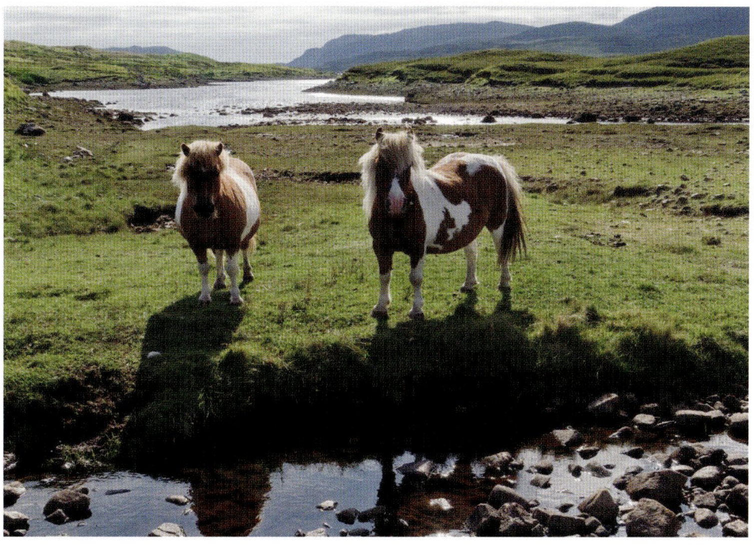

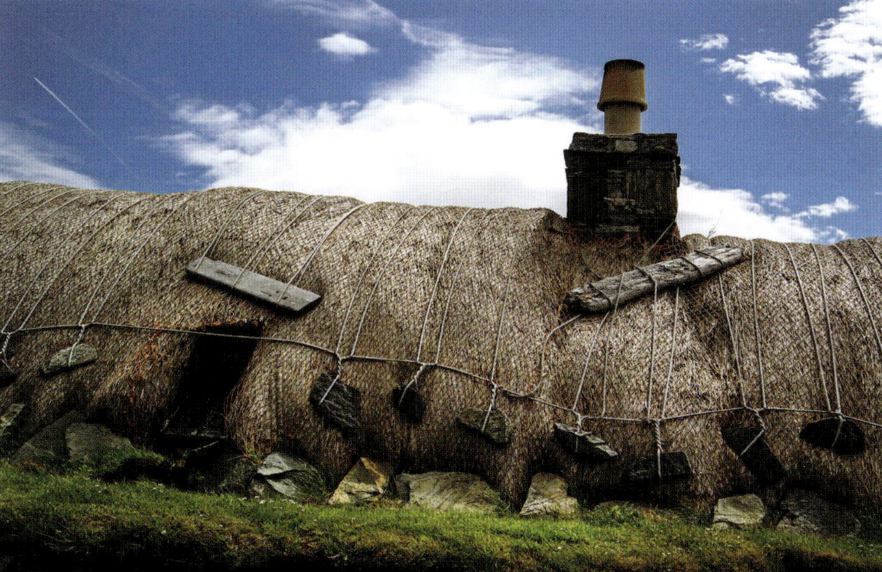

A marran grass thatch detail with storm proofing weights

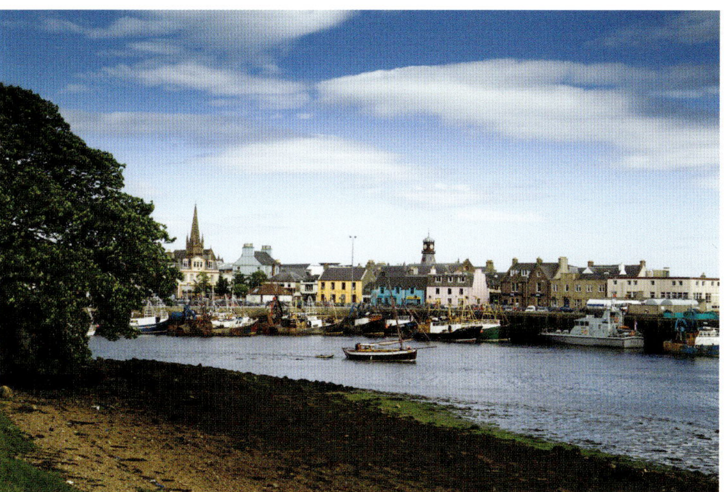

Stornoway Harbour

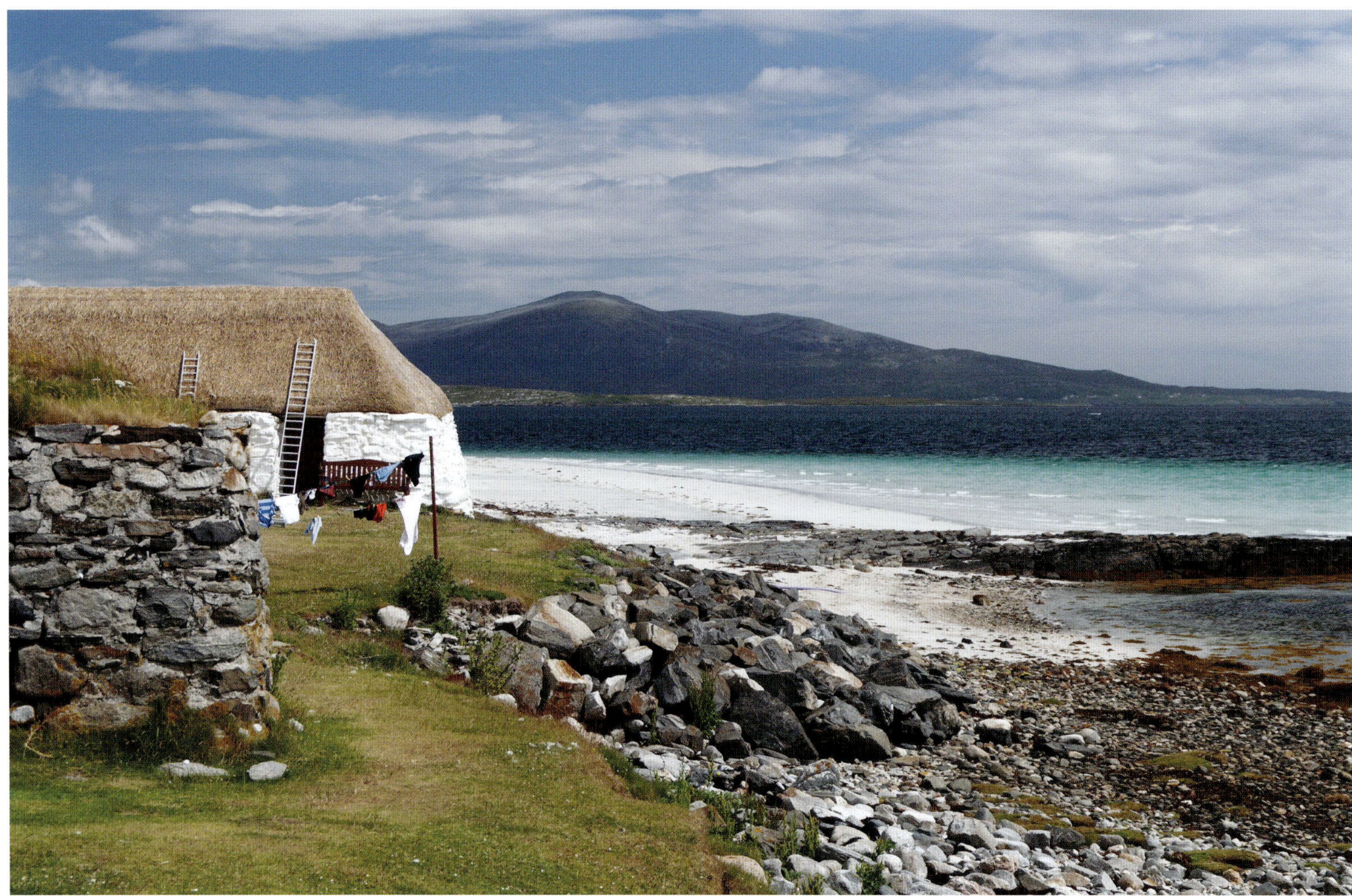

The thatched youth Hostel on Berneray overlooking the Sound of Harris

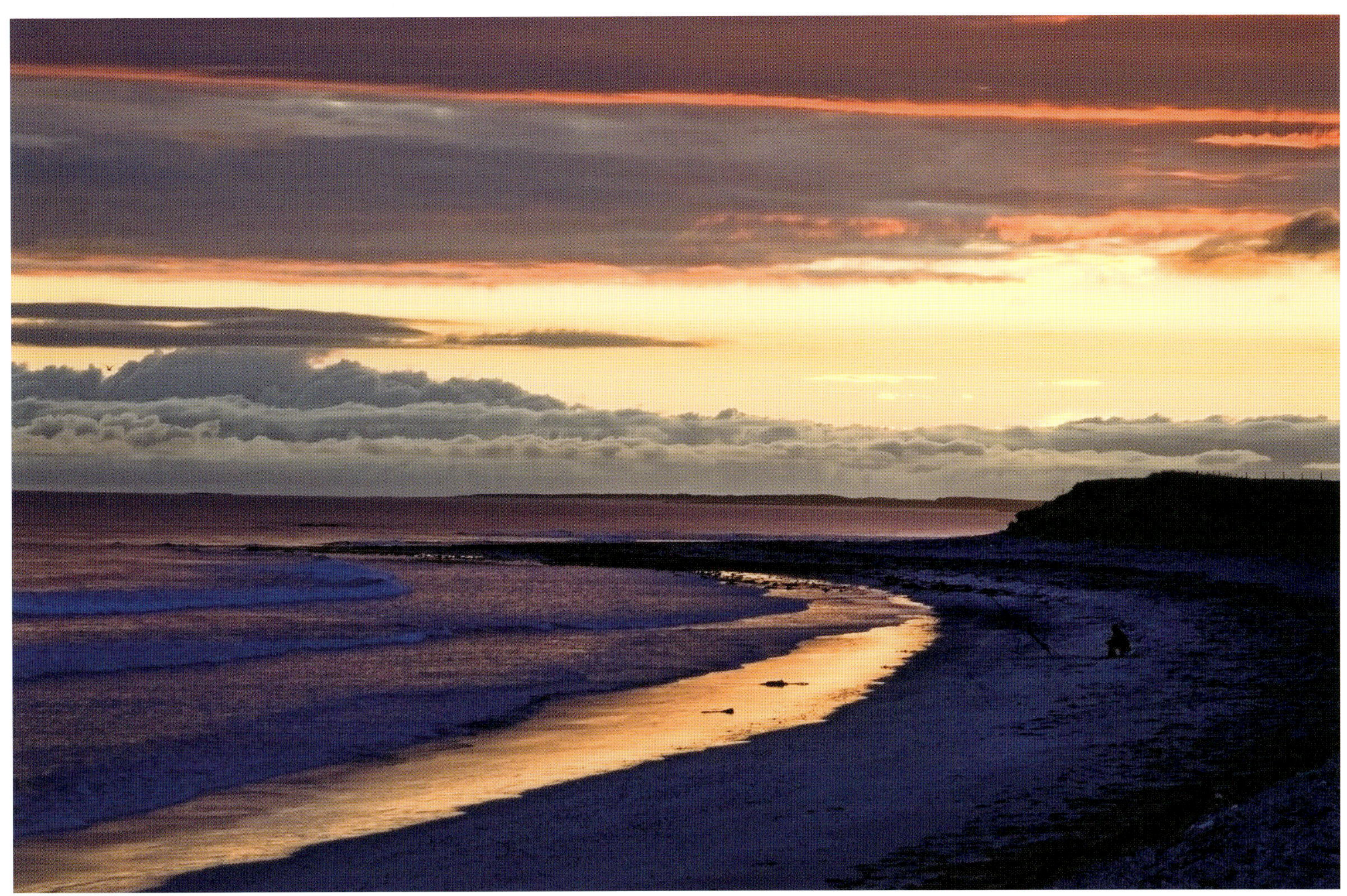

Another stunning sunset settles upon a lone fisherman at Balshare, North Uist.

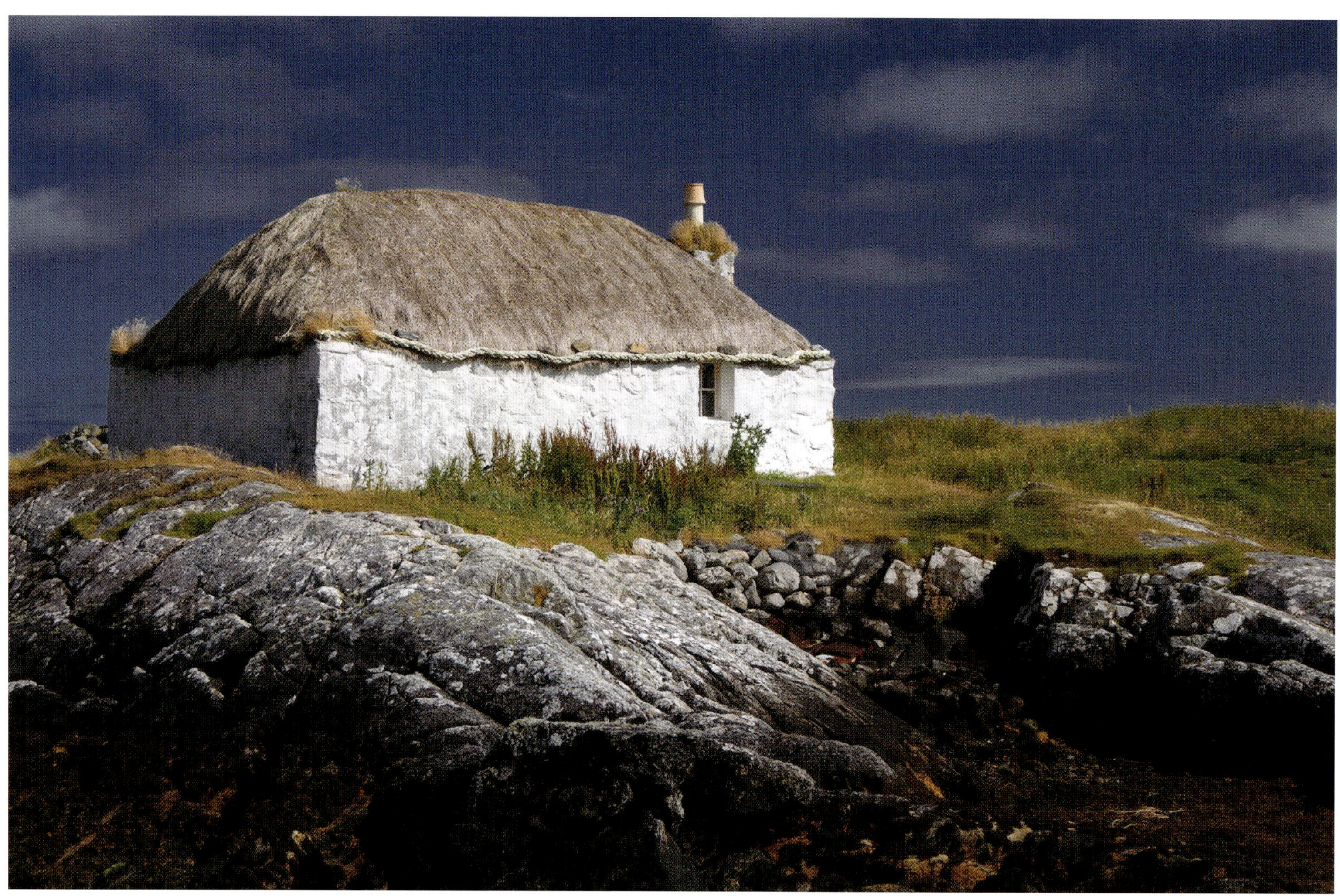

Traditional thatched byre, South Uist

Baleshare Beach looking south

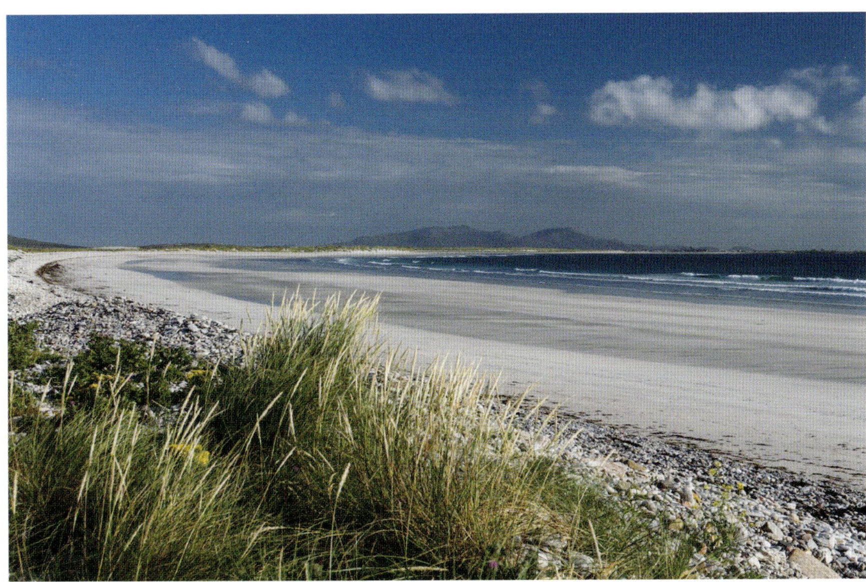

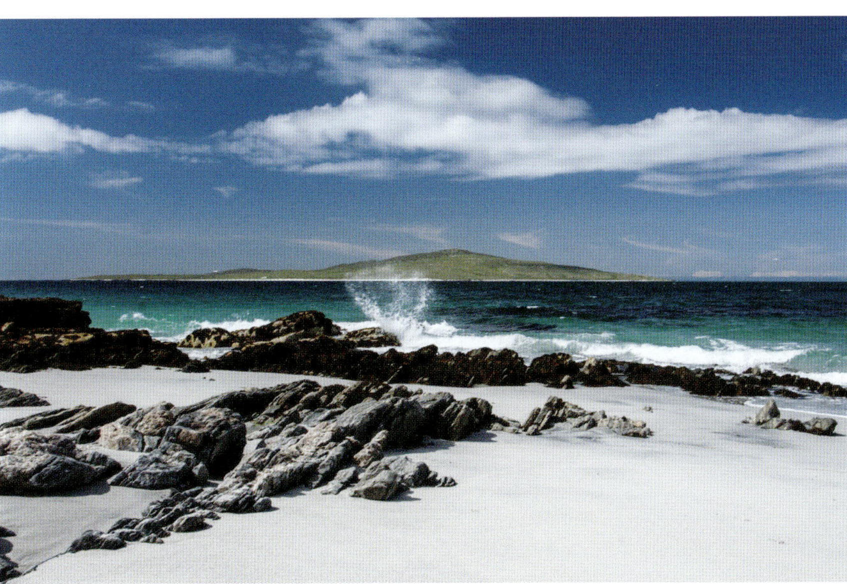

The north western point of Berneray, looking out to Pabbay

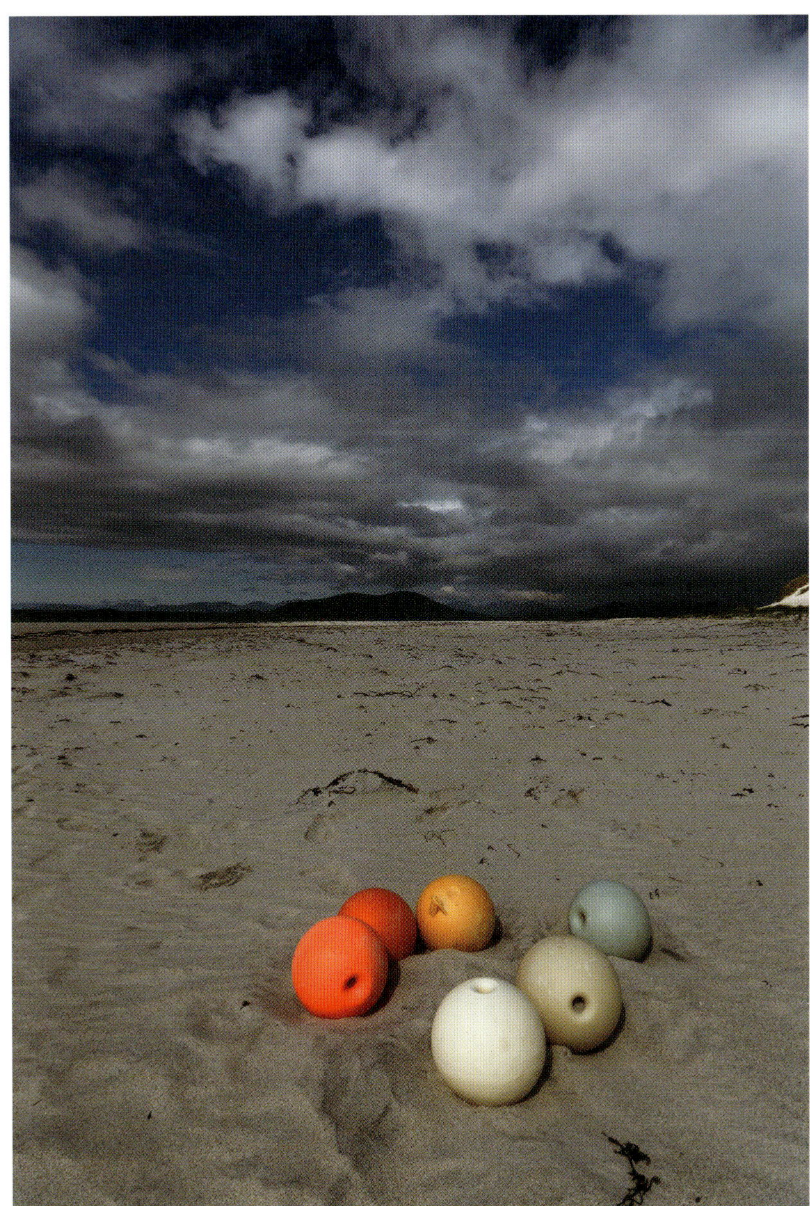

Random buoys on Berneray

A palate of rich colours offered by this remote bay on the Isle of Eriskay.

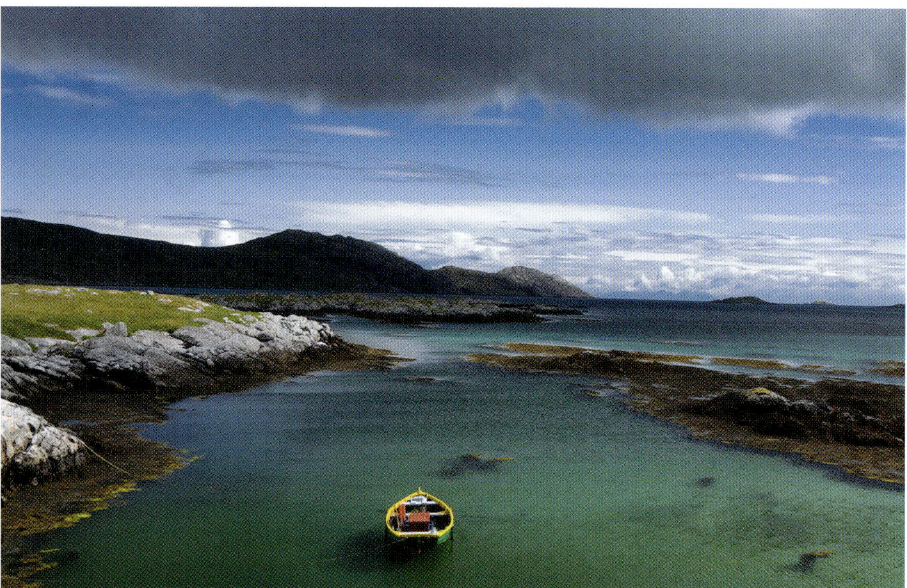

Ardmhor hamlet by Traigh Mhor, Barra.

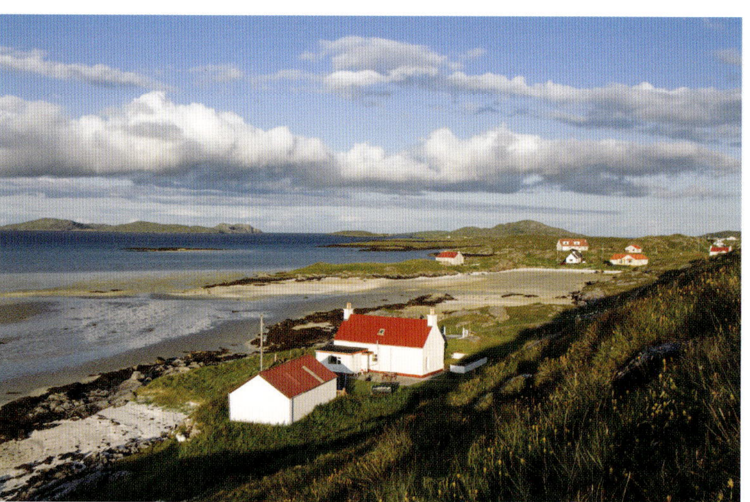

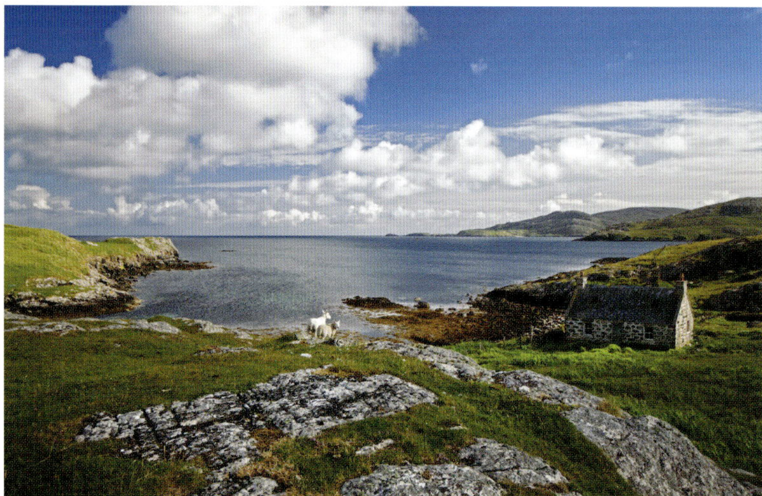

Crofters' world, Vatersay.

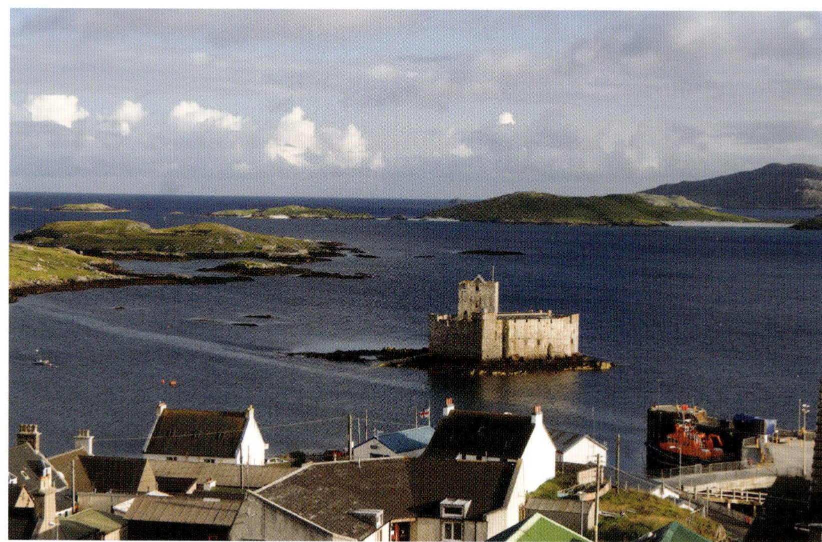

Kisimul Castle, Castlebay, Barra.

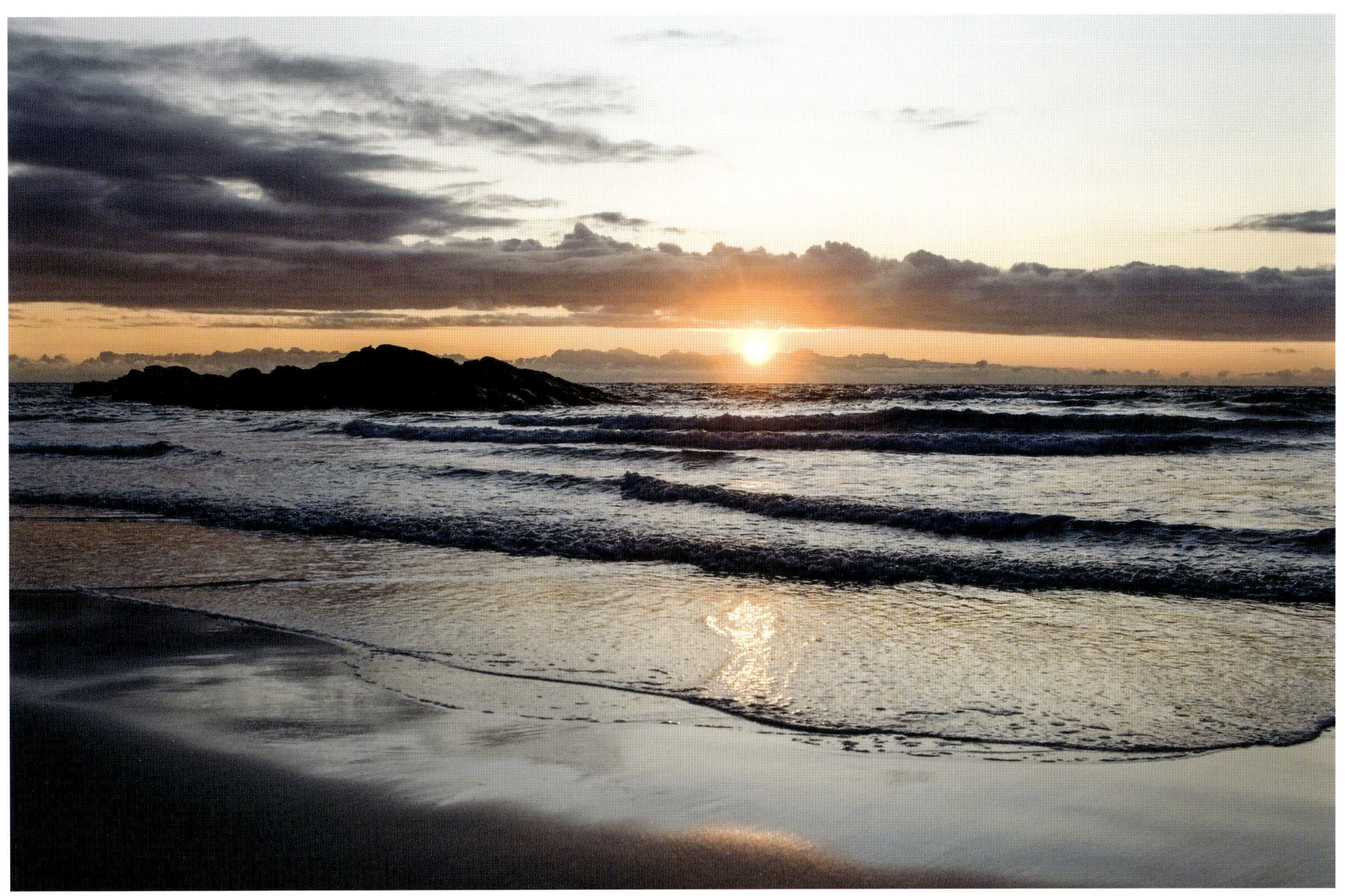

Sunset at Traigh Eais, on the Atlantic side of the famous airport beach on Barra

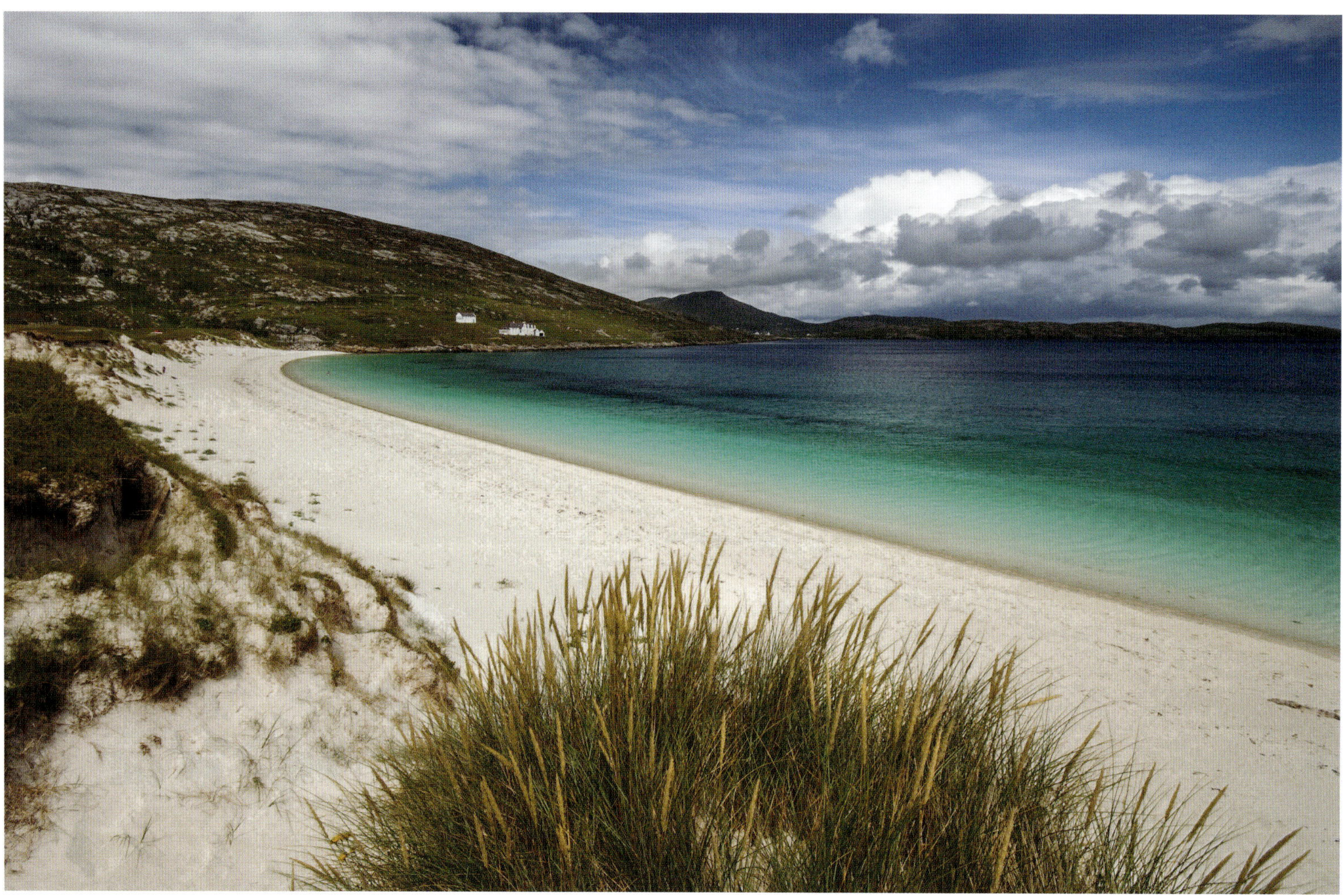

Vatersay Beach, a jewel of quintessential Hebridean dune habitat with turquoise sea.

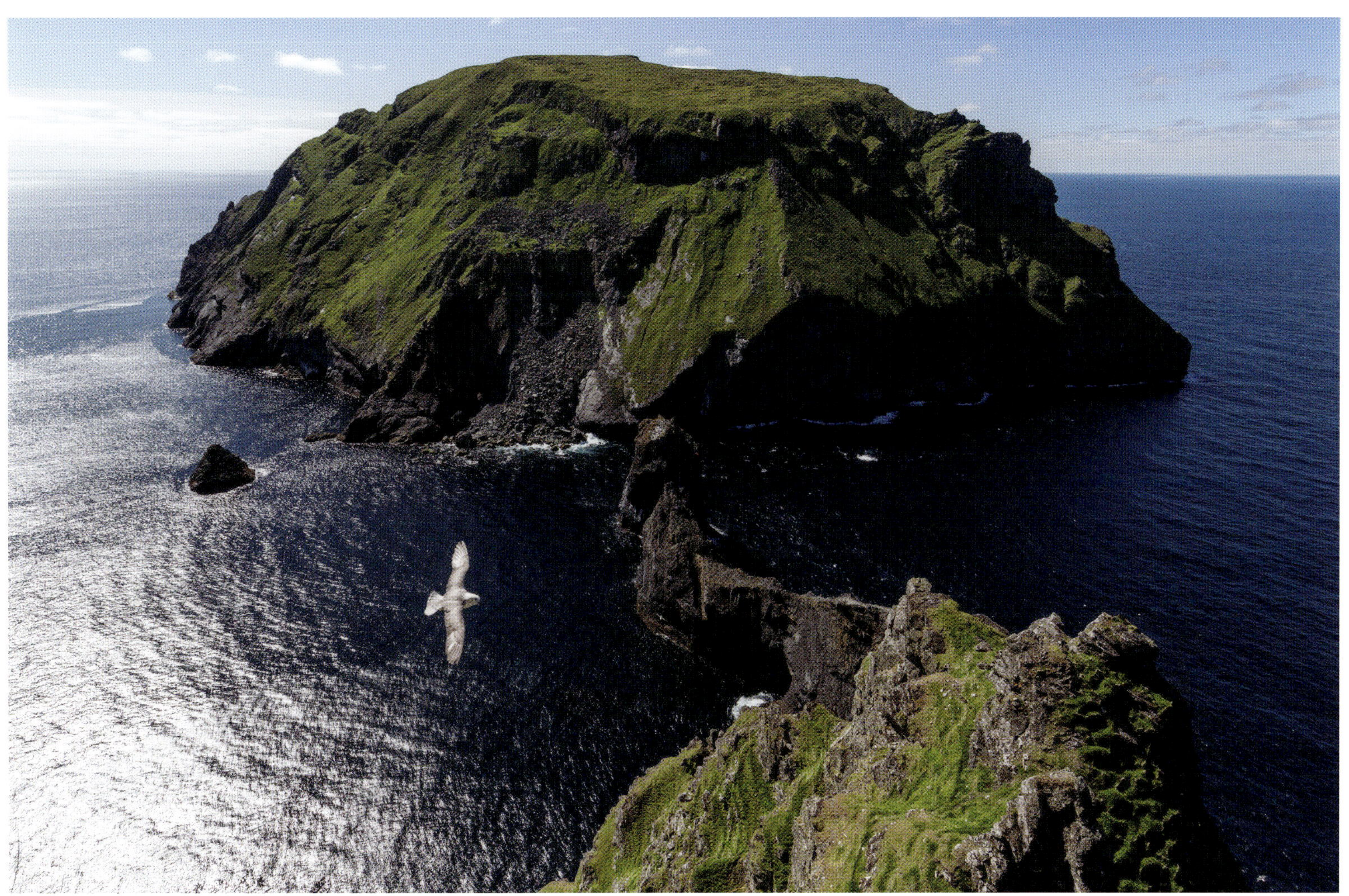

Fulmar soars across Soay, known as the 'Island of Sheep' .

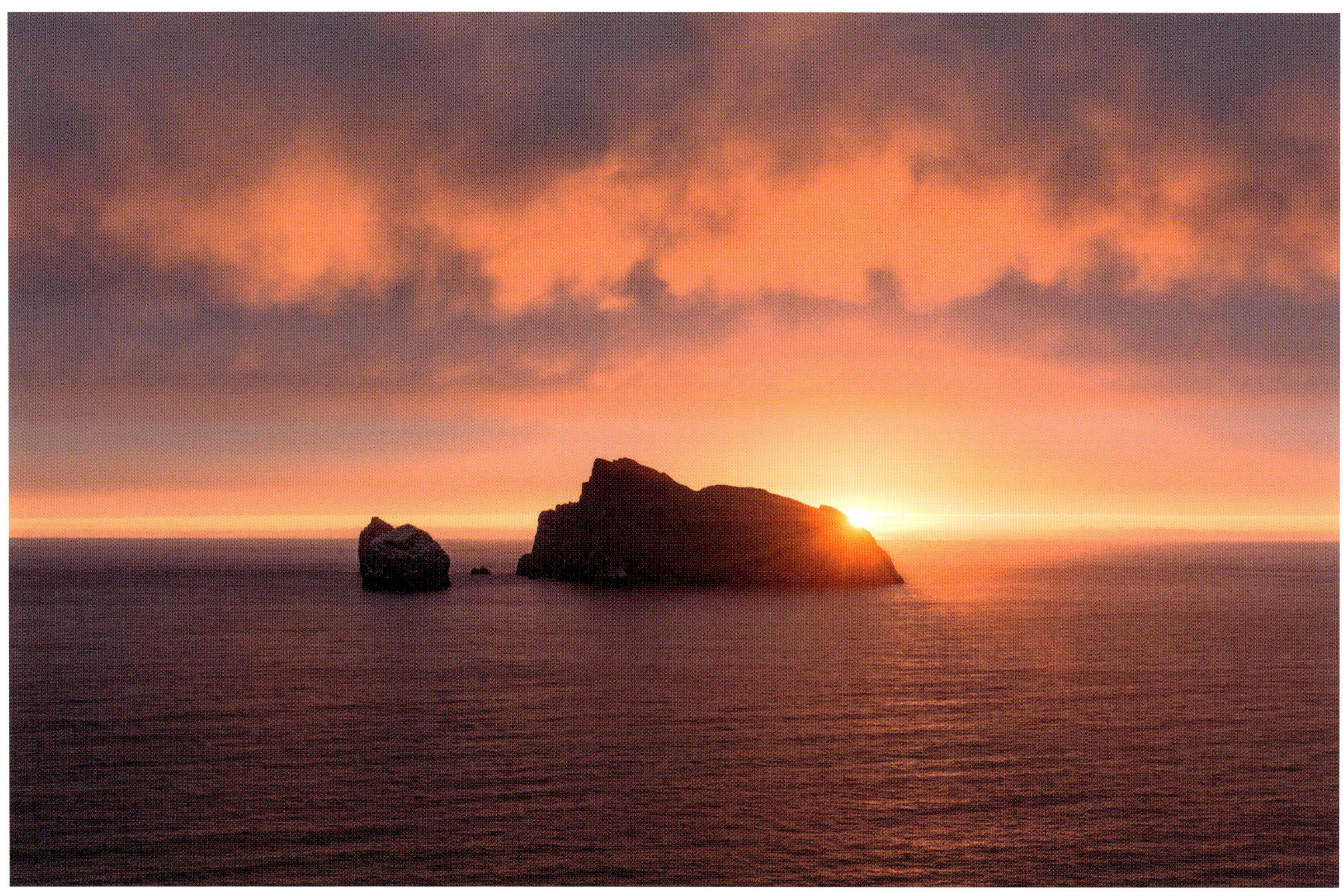

Boreray sunrise from the Gap

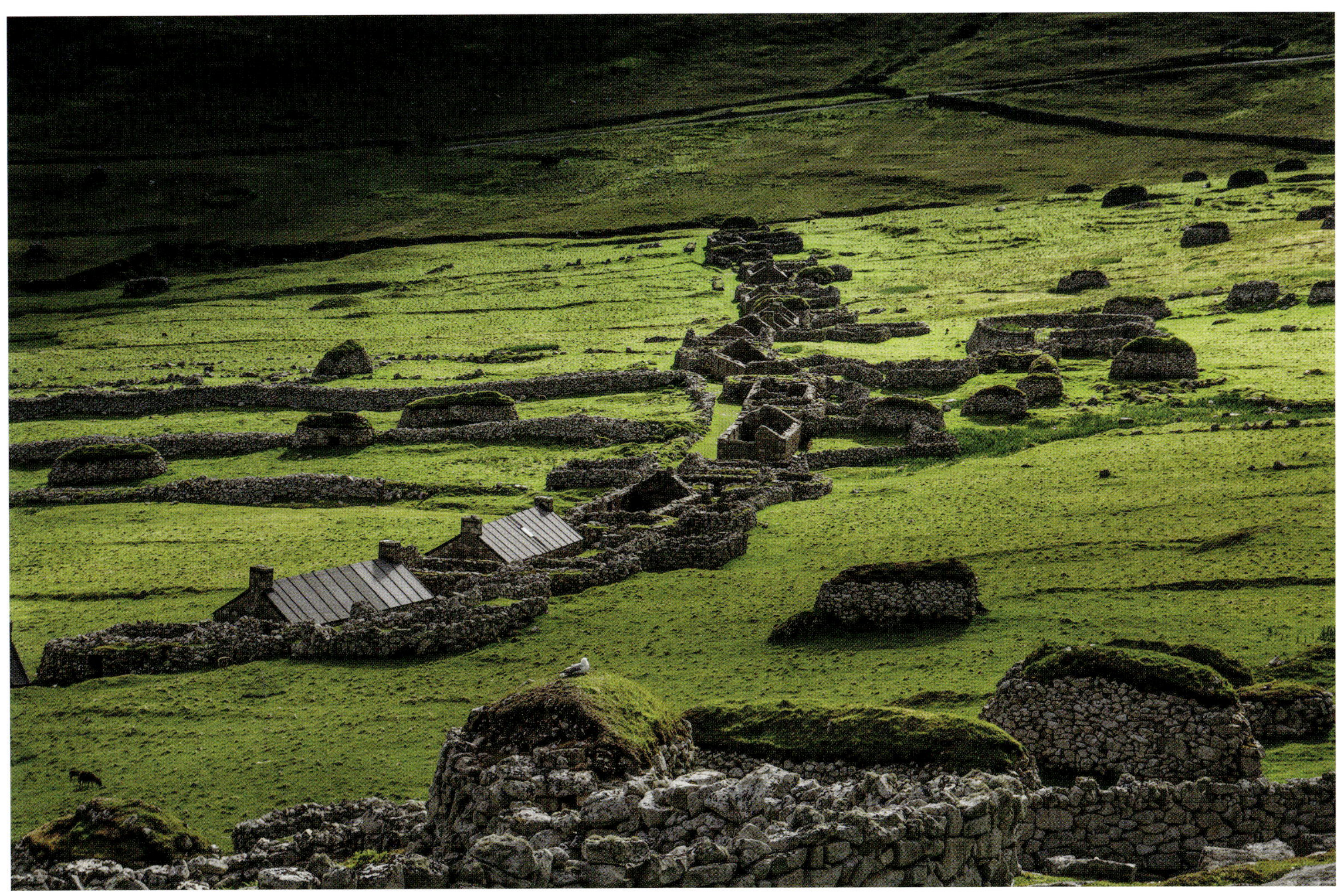

The part-restored village evokes wonder at the simplicity of times gone by.

Stacs Biorach and Shoaigh guard the channel between Hirta and Soay.

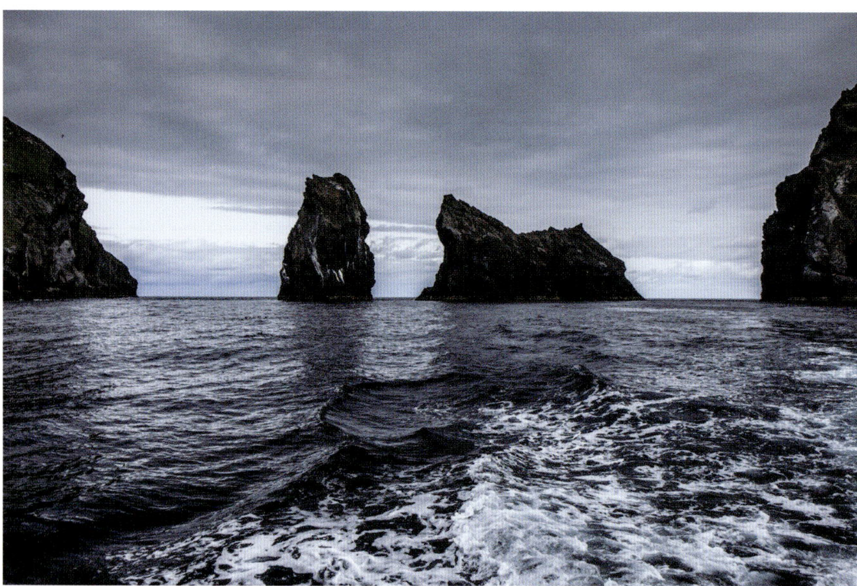

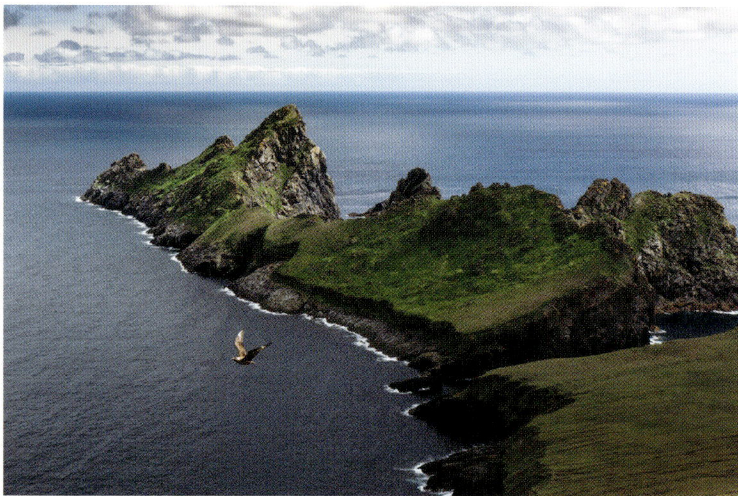

Dun, a bird reserve, extends from the Ba, caught here with a lone Bonxie.

Looking across fanks and cleits to Village Bay from the Gap, Hirta

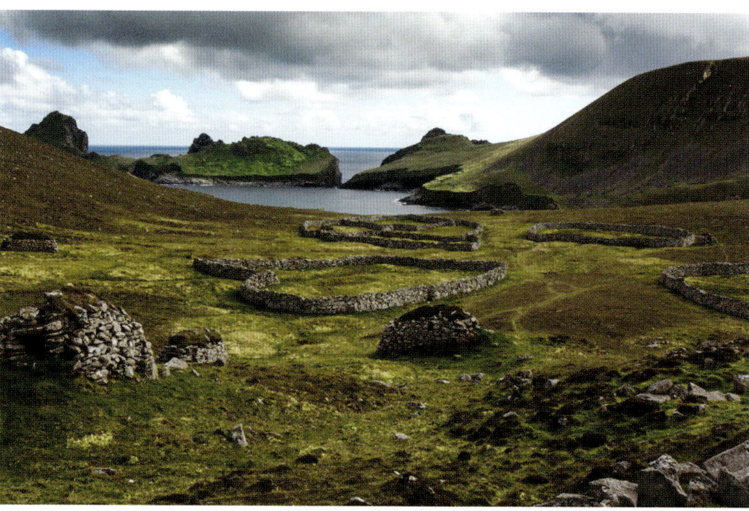

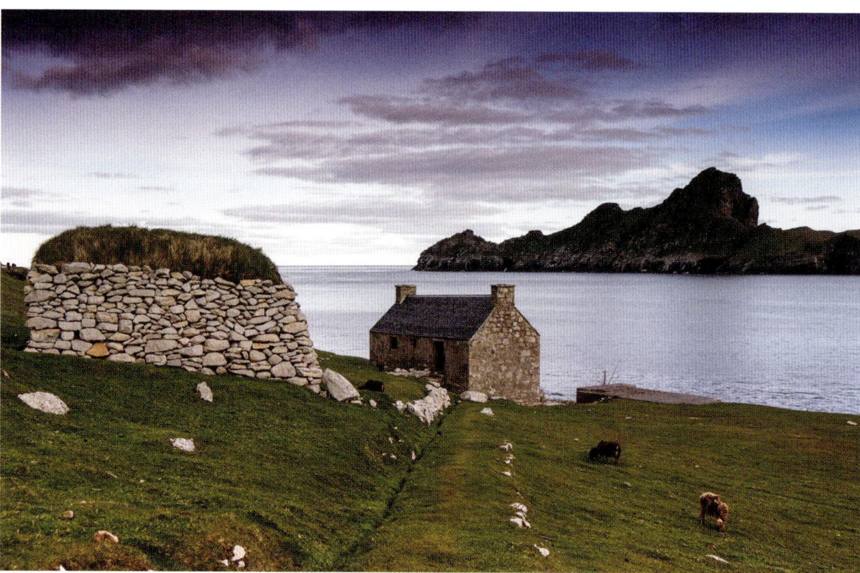

The Feather House and a giant cleit, Village Bay

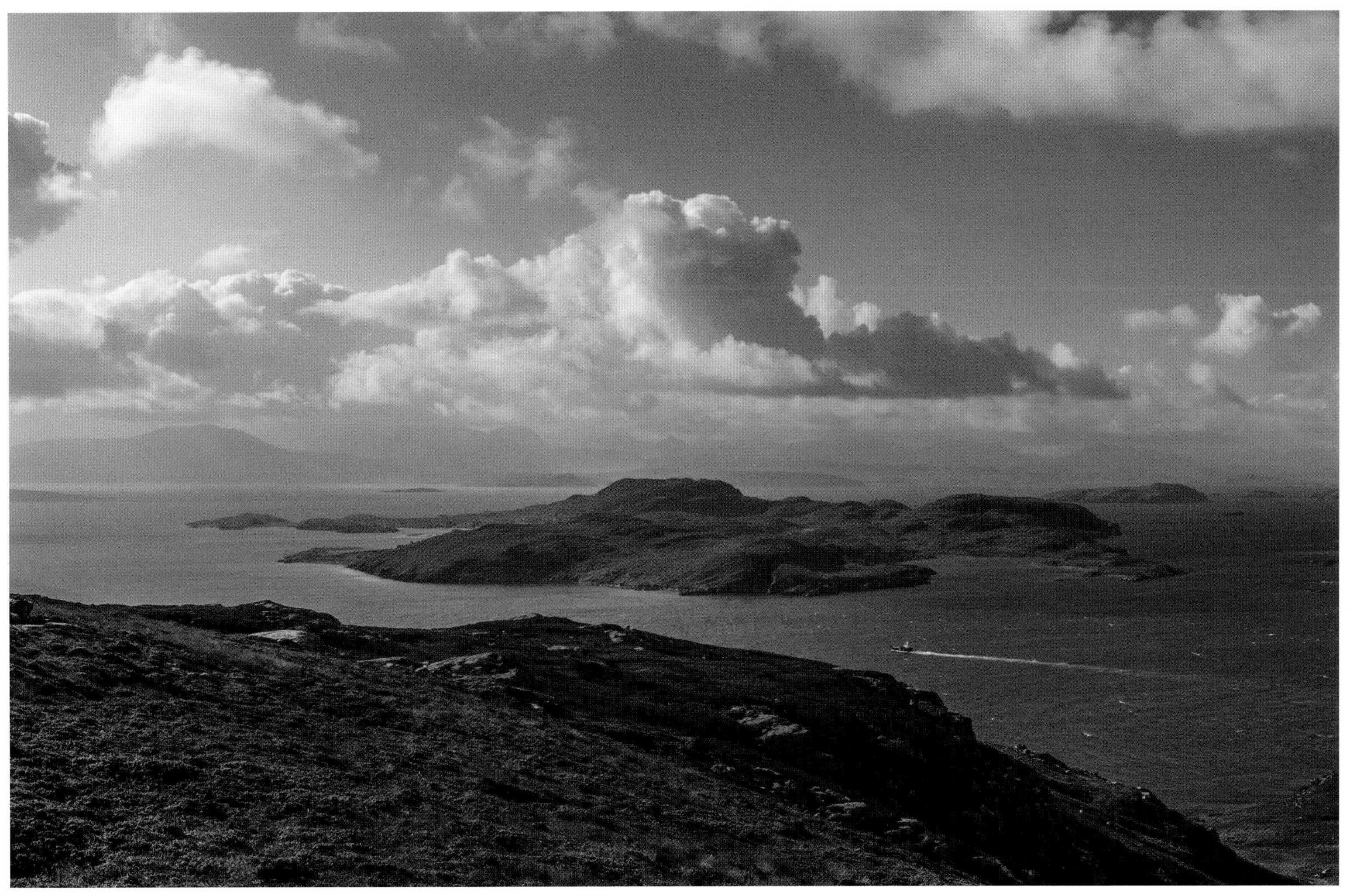

Tanera Mor, the principal inhabited part of the Summer Isles, by Achiltibuie, Assynt

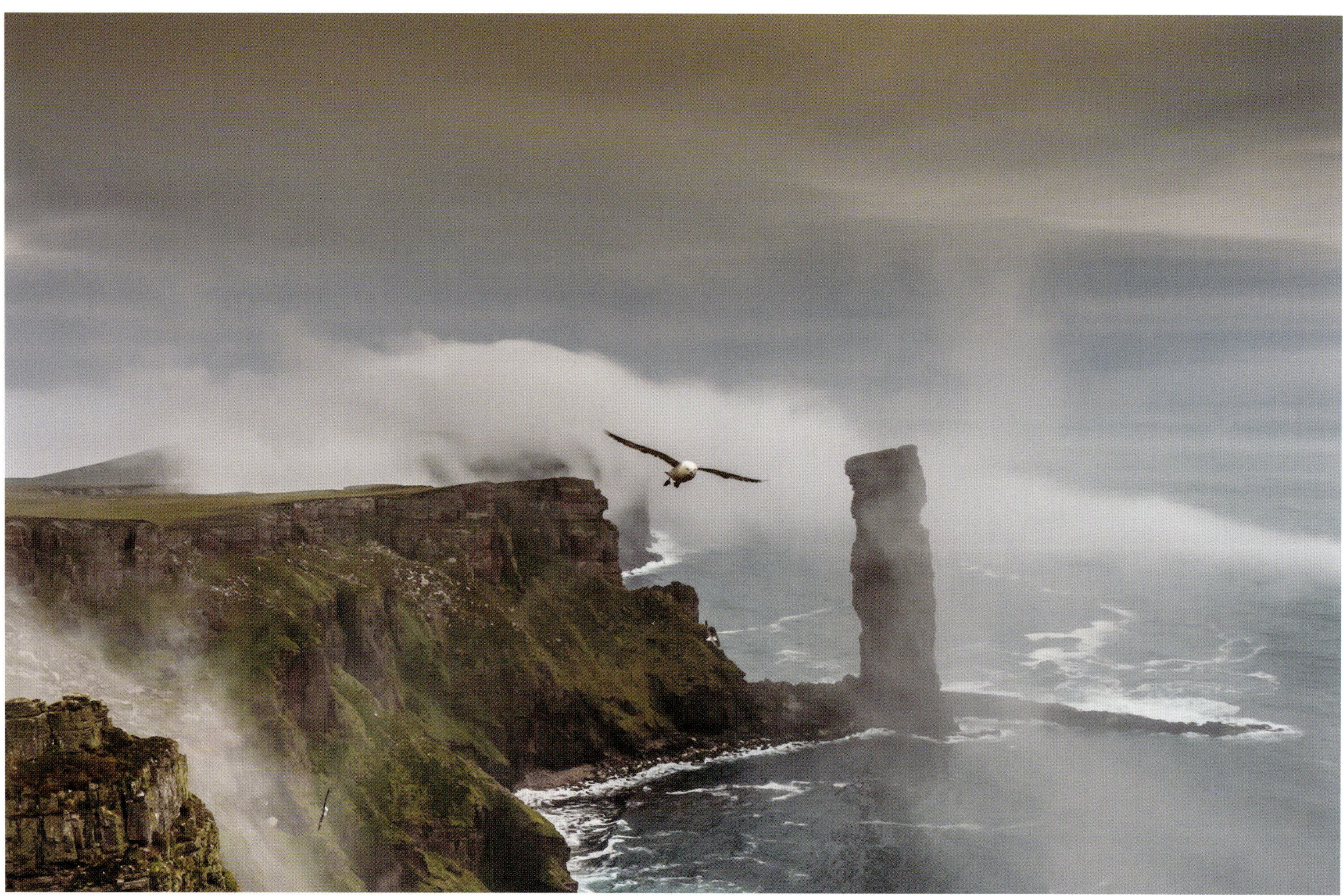

Swirling mists, a soaring fulmar and the iconic Old Man of Hoy

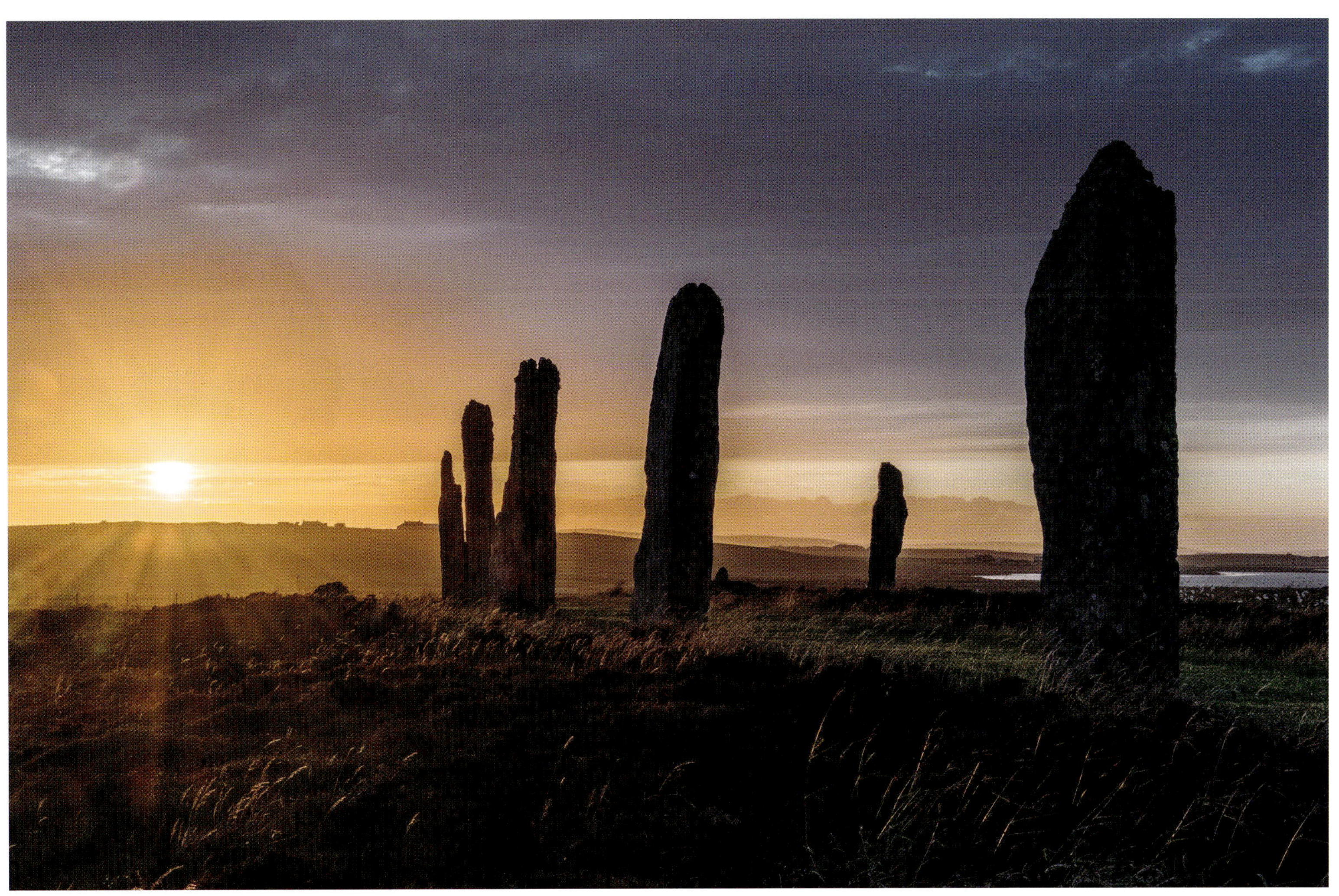

Solstice at the heart of Neolithic Orkney, the Ring of Brodgar, which is a World Heritage Site

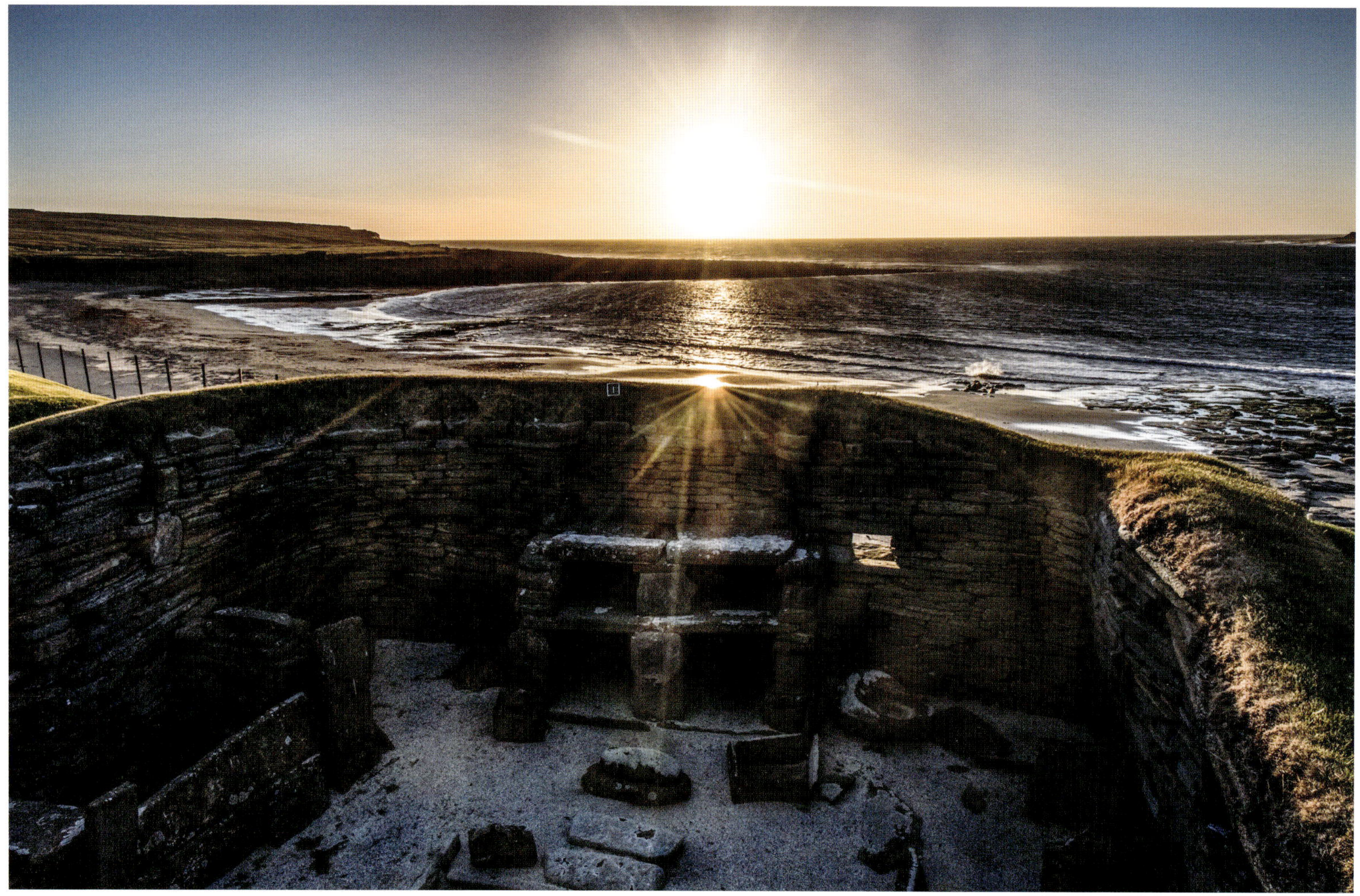

Sunset across Skaill Bay at Skara Brae. This Neolithic village,
also a World Heritage Site, dates back to 3180BC.

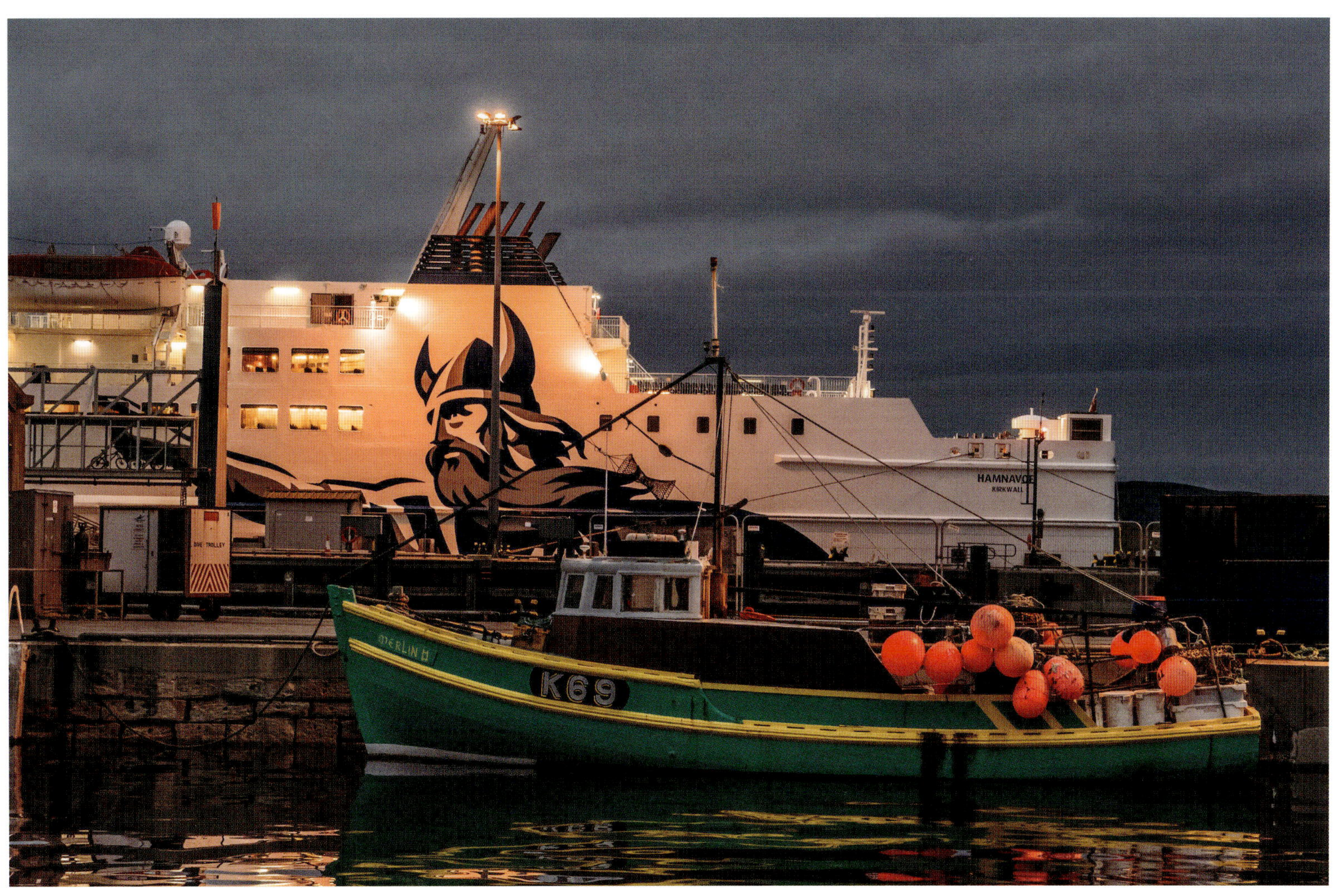

Sealink's Hamnavoe ferry at Stromness harbour shares an ambient dusk with a traditional inshore fishing vessel.

Sunrise at Harray Loch, by Brodgar

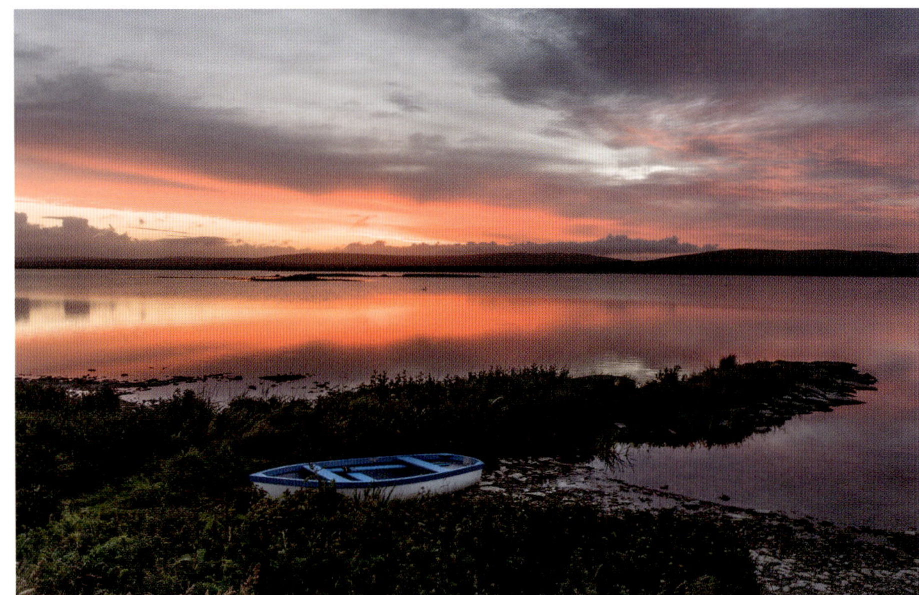

Alfred Street, Stromness

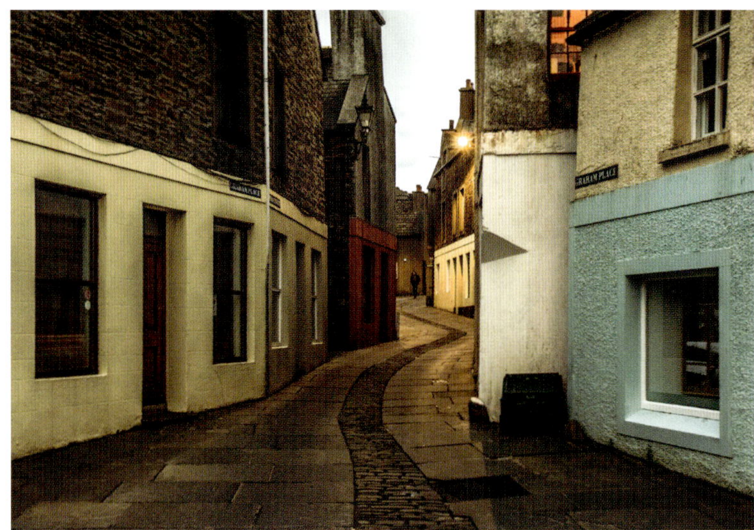

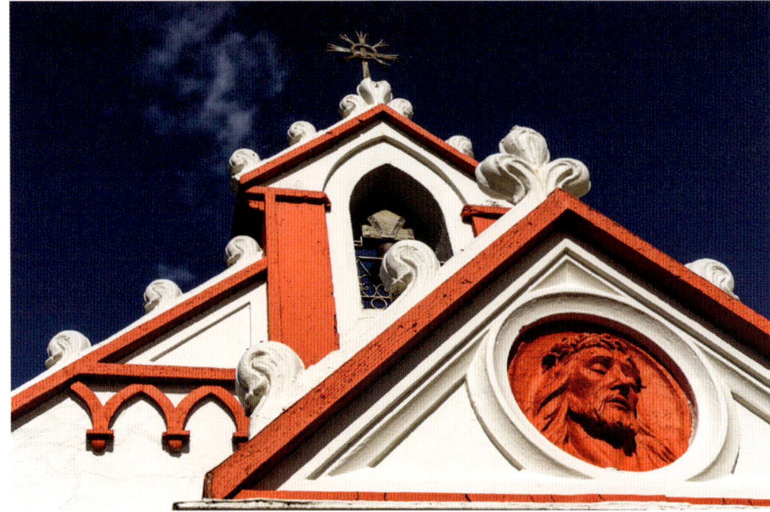

A roof detail from The Italian Chapel, built by prisoners of war during World War Two

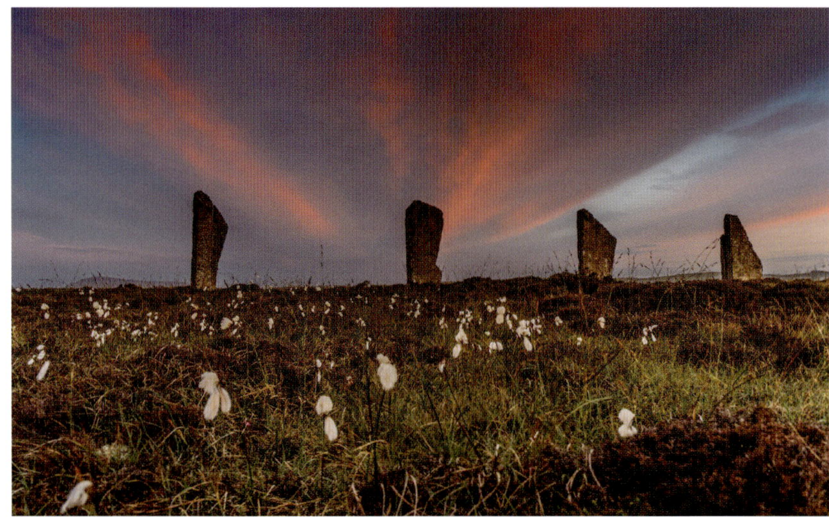

A dramatic skyline for the Ring of Brodgar

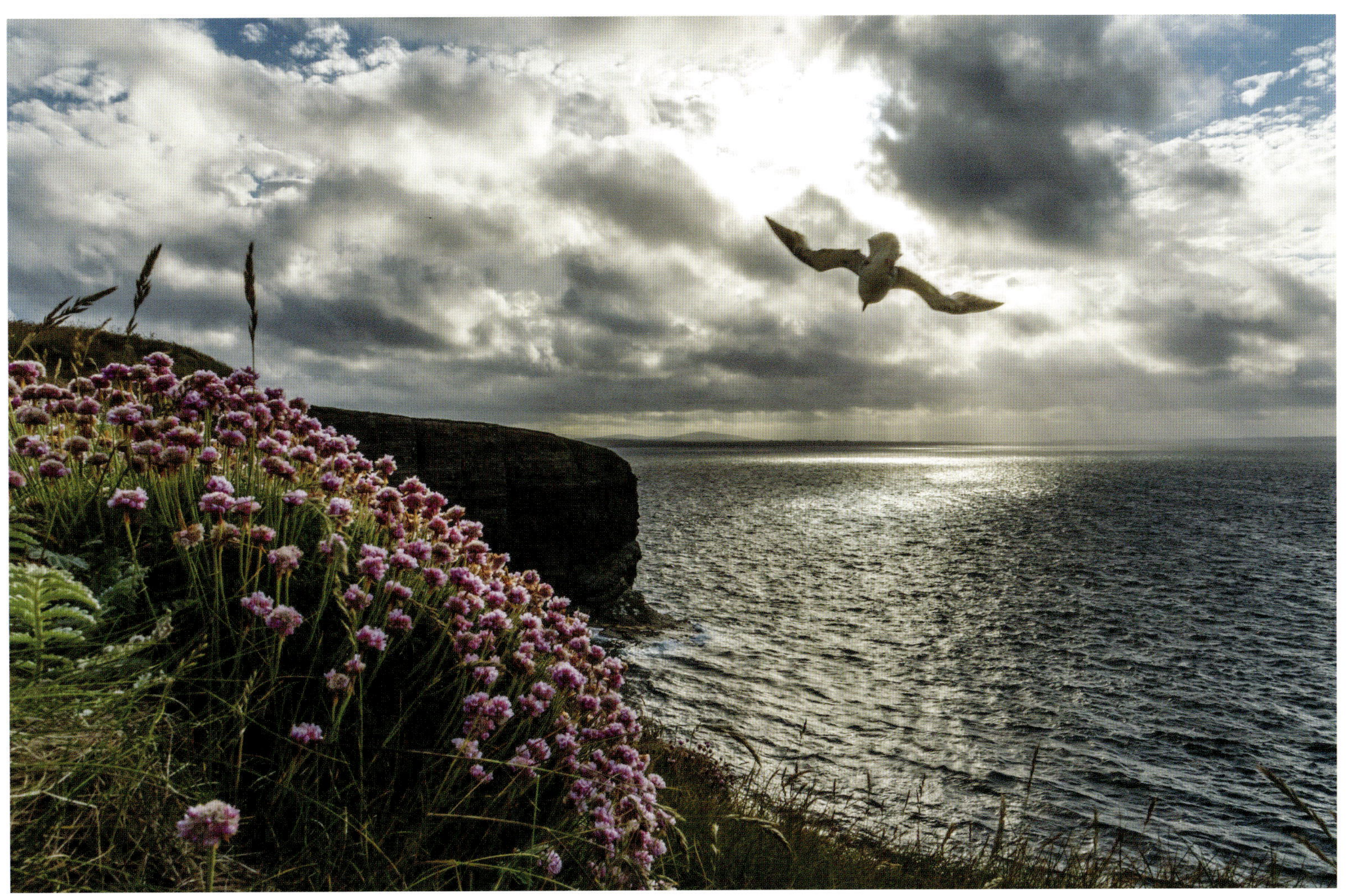

Thrift and fulmars characterise Mull Head Nature Reserve on the Deerness Peninsula.

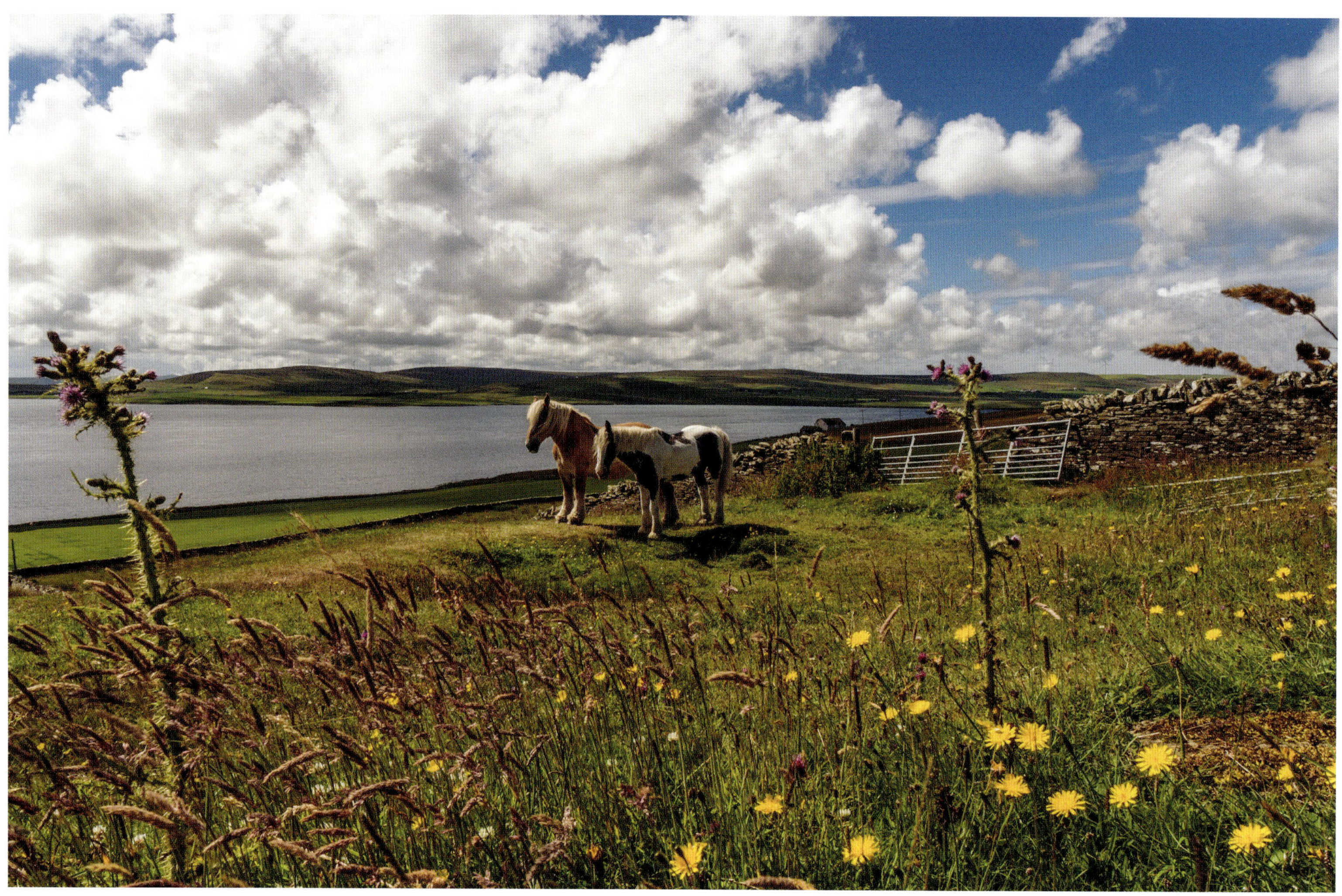

Contented Piebald and Bay horses on Rousay's west coast

A Shetland Pony enjoys the peace and quiet.

Pristine rock pool habitat on the east Cocast of Rousay, looking out to Egilsay

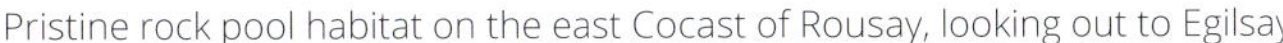

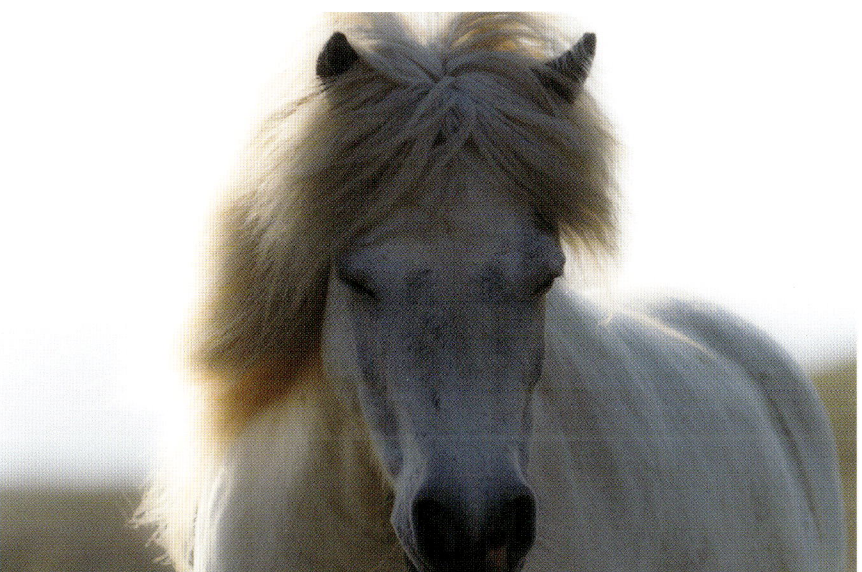

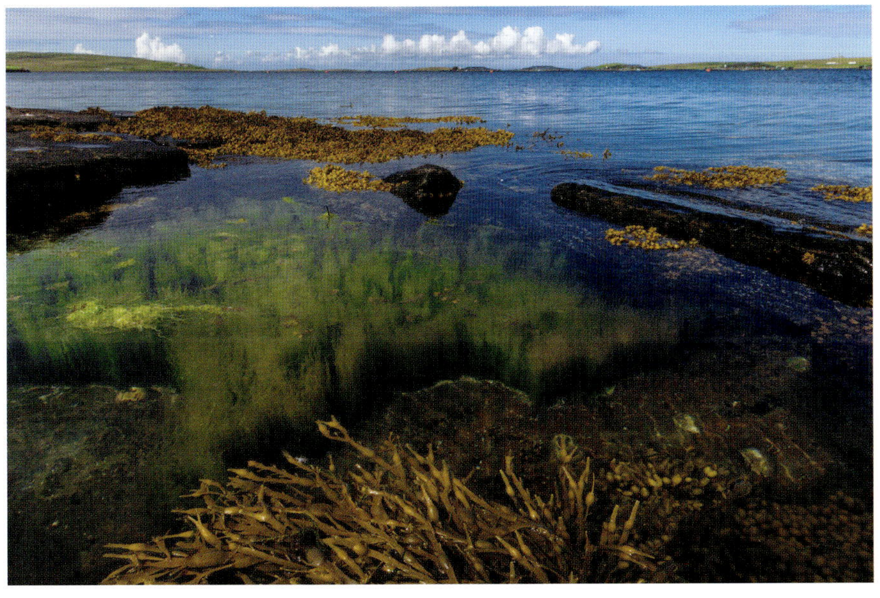

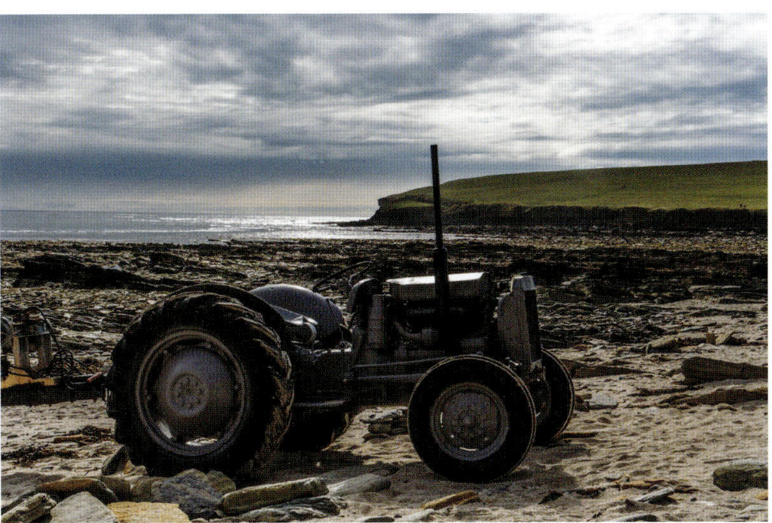

A cherished and working Grey Massey Ferguson at Birsay

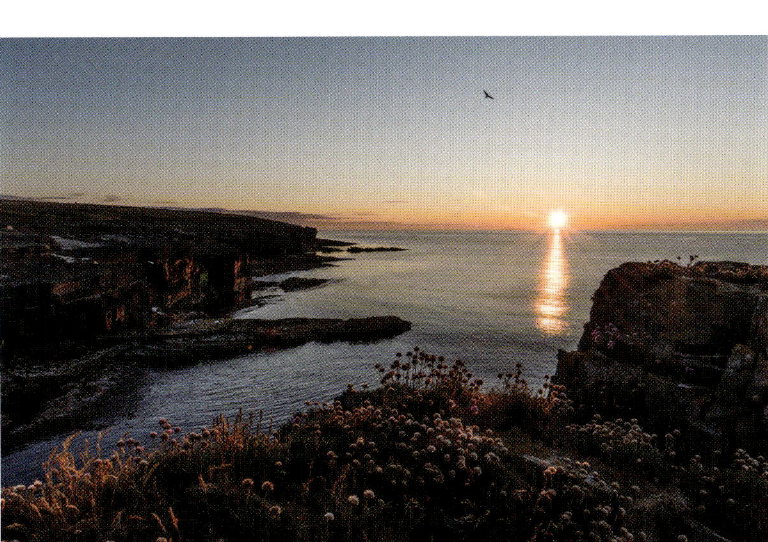

Deernes Peninsula at the break of dawn

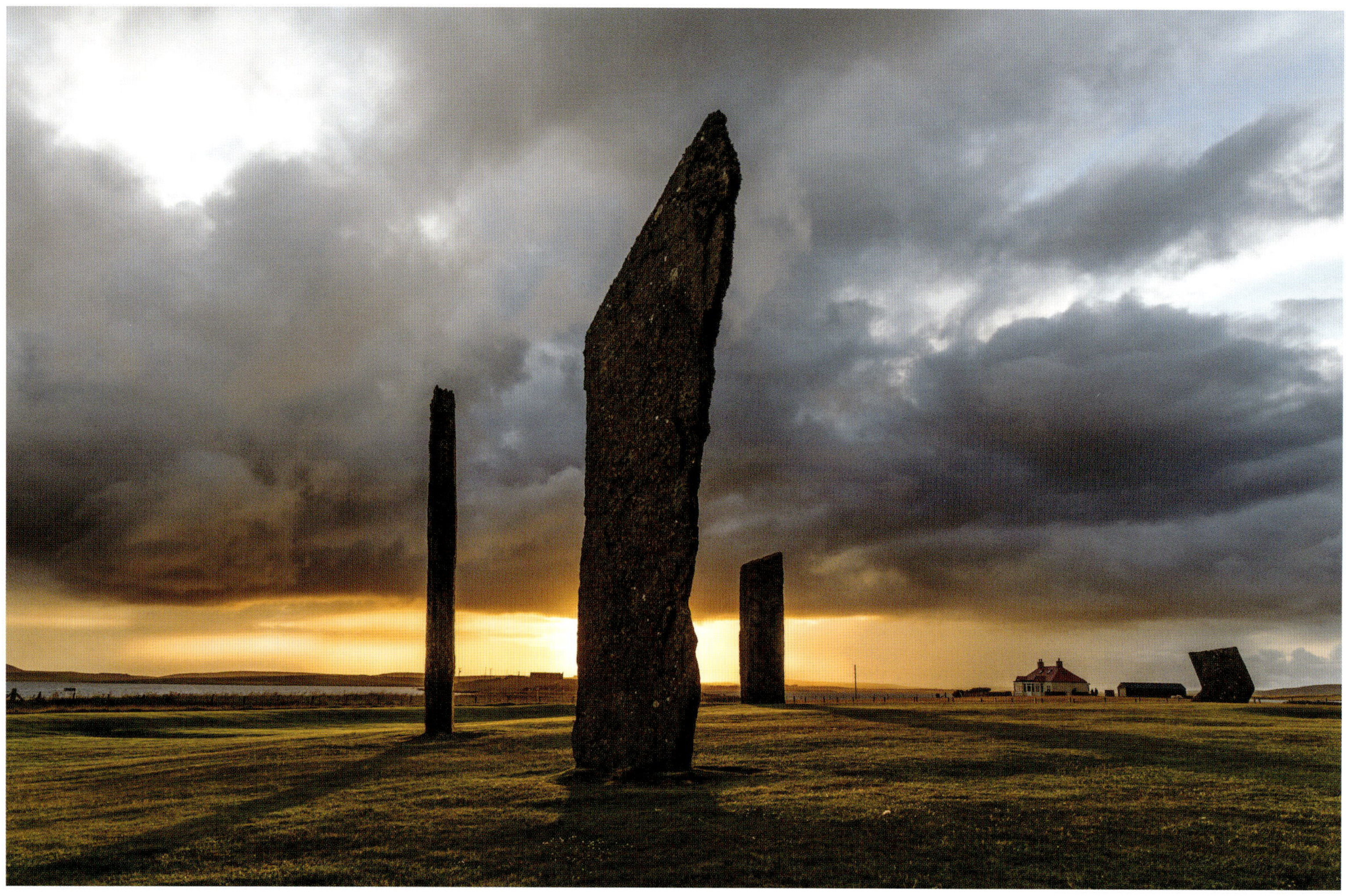

The Stones of Steness

Kirk, sheep and geology on Hoy

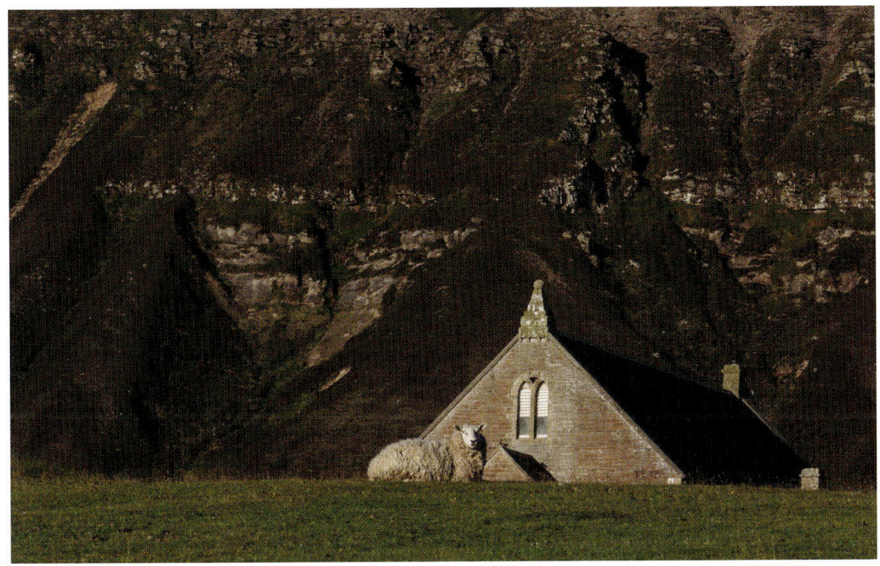

A small herd of free running Shetland ponies on Hoy

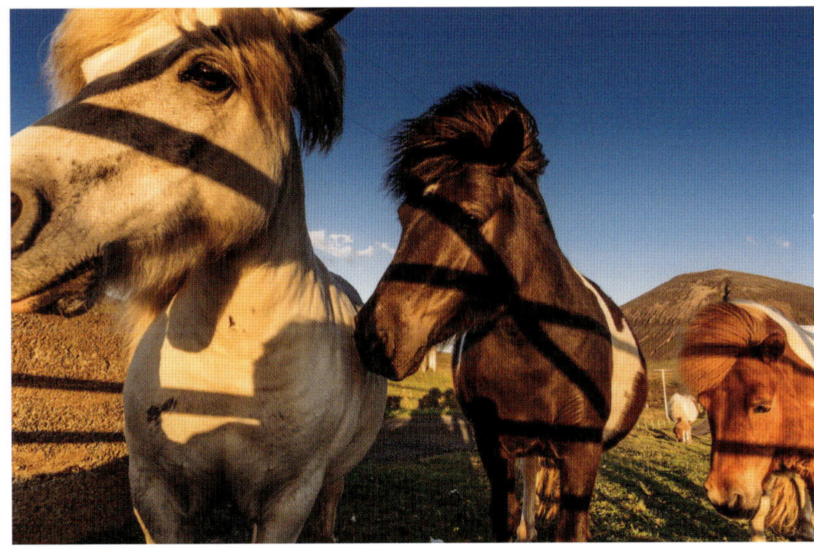

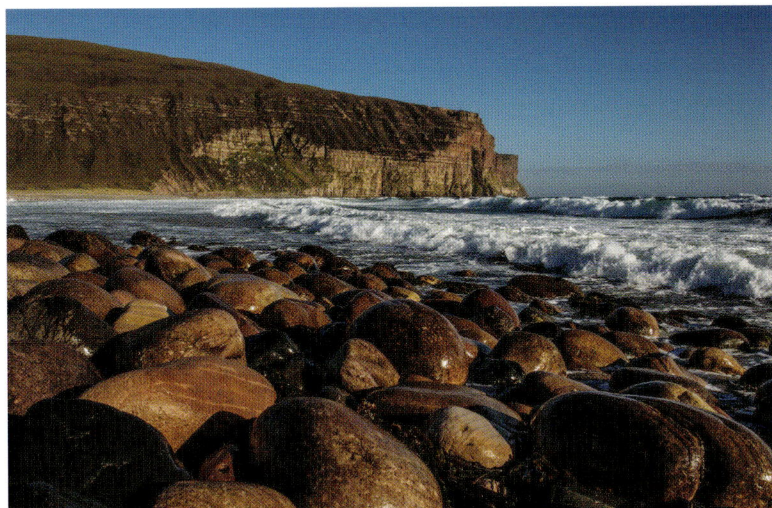

Rackwick Bay, Hoy

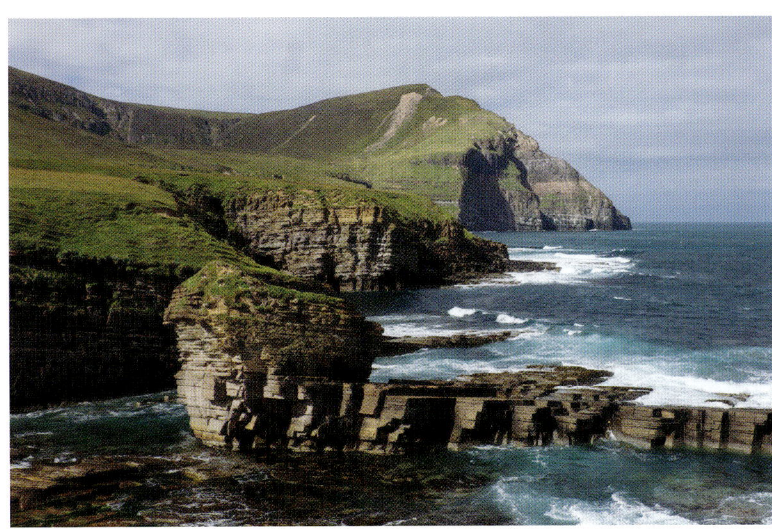

Hamar Hellia and Rami Geo, at the northern point of Hoy

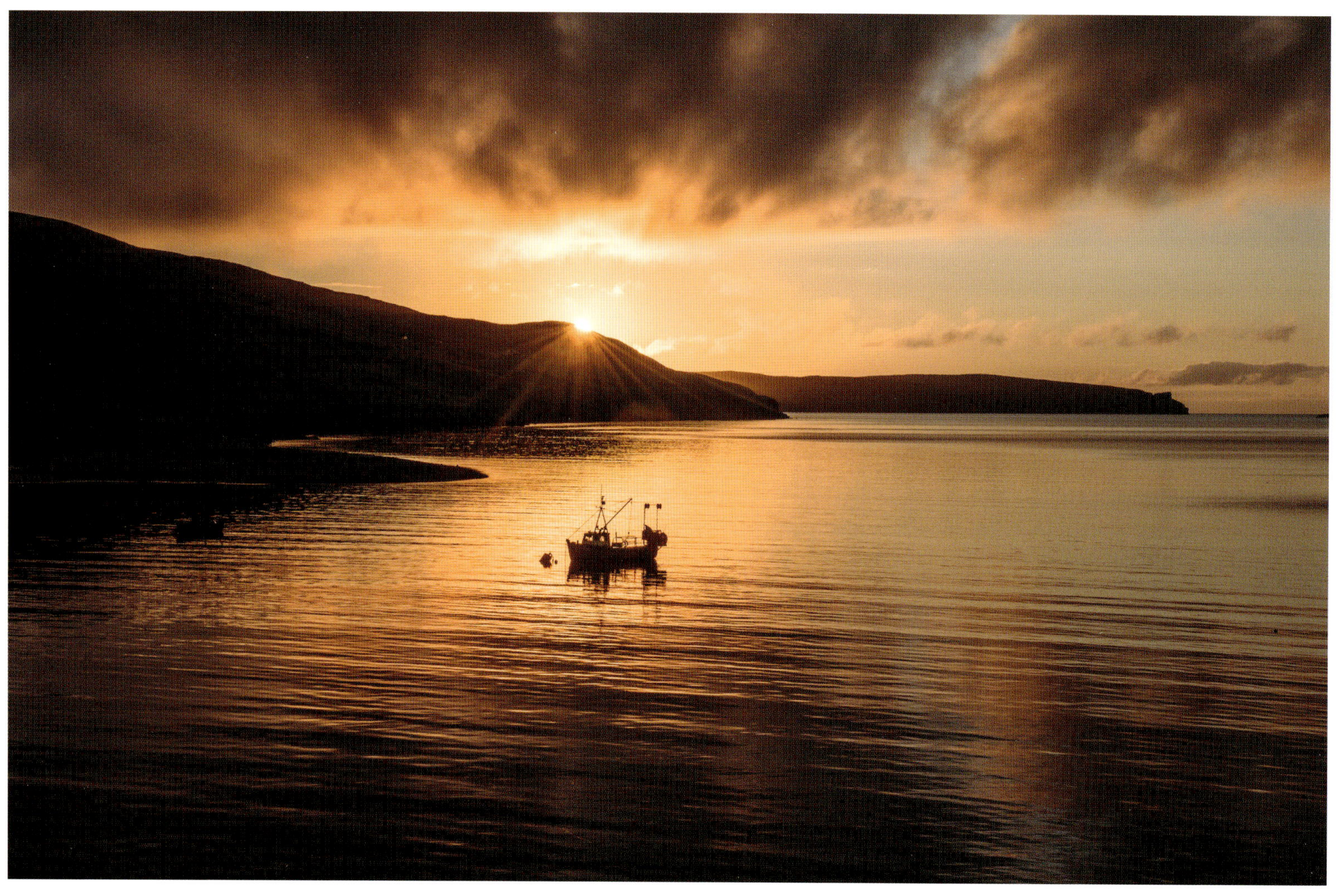

Ronas Voe sea loch at sunset

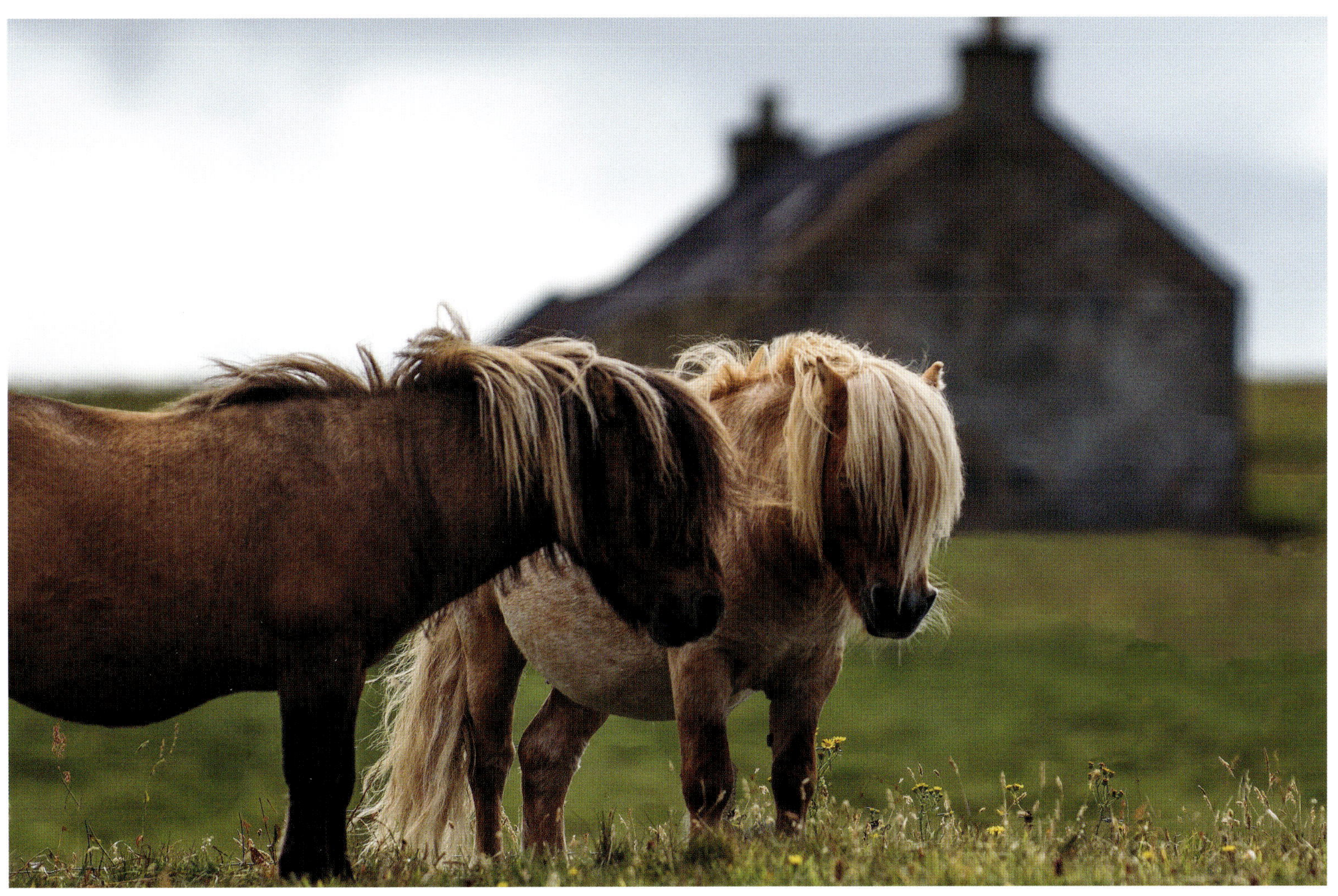

Lovable natives at West Sandwick, Yell

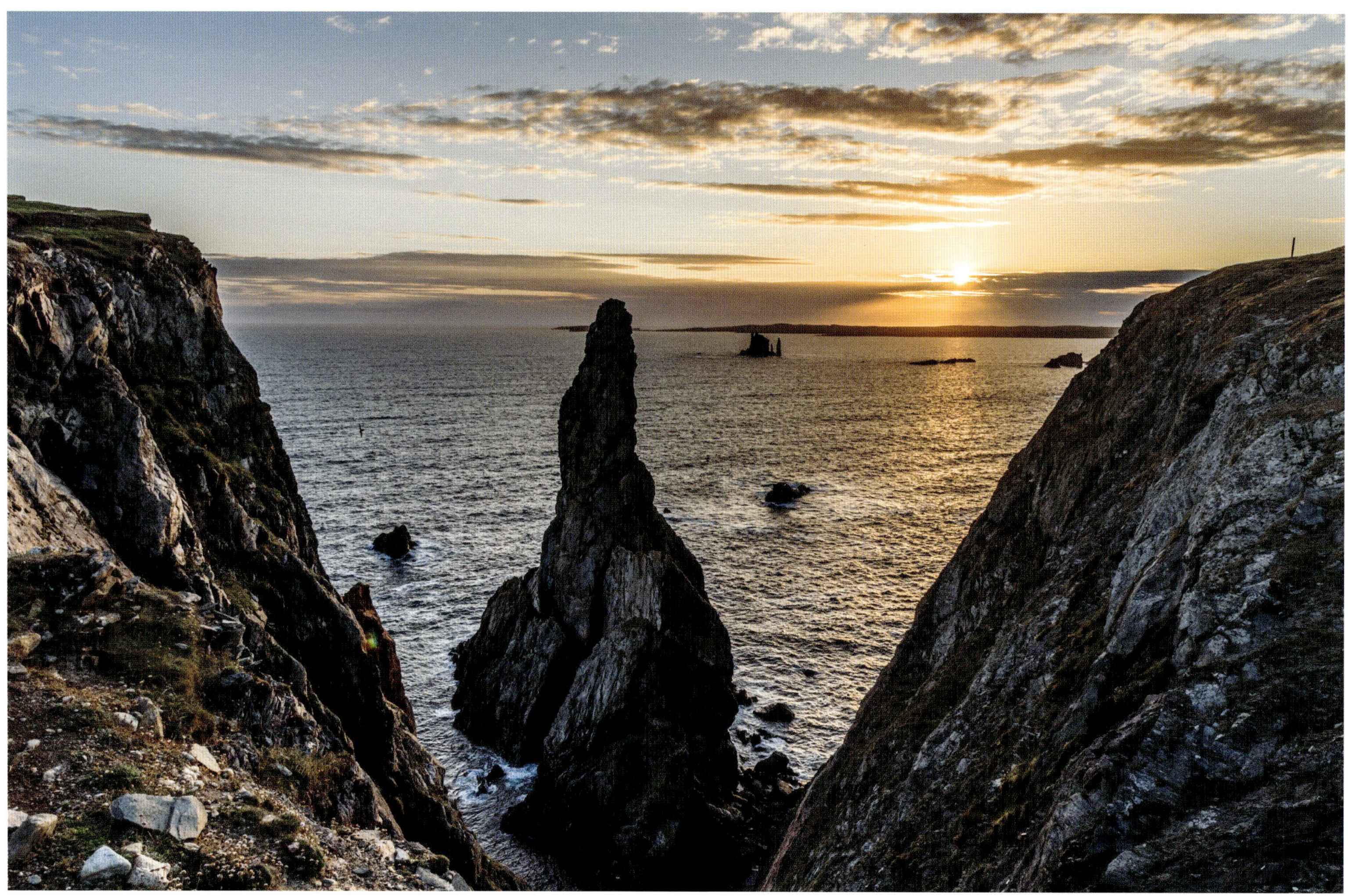

Echaness sunset from Ness of Hillswick, Mainland

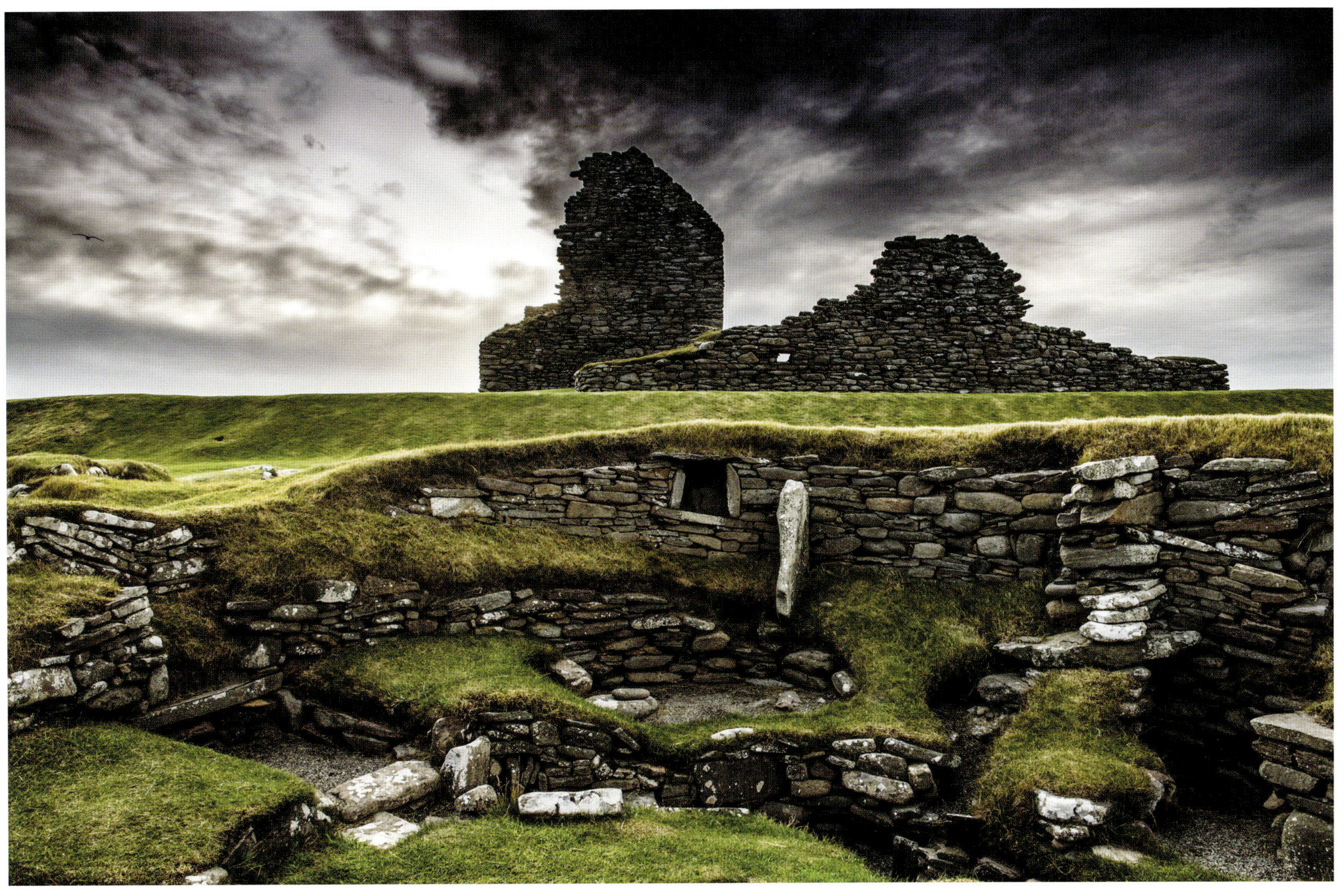

The prehistoric Norse settlement of Jarlshof, at West Voe, Sumburgh Point,
is Shetland's most significant archaeological site.

The Landmass of Saxa Vord by Hermaness, Unst

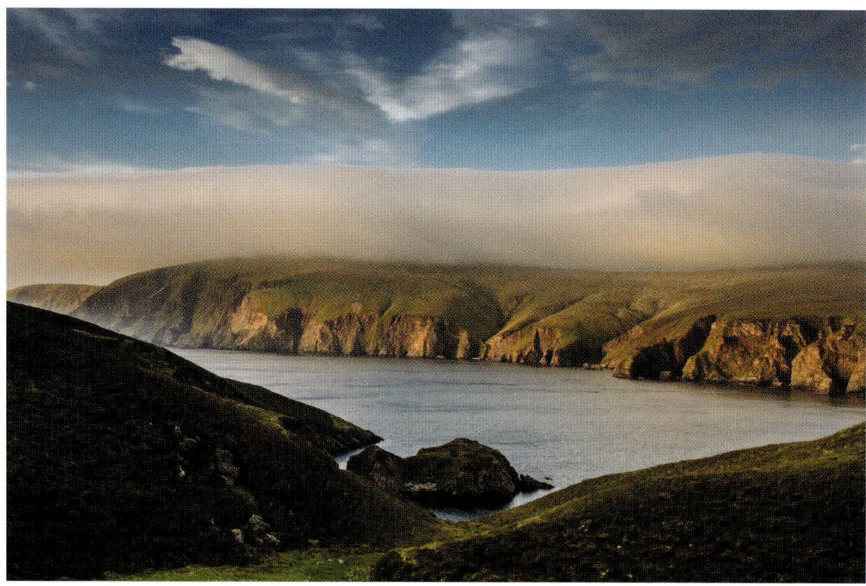

Cliffs at Stuis of Graveland by Grimister, Yell

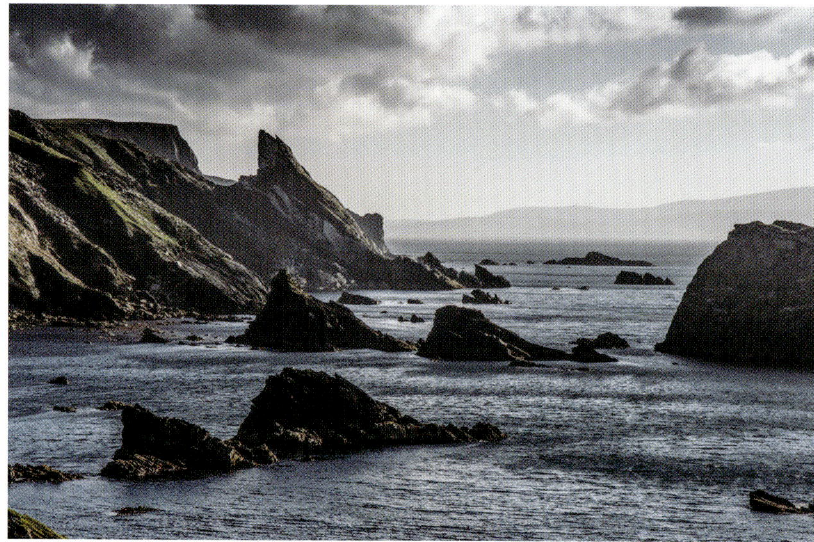

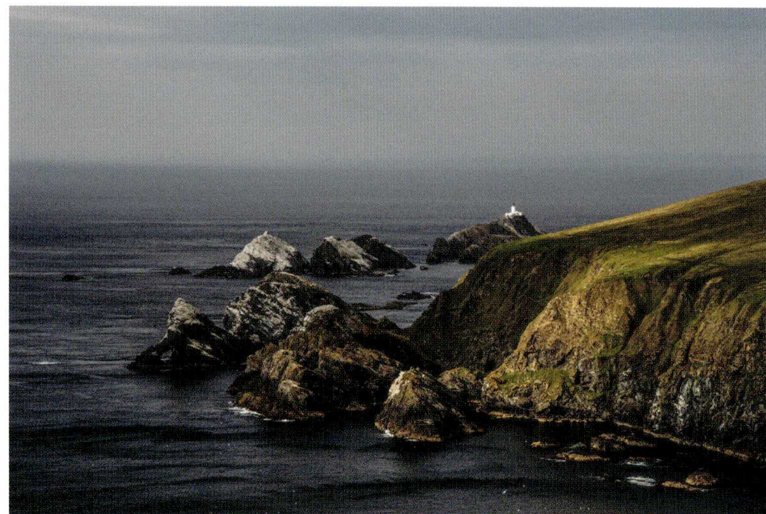

Muckle Flugga Skerries and Lighthouse, Hermaness Reserve, Unst

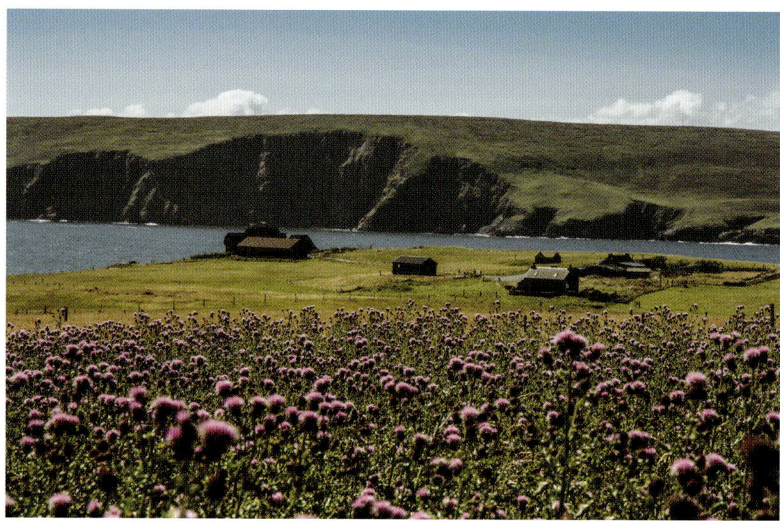

A meadow of thistles by Houbie, Fetlar

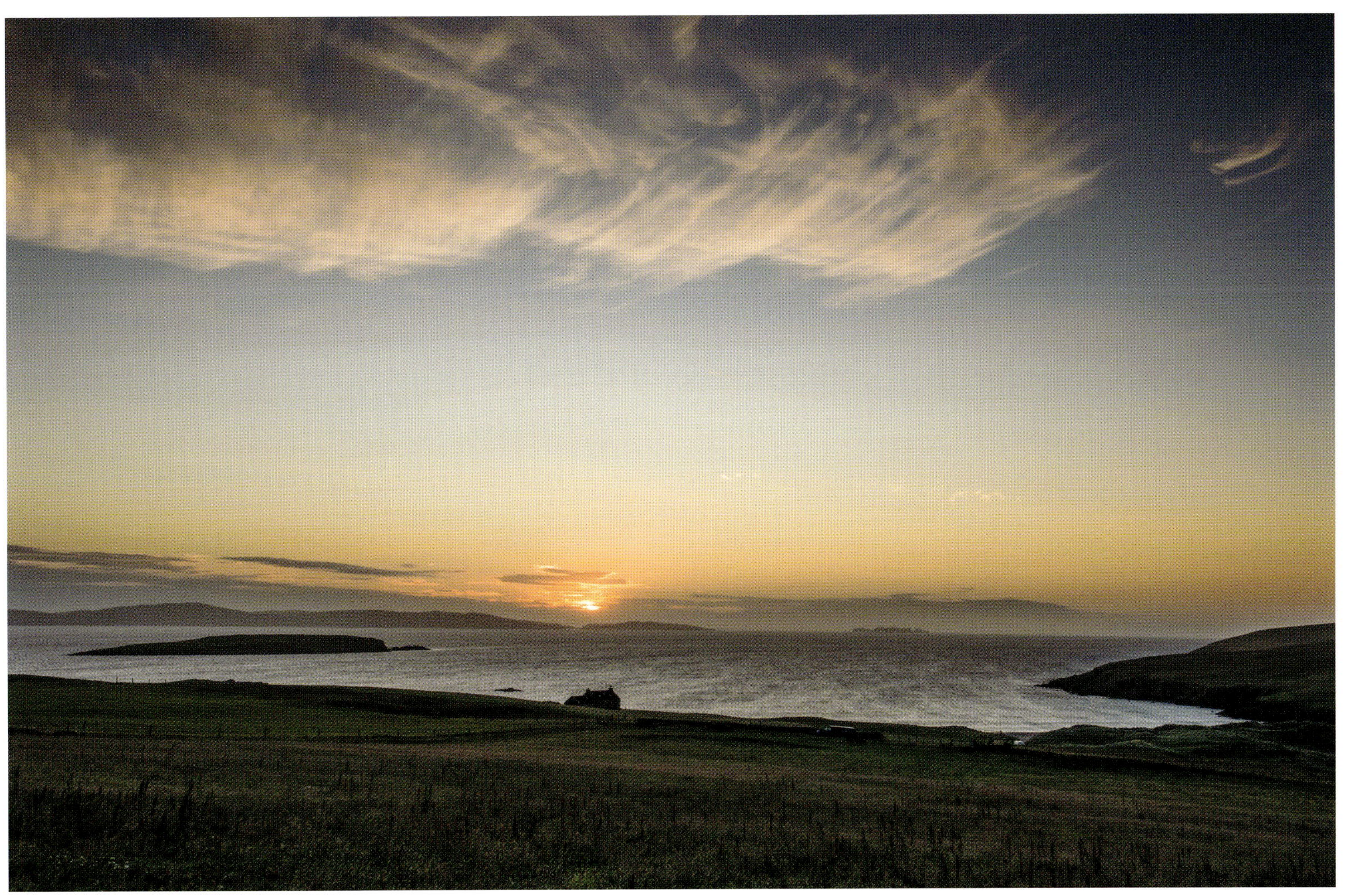

Lone cottage, west Sandwick, Yell

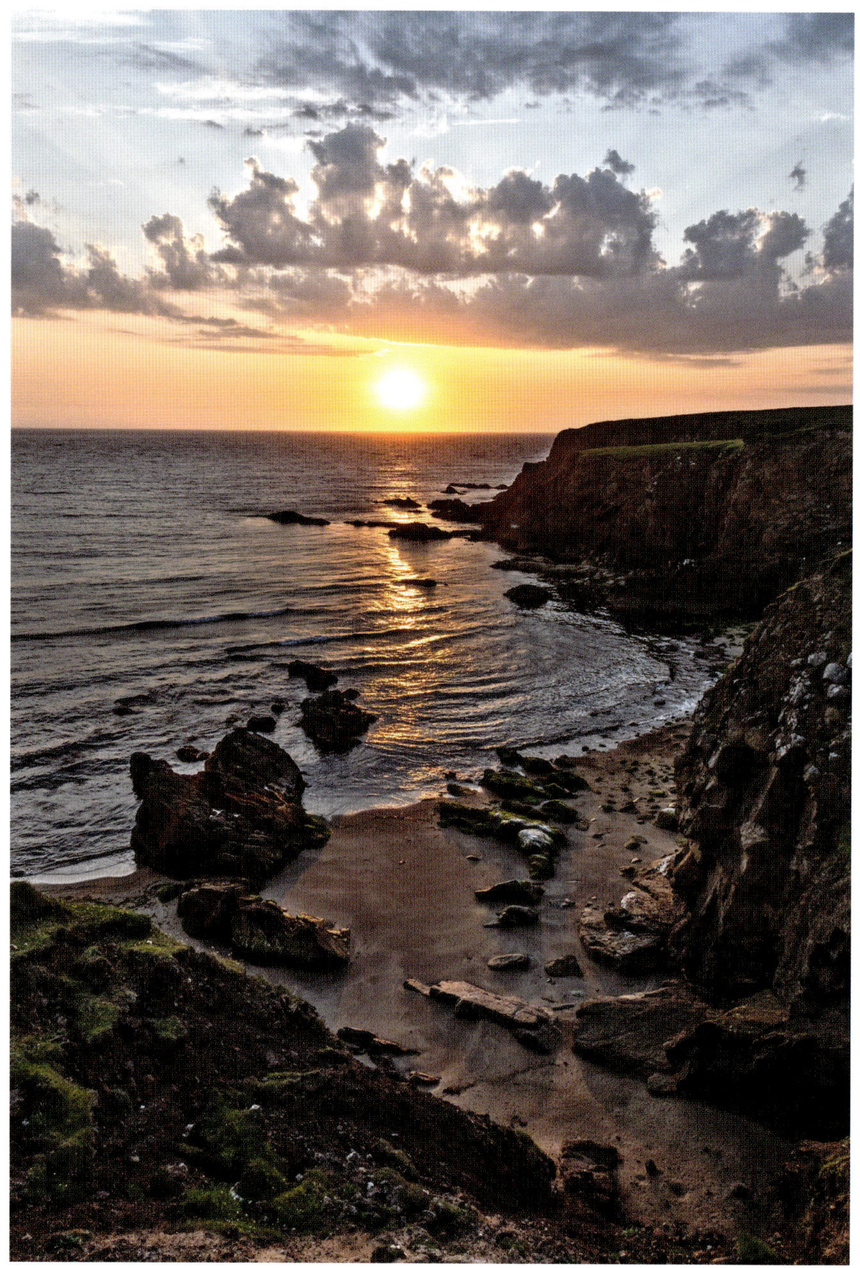

Sunrise at Skaw, the northern most point of the Unst

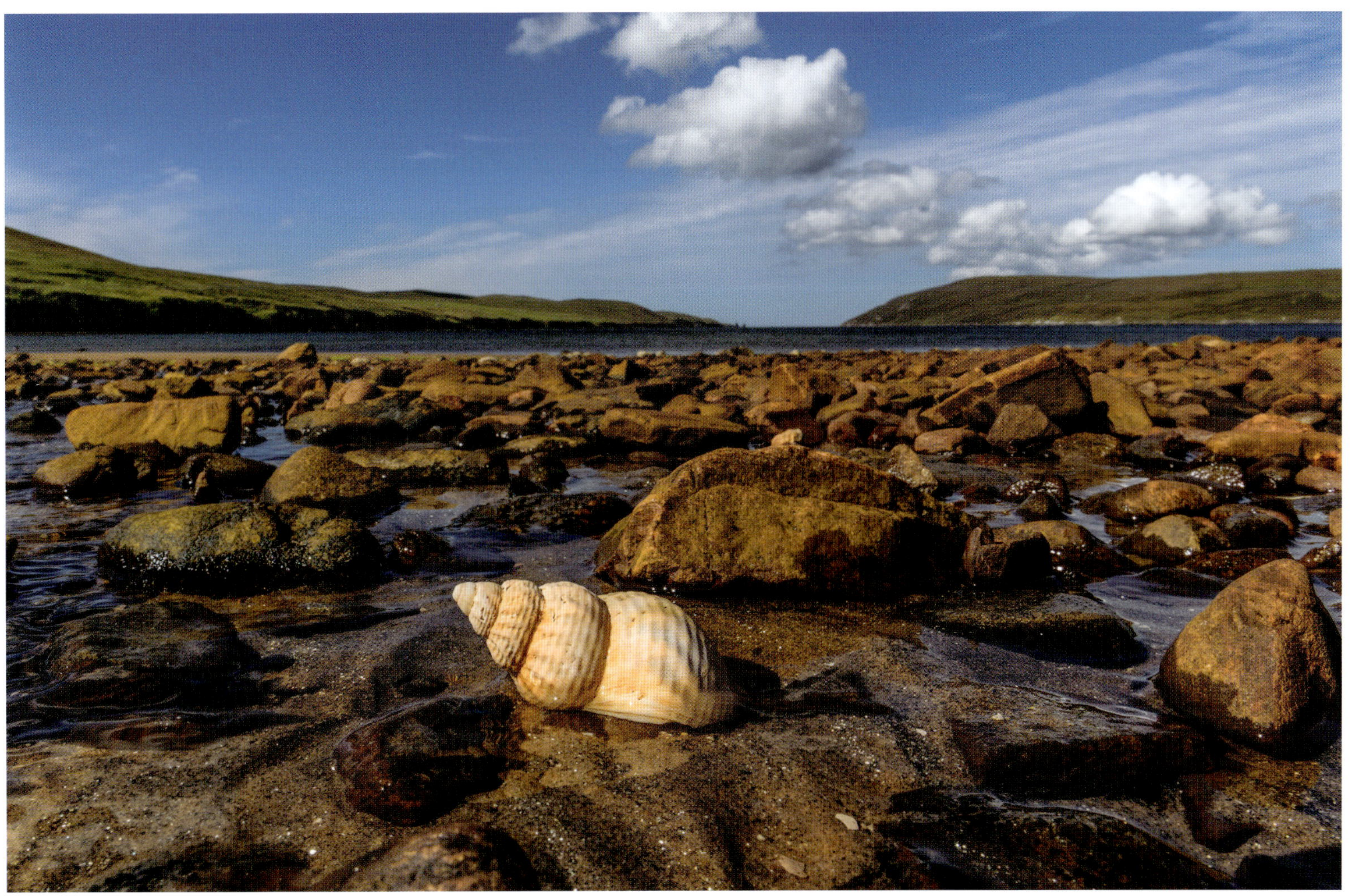

A giant whelk, Isbister shore, Mainland

The moon rising above Vidlin Harbour

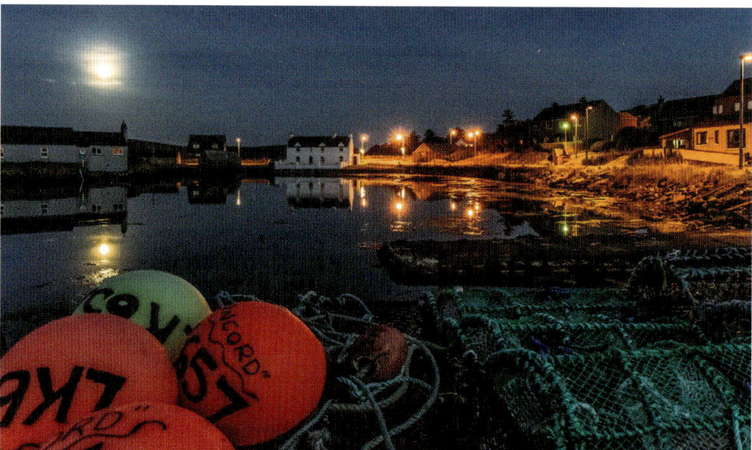

Dusk descends on the moorings at Vidlin.

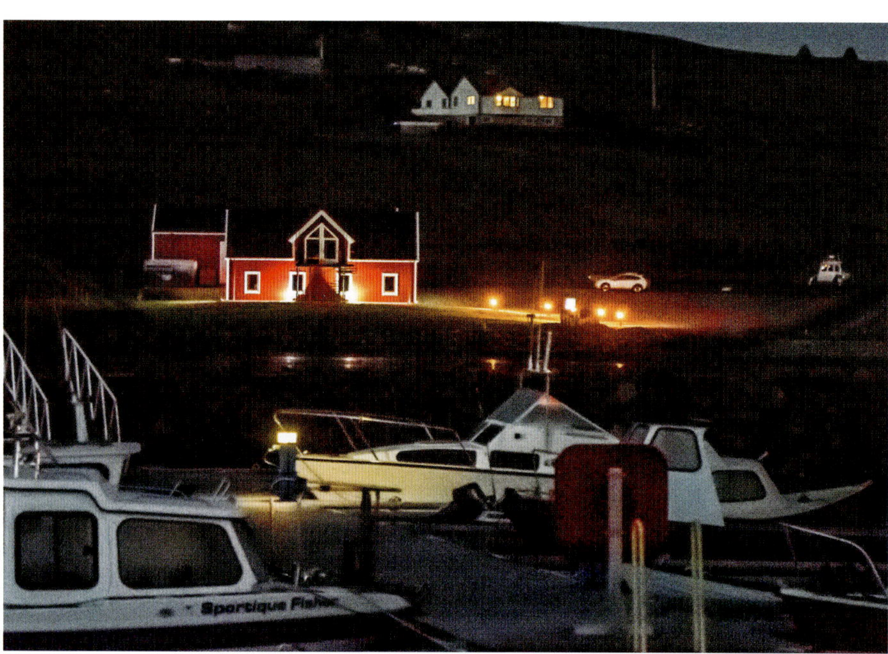

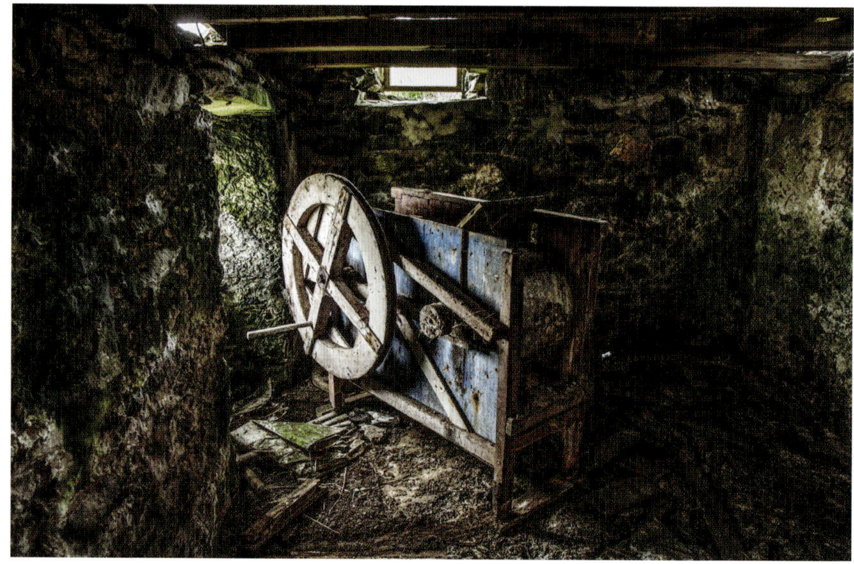

A hand-driven winnowing, or threshing machine, at West Sandwick, Yell

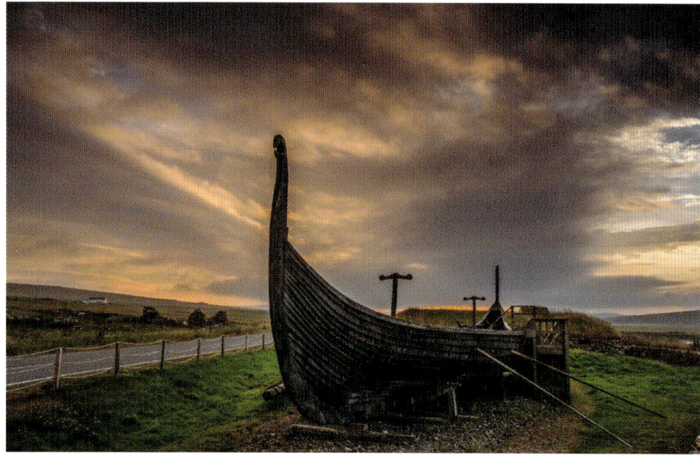

The Skidbladner, a replica Gokstad or Viking longboat, at Haroldswick, Unst

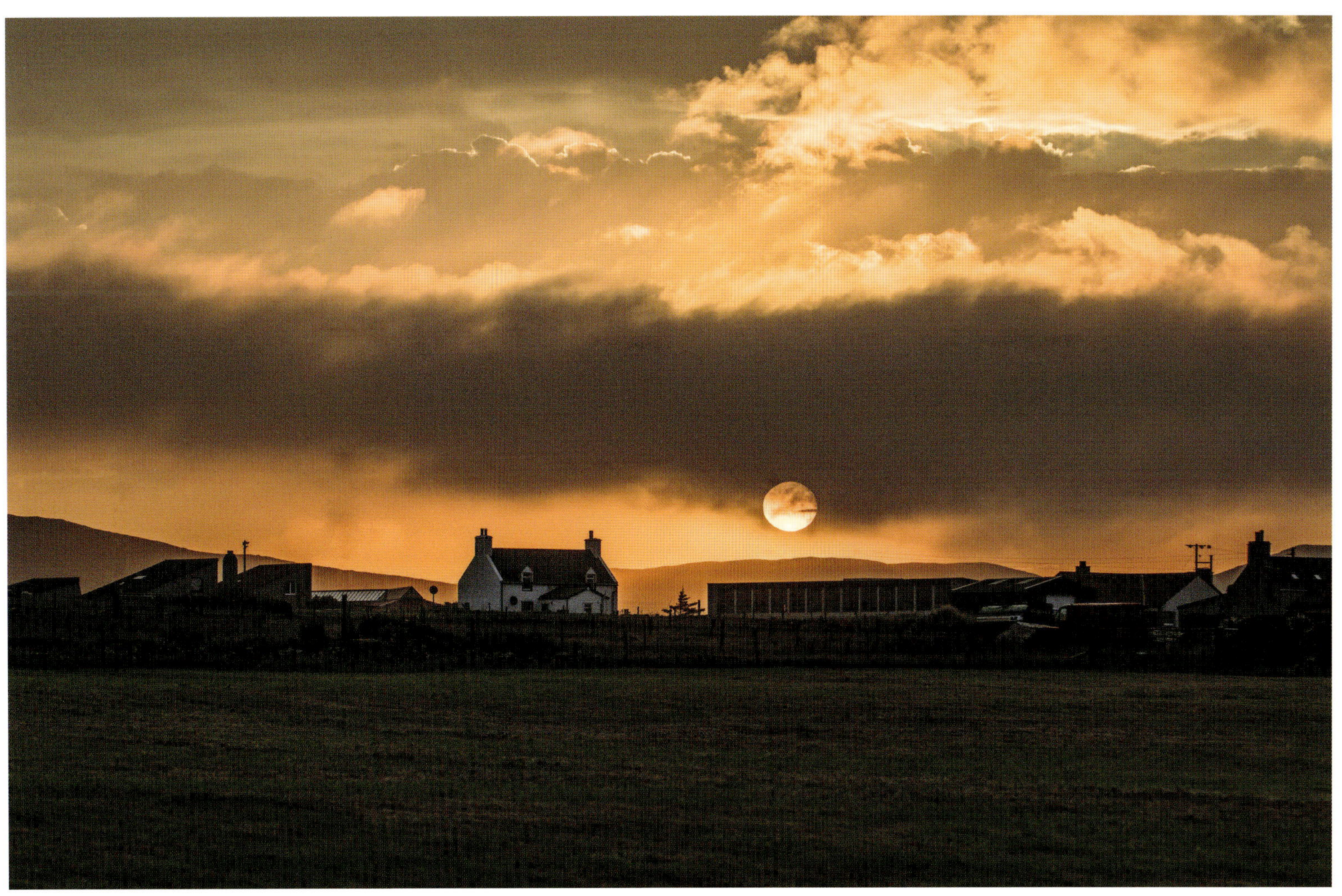

Sundown at Haroldswick, Unst

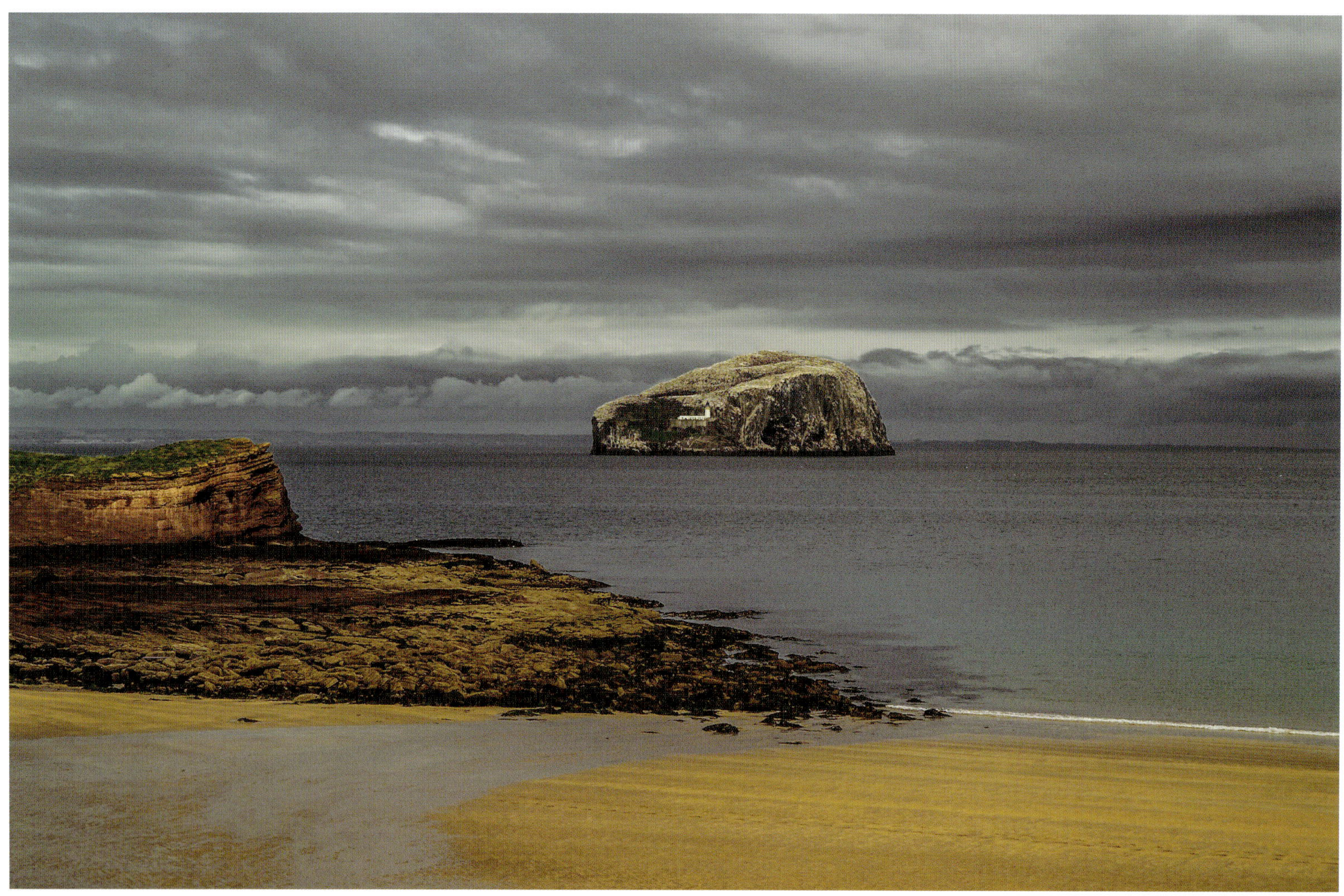

Bass Rock in the Firth of Forth seen here from East Lothian sustains the world's largest colony of Northern Gannets.